Gender Diversity and Sexuality in English Language Education

Also available from Bloomsbury

Engaging with Linguistic Diversity, David Little and Déirdre Kirwan
Initial English Language Teacher Education, edited by Darío Luis Banegas
Content Knowledge in English Language Teacher Education,
edited by Darío Luis Banegas
Researching Language Learning Motivation, edited by Ali H. Al-Hoorie
and Fruzsina Szabó
Social Networks in Language Learning and Language Teaching,
edited by Avary Carhill-Poza and Naomi Kurata
Teaching and Learning the English Language, Richard Badger
Language Learning Strategies and Individual Learner Characteristics,
edited by Rebecca L. Oxford and Carmen M. Amerstorfer

Gender Diversity and Sexuality in English Language Education

New Transnational Voices

Darío Luis Banegas and Navan Govender

BLOOMSBURY ACADEMIC
LONDON • NEW YORK • OXFORD • NEW DELHI • SYDNEY

BLOOMSBURY ACADEMIC
Bloomsbury Publishing Plc
50 Bedford Square, London, WC1B 3DP, UK
1385 Broadway, New York, NY 10018, USA
29 Earlsfort Terrace, Dublin 2, Ireland

BLOOMSBURY, BLOOMSBURY ACADEMIC and the Diana logo are
trademarks of Bloomsbury Publishing Plc

First published in Great Britain 2022
Paperback edition published 2024

Copyright © Darío Luis Banegas and Navan Govender and contributors, 2022

Darío Luis Banegas and Navan Govender and contributors have asserted their right under
the Copyright, Designs and Patents Act, 1988, to be identified as Author of this work.

Cover design: Charlotte James
Cover image © A-Digit/Getty Images

All rights reserved. No part of this publication may be reproduced or transmitted in
any form or by any means, electronic or mechanical, including photocopying,
recording, or any information storage or retrieval system, without prior
permission in writing from the publishers.

Bloomsbury Publishing Plc does not have any control over, or responsibility for, any
third-party websites referred to or in this book. All internet addresses given in this
book were correct at the time of going to press. The author and publisher regret any
inconvenience caused if addresses have changed or sites have ceased to exist, but
can accept no responsibility for any such changes.

A catalogue record for this book is available from the British Library.

A catalog record for this book is available from the Library of Congress.

ISBN: HB: 978-1-3502-1756-0
PB: 978-1-3502-1760-7
ePDF: 978-1-3502-1757-7
eBook: 978-1-3502-1758-4

Typeset by Newgen KnowledgeWorks Pvt. Ltd., Chennai, India

To find out more about our authors and books visit www.bloomsbury.com
and sign up for our newsletters.

Contents

List of Figures	vii
List of Tables	viii
Notes on Contributors	ix
Foreword	
Jane Sunderland	xiii
List of Abbreviations and Acronyms	xvi

	Introduction	1
	Dario Luis Banegas and Navan Govender	
1	Queer Critical Literacies and Initial Teacher Education: Transnational Moments	11
	Grant Andrews and Navan Govender	
2	An Intercultural Experience with a Gender Perspective between Post-secondary Students from Argentina and Canada	29
	Antonella Romiti and Jessie Smith	
3	Visually Significant Spaces: Mediating Queer Picturebooks for Deep Reading in Primary ELT	45
	David Valente	
4	Breaking the Heteronormative Prosody: What a Family Tree Tells Us about Gender and Sexuality in the EFL Classroom	65
	Germán Canale	
5	Exploring the Effects of Stereotype Threat on Men's Foreign Language Listening Performance in a Sample of Turkish University Students	85
	Gulsah Kutuk	
6	Dating as an Alternative Educational Site: An Analysis of a Female Bisexual International Student's Access to English Learning in Canada	105
	Liang Cao	
7	Multimodal and Critical Representations of Gender and Sexuality	123
	Shin-ying Huang	
8	Gendered Discourses in Global and Glocal ELT Textbooks	141
	Suha Alansari	

9	Gender, Sexuality and ELT Course Books: Where Are We Now? *Chris Richards*	159
10	Addressing Critical Perspectives in Language Teacher Education: Challenging Norms and Structures *David Gerlach*	175
11	Gender Diversity and Online English Language Teaching during the Covid-19 Pandemic in Bangladesh *Sayeedur Rahman and Mohammad Hamidul Haque*	193
12	New Transnational Voices on Gender Diversity in English Language Education: Moving Forward *Joanna Pawelczyk*	211

| References | 219 |
| Index | 247 |

Figures

1.1	A framework for queer critical literacies	18
3.1	*The Genderbread Person*	55
3.2	*The Gender Unicorn*	56
3.3	Character identities jigsaw piece	57
3.4	Model street party invitation	61
4.1	Illustration of family tree similar to the one used in Year 1	72
4.2	Sample questions for completing the task (oral discussion)	72
4.3	Family tree designed by a learner	74
4.4	Illustration of family tree similar to the one used in Year 2	76
4.5	Sample questions for task on family types (oral discussion)	77
4.6	Illustration of family tree similar to the one used in Year 3	78
4.7	Sample questions for awareness raising (oral discussion)	80
5.1	One-way ANOVA results for the English listening test scores across the groups	97
5.2	The Mediational Model – The difference between the self-as-target and group-as-target conditions	100

Tables

3.1	Ideas for *Julián at the Wedding*	60
4.1	Description of Task Enactment and Unit's Learning Goals in the Three School Years	71
6.1	Information of Xixi's Three Dating Partners	110
8.1	The Multimodal and Linguistic Constructions of Successful Globalized Women	146
8.2	The Multimodal and Linguistic Constructions of Regionalized Women	148
8.3	The Multimodal Construction of Localized Women	151
8.4	The Multimodal and Linguistic Constructions of Localized Men	154
9.1	Course Books Examined	167
9.2	Participants' Details	168
10.1	Relational Types of Language Teacher Educators	183
11.1	Profile of the Participants	199

Notes on Contributors

Suha Alansari completed her PhD at Warwick University, UK, in 2019. She is now an assistant professor at King Abdulaziz University in Jeddah, Saudi Arabia. Her research interests include multimodality, gender, ELT textbooks and cultural globalization.

Grant Andrews is Lecturer at the Wits School of Education in Johannesburg, South Africa. His research interests include queer visual and literary culture in South Africa, and questions of gender and sexuality in education. He is currently working on a project studying queer visualities and queer theory in South Africa.

Dario Luis Banegas is Lecturer in Language Education, Moray House School of Education and Sport, University of Edinburgh, UK, and Associate Fellow with the University of Warwick, UK. He is an active member of teacher associations in the UK and Latin America. With Bloomsbury, he has edited *Initial English Language Teacher Education* (2017) and *Content Knowledge in English Language Teacher Education* (2020). He co-edited the volume *International Perspectives on Diversity in ELT* (2021) and a special issue on comprehensive sexuality education in ELT for the *ELT Journal*. His main teaching and research interests are: social justice in language education, action research and initial English language teacher education.

Germán Canale (PhD in SLA, Carnegie Mellon University, United States) is Associate Professor at the Institute of Linguistics, FHCE, Universidad de la República, Uruguay. His research interests include: discourse analysis, multimodality and learning, educational media and textbook studies, foreign language policies and education. His latest book is *Technology, Multimodality and Learning: Analyzing Meaning across Scales* (2019). He has published in *Language, Culture and Curriculum*; *Sociolinguistic Studies*; *Spanish in Context*; *Sociocultural Pragmatics*; *The L2 Journal*; among others.

Liang Cao (he/him) is a PhD candidate in the Faculty of Education at Simon Fraser University in Canada. His research draws on interdisciplinary scholarship in applied linguistics, sociolinguistics, queer studies and migration studies. His ongoing dissertation project explores adult queer migrants' English learning experiences in non-conventional educational settings in the Greater Vancouver Area in Western Canada.

David Gerlach is Full Professor at the University of Wuppertal, Germany. His research and teaching focus on professional development of language teachers, critical literacy and critical pedagogy, learning difficulties and inclusive language teaching. Lately, together with colleagues, he has been involved in conceptualizing a more critical perspective for the language teaching practice in Germany and wants to extend this to the practice of language teacher education within the German structures.

Navan Govender (he/they) is Lecturer at Strathclyde University, Glasgow, UK, who leads the Professional Graduate Diploma in Education (PGDE) English specialism. Navan's research focuses on critical literacies, its intersections with various critical and queer pedagogies, and the implications for practice across English education and teacher education: from multimodality and transmodality, to (a)gender and (a)sexual diversity and decoloniality. Their most recent publication includes: Govender, N. (2020). Critical transmodal pedagogies: Student teachers play with genre conventions. *Multimodal Communication*, 9(1), DOI: https://doi.org/10.1515/mc-2019-0009.

Mohammad Hamidul Haque is currently working as a faculty of English Language and Linguistics at American International University – Bangladesh. He worked as a consultant in the British Council and UGC Bangladesh-sponsored project TELSHEB and developed *English for Academic Purposes* coursebook as an author for undergraduate level. He was also a master trainer for trials and implementation of the coursebook in the universities. His area of interests includes Second Language Acquisition and Teaching, English Linguistics and related fields.

Shin-ying Huang is Professor in the Department of Foreign Languages and Literatures at National Taiwan University in Taiwan. Her research interests include critical literacies, multimodal literacies, and critical and multimodal discourse analysis. Her research has been published in international journals such as *Language Learning & Technology*; *Gender and Education*; *English Teaching: Practice & Critique*; *Journal of Adolescent & Adult Literacy*; *Language, Culture and Curriculum*; *TESOL Journal*, among others. She was a visiting scholar in the Department of Second Language Studies at the University of Hawaii at Manoa, United States from 2017 to 2018.

Gulsah Kutuk is Visiting Research Fellow at Liverpool John Moores University, UK. She holds an MA in English Language Teaching and Applied Linguistics (King's College London, UK) and a PhD in Education (Edge Hill University, UK). She is originally from Turkey where she worked as an EFL tutor and taught academic and general English for about three years at two different universities.

Currently, she conducts research in a variety of areas of TESOL including gender stereotypes and the role of emotions in teaching and learning EFL. She has also been an active member of professional organizations such as British Association for Applied Linguistics (BAAL) and presented her research in various national and international conferences including the Psychology for Language Learning (PLL) conference.

Joanna Pawelczyk is Associate Professor of Sociolinguistics at the Faculty of English, Adam Mickiewicz University in Poznań, Poland. Her main research interests are in the area of language, gender and sexuality including gender in the professional organization, qualitative research methodology as well as gender and interaction of psychotherapy.

Sayeedur Rahman is Professor and former chairperson of the Department of English Language at the Institute of Modern Languages (IML), University of Dhaka, Bangladesh. He received his PhD in English Language Teaching from Jawaharlal Nehru University, India, as an ICCR scholar. He has extensively worked as an ESL/EFL teacher, researcher and consultant for more than twenty years and has published widely in the areas of SLA and sociolinguistics.

Chris Richards is originally from Cardiff (Wales), where he trained as a high school English teacher after graduating with a Master of Arts in English. He began working in Birmingham and then in South East Wales. In 2016, he relocated to Spain and began teaching English and preparing students for Cambridge and Trinity exams. He completed his MEd in Applied Linguistics in 2019 and, later that year, began working as a teacher mentor for a private language academy in Madrid. He continues as an independent researcher.

Antonella Romiti is Instructor in Academic Reading Comprehension in English courses at Universidad Nacional de General Sarmiento, Buenos Aires, Argentina. She has also taught at different teacher training colleges in Buenos Aires. She did a postgraduate specialization in African American Literatures, and is currently doing an MA in World and Compared Literatures in the University of Buenos Aires (UBA), Argentina. She is on the Board of UNGS Faculty Trade Union. She is also interested in elementary and high school education policies in Buenos Aires.

Jessie Smith is Coordinator of and Instructor in the Latin American Studies Program, in the department of Interdisciplinary Studies, at Langara College in Vancouver, Canada. She did her MA in political economy at the Institute of Political Economy at Carleton University, Ottawa, Canada. She was on the Board of the Langara Faculty Association (faculty union) for seven years, and continues to push for progressive policies to support faculty and students in public postsecondary institutions in Canada.

David Valente is a Nord University, Norway, research fellow in English language and literature subject pedagogy. His PhD research explores the development of intercultural citizenship education through children's literature in primary English language education. David has over twenty years' experience in English language teaching and is coordinator of the IATEFL Young Learners and Teenagers Special Interest Group. He is also a review editor for the *Children's Literature in English Language Education* journal https://clelejournal.org/.

Foreword

There are many reasons why this book is needed, and why it is needed now. Primarily, a huge number of socially and sexually diverse students of a great range of ages pass through our English language classrooms, for many years. These students include children who are very much learning about the still highly gendered world, teenagers who are rapidly developing as sexual beings, and adults who may still be wondering exactly who they are and how they should be relating to people. And here they are in the very personal place that is the language classroom – personal because their learning materials, and most probably the teacher, will frequently focus on personal things: individuals' likes and dislikes, their activities, their past, their future plans, their families.

This may be fine for the student who finds the above liberating, even enabling of a new identity along with the new language. It may also be fine for those students whose gender and sexual identity and personal life correspond to the likely heteronormative stance of the teacher, and the almost certainly heteronormative stance of the global textbook. But what of the teenage girl who has no boyfriend to talk about in a class or group discussion on 'Going Out', and has no interest in getting one? Or the student experiencing cognitive dissonance during an exercise on third-person pronouns because they identify as non-binary? Or the one who does not identify with the gender assigned to them at birth, who is told in a lesson on 'Congratulating People', to design a Congratulations card for the birth of either a new baby girl *or* a new baby boy? Our classrooms are hugely diverse, but many students will keep some of their multiple identities close to their chest, and the teacher is likely to be aware of only a small fraction of the many students who pass through their hands who are not heterosexual or who do not identify with the gender assigned to them at birth.

The foreign language textbook is particularly problematic. Decades of research on representation – text and illustrations – in mainly English as a foreign language (EFL) textbooks have found these to contain more male than female characters, to show those males involved in a greater range of occupational and other activities than females, and to reproduce a range of gendered stereotypes, for example, in the carrying out (or not) of domestic work. And if we see such representation also as potential social construction, we can also see it as limiting the aspirations of all students – of course, in conjunction with other such representations/constructions. This is not to say that students cannot think for themselves and 'consume' these representations critically, or that the teacher will not ask the students to critique what they are presented with – but there is no guarantee that either will happen.

But if female students look in vain for sets of textbook representations which are not gendered in this way, what about gay students or those who do not identify as cis? For them the issue is not so much how they are represented but almost always that they are not represented at all. Given market forces, the PARSNIPS principle for textbook content (no politics, alcohol, religion, sex, narcotics, -isms or pork; see Aldridge-Morris 2016) means that mainstream global EFL textbook writers and illustrators play it very, very safe – to the extent that the textbook content is likely to lag behind the legislative and curriculum edicts of a country in which they are used.

The language classroom is gendered in yet another way: unlike first languages, second languages and even subsequent languages, spoken in the community, foreign languages are distinctly feminine, in that when they are to be selected in education, they almost always attract more female than male students, teachers tend to be women and female students tend to get the better grades, including IELTS scores. Is this because, as some believe, 'girls are simply better at foreign languages'? Does this essential belief then translate into 'boys are better at particular other subjects'? And how does this impact on career paths? *Gender Diversity and Sexuality in English Language Education: New Transnational Voices* addresses the above issues in a highly grounded way. The contributors are experienced practitioners, many with transnational experience under their belt. Transnationality is of course highly characteristic of foreign language education: while many in the profession work away from the country of their birth, their close colleagues are working in their home countries (but may also have spent time abroad). Such professional groupings and networks in which these teachers from different backgrounds crucially share professional challenges offer fertile ground for increasing mutual understanding, and for informal professional and personal development in our ever-changing, globalizing world.

Each chapter is contextualized – geographically, politically and in an actual classroom (or learning) setting. No chapters confront us with depressing, dead-end analyses associated with the heteronormativity of classroom interaction or learning materials which offer no way forward; indeed, the majority rather look at how such hetero- (and cis-)normativity can be addressed, at a local, individual classroom level, often 'queering the pitch' in a most constructive way. This book thus joins Joshua Paiz's (2020) *Queering the English Language Classroom: A Practical Guide for Teachers* in this endeavour. While the Ministry of Education edicts may be hard to change, in many classrooms, as long as they are textbook- or curriculum-related, topics can be freely chosen, and reflective critique encouraged. In principle – and this is probably true only of language classrooms – *any* topic is valid when it comes to the practice of speaking, listening, reading and writing. Further, debate and discussion – for example, to practice 'Expressing a Point of View' – in whole class, groupwork and pairwork are valid pedagogic activities.

Of course, a classroom which explicitly takes on board social inclusion and diversity in their widest senses does not do so only for the benefit of our LGBTQI+ students but for all classroom participants. Gender and sexual identity are relevant to all. Members of 'majority groups' may not experience 'identity' in the same way that minority groups do, but such normativity – its manifestations, its benefits for some, its difficulties for others – is precisely what needs addressing. It would be foolish to deny that this will frequently be challenging for the foreign language teacher, especially given the regressive political climate still or newly evident in many countries today, and because of this, teachers' approaches need to vary with socio-cultural contexts as well as with institution. Small steps, which require seeing a language teacher as an educator *beyond* our subject, but a teacher, we can agree, has huge potential influence.

A final point: the new and exciting transnational voices that have contributed to *Gender Diversity and Sexuality in English Language Education* primarily address teachers. But teachers may also be or may become researchers, and here the richly diverse foci of the twelve chapters, together with the substantial lists of references, provide both stimuli and starting points for further work. Interesting times.

Jane Sunderland
August 2021

Abbreviations and Acronyms

ACDP	African Christian Democratic Party
ANOVA	One-way analysis of variance
ARCE	Academic reading comprehension in English
BAME	Black, Asian and Minority Ethnic
CDA	Critical Discourse Analysis
CEFR	Common European Framework of Reference
CLIL	Content and language integrated learning
COIL	Collaborative online international learning
CoP	Communities of practice
CPD	Continuing professional development
CSE	Comprehensive sexuality education
EAL	English as an additional language
EDI	Equality, diversity and inclusion
EFL	English as a foreign language
ELT	English language teaching
ESL	English as a second language
GDI	Gender-related Development Index
GE	Global Edition
GELC	Global English language coursebook
GVA	Greater Vancouver Area
HDI	Human Development Index
ITE	Initial teacher education
IWB	Interactive whiteboard
L2	Second language
LDC	Least developed country
LGBT/LGBTQ+/ LGBTQI+/LGBTIQ	Lesbian, gay, bisexual, transgender/queer, intersex and other nonnormative gender and sexual identities
LPP	Legitimate peripheral participation
M	Mean
MANOVA	Multivariate analysis of variance
MEE	Middle Eastern Edition

OECD	Organisation for Economic Co-operation and Development
PELT	Primary English language teaching
PET	Preliminary English Tests
PRC	People's Republic of China
QCL	Queer critical literacies
RP	Represented Participant
RSHP	Relationships, sexual health and parenthood
SD	Standard deviation
SE	Special Edition
SIG	Special Interest Group
SLA	Second language acquisition
SOGIE	Sexual orientations, gender identities and gender expressions
SPSS	Statistical Package for the Social Sciences
ST	Stereotype threat
STEM	Science, Technology, Engineering and Mathematics
TEFL	Teaching English as a foreign language
UCLES	University of Cambridge Local Examinations Syndicate
UNDP	United Nations Development Programme

Introduction

Dario Luis Banegas and Navan Govender

Almost three years ago, we, the editors of this volume, met at a café in the city centre of Glasgow (and yes, it was cold and raining) to discuss the possibility of working together on a project that combined our experience on a shared professional and personal interest: gender and sexuality in education. Specifically, we were interested in contributing to the conversation on diversity and inclusion around gender and sexuality since there is a need in the language education field to understand how this issue is present (or absent) in practice, the curriculum and institutions. As two academics in the field of (language) education, we agreed to edit a volume which brought together international research-informed accounts of how gender and sexuality are explored, enacted and mobilized in English language education, where English is an Lx, that is, a first, second, third language and so on, without connotations of inferiority (Dewale 2018).

With that idea in mind, we released a call for contributions which we shared among our professional contacts and social network profiles. We were surprised to receive so many proposals from almost every continent. The authors included in the volume were selected against the following criteria: (1) geographical representation, (2) types of institution (tertiary and university levels), (3) rationale and data included in the abstract, (4) experience as lecturers in including a gender perspective in their teaching practice, (5) authors' record of publications and ideological and epistemological stances on English language education, (6) experience as teacher educators and course developers following a bottom-up/critical/socio-cultural approach, (7) involvement in research forums, publication venues and professional associations and (8) reader-friendly writing style. These criteria allowed us to include contributions from diverse contexts (e.g. Argentina and Taiwan) and authors who are new to the publishing market and/or based at tertiary institutions and Ministries of Education. Notwithstanding, by relying solely on the contributions received, this volume does not interrogate the full spectrum of gender and sexuality diversity. For example, we must acknowledge that the volume does not offer coverage of transgender, two-spirit and non-conforming issues as other recent volumes robustly do (e.g. Paiz & Coda 2021; Pakuła 2021; Rousselle 2020).

The aim of this volume is to collect teaching-informed research studies as well as research-informed teaching accounts which explore the teaching of English that engages with (a)gender and (a)sexual diversity. Informed by critical theories, critical literacy, post-structuralism, queer theory and indigeneity/(de)coloniality, the critical perspectives in this volume consider gender and sexuality as dimensions of human life and aim to promote sexual, gender, emotional and relational well-being together with the construction of cultural horizons and citizenship. This volume also represents a broad range of perspectives and contexts that contribute to the increasing internationalization of higher education and their teacher education provisions. This edited volume provides original research accounts in English language education in diverse settings: Argentina, Bangladesh, Canada, Germany, Saudi Arabia, South Africa, Spain, Taiwan, Turkey, the UK and Uruguay. The geographical settings some contributions come from and the incorporation of new professional voices in the generation and dissemination of knowledge in teacher education make this volume unique. In this regard, the voices and contexts amalgamated in the chapters move away from only representing WEIRD (Western, educated, industrialized, rich, democratic) settings.

In the sections below, we offer a brief conceptualization of the overarching areas that provide the content and context of this volume: (1) English language teacher education, (2) transnationality and (3) gender.

English Language Teacher Education

English language teacher education programmes around the world are usually organized around general knowledge, pedagogical content knowledge and subject-matter/content knowledge (Banegas 2017). Such programmes exhibit a tendency to favour linguistics-based knowledge as well as pedagogical tools and resources for effective teaching. Recent publications discuss the need to transform the language teacher education knowledge base by adopting a field-driven change perspective to respond to current pedagogical demands, learners' and teachers' identities, and interdisciplinarity (Freeman 2020; Le 2020). In addition, Johnson and Golombek (2020) highlight that while language teacher education pedagogy needs to remain theoretically informed, it needs to be locally situated to cater for the particularities and possibilities that each complex context offers. In line with these new demands, there have also been studies and pedagogical experiences which address broad social issues with the aim of raising social and critical awareness and dismantling hegemonic ideologies deep-seated in teacher education (e.g. Hawkins 2011; Lamb, Hatoss & O'Neill 2019). As a response to this tendency, a few studies have explored gender in teacher preparation (and development) from a critical pedagogy lens (e.g. Banegas & Gerlach 2021; Mojica & Castañeda-Peña 2021). However, there is still a predominance of research literature and practice that focuses on language teaching and learning from a context-knowledge perspective overlooking how English language education is implicated in (re)producing or transforming certain social norms such as those related to (a)gender and (a)sexual diversity.

While, on the one hand, the market offers books for the study of linguistics, grammar, and phonetics and phonology (i.e. the content of English language education), there are few to no books which can help teacher educators and (student) teachers design and deliver modules and lessons in ways that critically engage with the issues of (a)gender and (a)sexual diversity already embedded in them. On the other hand, the literature available on the intersection between language and gender and/or sexually diverse identities predominantly tends to focus on linguistics, sociological studies, literary enquiries or cultural studies that explore how gender and sexual diversity are performed and experienced in educational contexts (e.g. Paiz & Coda 2021; Pakuła 2021; Sauntson 2018). In these cases, (a)gender and (a)sexual diversity are explored in relation to broad concepts such as intersectionality or modern foreign languages rather than being situated in English language, literacy and literature-specific contexts that reveal the connections between language, meaning-making, identity and power. The particularities of the English language classroom and its role in confronting, negotiating and transforming relations of power and identity through language and literacy can often be left unexplored. This is a noticeable gap particularly when considering the relationship between language, literacy, identity and power as intrinsic to any English classroom. As a response to this niche, this edited volume attempts to provide readers with informed accounts of how teachers and teacher educators in English language education design, implement and navigate the slippery interconnections between subject-matter knowledge and identity in their particular contexts.

(A)gender and (A)sexual Diversity

What's gender got to do with English language teaching? This is perhaps a recurring question, and one that raises the issue of whether or not (a)gender and (a)sexual diversity is in fact a concern for English language, literacy and literature classrooms. Our position within this volume is: yes, this is certainly an issue that intersects with subject knowledge, pedagogy and the social impact of language and language education. Banegas, Jacovkis and Romiti (2020: 2), for example, make it clear that teacher education institutions 'are part of society and as such they are compelled to engage with the wider communities in which they are inserted'. However, what it means to be and do (a)gender and (a)sexuality can vary significantly in conceptualization, performance, representation, cultural appropriateness and material experiences across global contexts. This is perhaps further complicated by increasingly transnational and decolonial movements where differing perspectives might intermingle in the same physical or online spaces.

While this volume seeks to bring together some of these emerging and established voices on gender, criticality and English language teaching from across transnational perspectives, it is perhaps also vital that we unpack what we, as the editors, understand by a gender perspective:

> We all have a relationship with the notion of gender because we were ALL labelled at birth. Even if you are intersex, the doctor told your parents you were male or female and, from that moment on, a massive cartoon anvil of gender expectations landed on your head. (Dawson 2021: 18)

According to Dawson, as well as others in gender studies, queer theory, the broad range of feminisms and studies in masculinities, gender is a social construct that is typically conflated with sex (anatomical and physiological bodies) and sexuality (the presence or absence of desire and sexual attraction). That is, sex-gender-sexuality are often perceived as interlocked within a normative and linear relationship (Butler 2004, 2007). For example, female bodies are normatively perceived to necessitate femininity, which necessitates a heterosexual desire for male bodies in the Western world. Seeing the world through gender binaries, these normative and often hegemonic constructions of gender are only a small part of the story. Instead, there are multiple possibilities for thinking about and doing gender that often get marginalized, under- or misrepresented, or silenced altogether. Furthermore, postcolonial and non-Western perspectives offer a broader picture of (a)gender and (a)sexual possibilities.

These normative understandings are inherently (but not equally) oppressive to queer and heterosexual communities, cisgendered and transgendered communities, and (non-)conforming and non-binary communities alike. That is, how normativity circulates through discourse (Gee 1989) and discursive practice in and out of the classroom contributes to shaping public imagination, how gender is policed and regulated using heteronormative and heteropatriarchal 'ideals', and the kinds of representation we have access to (Govender 2018, 2019; Sunderland 2000). If English language teaching and learning is to better reflect the identities and experiences of teachers, learners and society at large, then practices of representing and talking about (a)gender diversity are necessary components of pedagogy. In these pedagogical repertoires, teachers and learners might foreground the active interrogation of how gender is constructed through different language practices, modes and genres, and the social and psychological effects of these practices.

It therefore becomes useful to note differences in gender identity, gender presentation or performance, and the discursive construction of gender through language and other semiotic modes. While gender broadly refers to those 'cultural meanings ascribed' (Wood & Eagly 2009: 109) to bodies, gender identity refers to whether or not, and perhaps how, those cultural meanings are taken up or transformed by individuals' understandings of themselves (Miller 2015). These understandings of self might then be made visible, or not, through various forms of gendered performance and/or (re)presentation, as individuals navigate personal, emotional, social, cultural, institutional, political, historical and other regulatory forces (Butler 2004; Connell 2005). Herein lies the role of power of English language and literacy education. By unpacking how heteronormativity, heteropatriarchy and cisnormativity become established as powerful forms of identity through discourse, as well as through an exploration of non-normative discursive representation, English language teachers and learners might then deconstruct and reconstruct gender in more socially just and empowering ways (Govender & Andrews 2021).

Take, for example, the experiences of poet, activist and performer Alok Vaid-Menon:

> I didn't have access to representation that looked like me from anywhere, and so I turned to the internet to find it and then recognized it was less about finding and more about creating. (Vaid-Menon cited in Lehner 2019: 58)

The lack of equitable and affirming representations of (a)gender and (a)sexually diverse people is not just a matter for cultural studies, gender studies, queer theorists and feminists. It is an educational and pedagogical matter that sits within the remit of educational policymakers, those in governance, school and higher education management, teachers, teacher educators and lecturers alike, and the children and young people that education is meant to serve. English language and literacy education is well-positioned to engage with issues of power, access, diversity and (re)design (Janks 2010) and build both teachers' and learners' capacity to produce texts that better represent the diverse lives they lead. Furthermore, how (a)gender identity intersects with (a)sexualities, race/ethnicity, language variety, ability and neurodiversity, class and socio-economic status, age, employment, faith and/or tradition, post- and decoloniality, and the many other dimensions of human experience (Hill Collins 2019) matter for the ways in which language and other sign systems might be harnessed to construct a more socially just and critical future.

Transnational Voices

In this volume, we discuss (a)gender and (a)sexuality diversity in English language education by bringing together experiences from transnational voices. We have adopted the notion of *transnationality* to account for deeper interrelational processes across situated lived experiences in the broad context of higher education. According to Mayhew (2015), transnationality is multifaceted and dynamic. For example, in the area of business, the term refers to international cooperation within and beyond those generated by nation-states, and it may entail working with neighbouring countries or within a region as countries and institutions share similar concerns or interests. While transnational approaches continue to emphasize the powerful role and power struggles between nation-states (Amelina, Boatcă, Bongaerts & Weiß 2021), in this volume we take a different angle as we do not seek to represent nation-states or global trends. On the contrary, we prioritize underrepresented voices, approaches and lived experiences.

We mobilize the term *transnationality* to refer to educators' actions, practices, contacts and beliefs that transcend national, cultural and ideological borders (Anzaldúa 2012; Francois 2016). In this sense, transnational educators may have migrated to other contexts for personal and professional reasons (e.g. a South African academic working in UK teacher education) and/or be involved in the teaching of English in contexts where the language does not play a dominant role in everyday life (e.g. an educator based in Uruguay teaching English, a

Welsh educator teaching English in Spain). As educators navigate the cultural geographies of transnationality and inhabit fluid transnational spaces, they contribute to a complex and multidirectional flow of cultural and socio-economic capital (Blunt 2007) which includes their lived experiences, positionalities and cognitions about what (English language) teacher education involves.

On the one hand, these transnational voices seek to integrate into the global conversations on English language teacher education. On the other hand, they do so by enacting locally responsive pedagogies that bring in differentiation to the learning experience. In this regard, their conceptualizations and practices around gender in education may differ as they have different context-responsive trajectories in relation to how gender inequality, inequity and (lack of) diversity are addressed in the wider systems of education, cultural practices and society.

As such, transnationality resonates with this volume's aim to value plurality: including the plurality of gender and sexual identity, presentation and performance, and discursive construction in and through English language teaching. From this poststructuralist viewpoint, meaning-making in the English language classroom thrives on harnessing difference and diversity as productive resources for (re)reading and (re)designing the world in more equitable and culturally sustainable ways. To end with Gloria Anzaldúa's (2012) words from *Borderlands/La Frontera: The New Mestiza*,

> At some point, on our way to a new consciousness, we will have to leave the opposite bank, the split between the two mortal combatants somehow healed so that we are on both shores at once and, at once, see through serpent and eagle eyes. Or perhaps we will decide to disengage from the dominant culture, write it off altogether as a lost cause, and cross the border into a wholly new and separate territory. Or we might go another route. The possibilities are numerous once we decide to act and not react. (100–1)

Structure of the Book

The chapters in this edited volume are organized into three parts: (1) Teaching for gender and sexuality diversity, (2) Navigating gender and sexuality diversity and (3) Interrogating resources for gender and sexuality diversity. The sections represent three interdependent areas of inquiry: how educators design pedagogies and curriculums around gender and sexual diversity; how students and teachers navigate issues of gender and sexual diversity in practice; and how issues of gender and sexual diversity emerge in the materials for teaching and learning English. All the chapters lie at the intersection of research-driven practice and practice-driven research. Readers will notice that some authors use previously gathered data (e.g. Chapter 11) or new data sets (e.g. Chapter 12).

In Chapter 1, Andrews and Govender draw on autoethnographic methods to analyze how they enact a queer critical literacies approach in their UK- and South African-based initial teacher education programmes. In their sharing and discussion of critical moments in English language and literacy education, they unpack the queer politics of Johannesburg and Glasgow and reflect on how their contexts of working and living influence their practice.

In Chapter 2, Romiti and Smith describe a collaborative online international project that brought together higher education students in Vancouver (Canada) and Buenos Aires (Argentina). The project concentrated on the use of the arts as a form of social change to understand gender in the Americas. In the chapter, the authors discuss students' coursework and insights and put forward a series of pedagogical suggestions.

In Chapter 3, Valente explores the mediation of picturebooks with gender-queer characters in the context of primary English language teaching. Drawing on critical visual literacy and deep reading approaches as key theoretical underpinnings, the chapter demonstrates how picturebooks enable children to discover gender diversities in ways which are congruent with their affective and linguistic needs as primary learners of English around the world.

In Chapter 4, Canale draws on ethnographic data to describe a teacher's journey on introducing issues of heteronormativity in her English language class with teenage learners in Montevideo, Uruguay. The chapter highlights the complex dynamics between imposed heteronormativity and teacher and learners' attempts to negotiate social reality. Implications show the importance of education as civic engagement by addressing language learning as a space/process for defying heteronormativity.

In Chapter 5, Kutuk takes a quantitative approach to examine whether the negative stereotype that women are better at English language learning than men had an impact on a group of Turkish men learners' English listening performance through their self-efficacy and anxiety. As expected by the author, when compared to the control group, the participants in the two experimental groups performed worse. The findings suggest that gender stereotype threat might influence men's English listening performance.

In Chapter 6, Cao explores Chinese, cisgender female, bisexual, international student's English learning experiences in her three dating relationships in

Canada. Combining the theoretical frameworks of legitimate peripheral participation and language ideology, the author analyzes how the participant's access to English learning and identity construction was critically shaped by heteropatriarchy and the ideologies of linguistic nationalism and standard English in dating practices.

In Chapter 7, Huang examines Taiwan-based students' multimodal self-representation regarding gender and sexuality in a series of English language learning activities. Findings show that the interplay between the visual and linguistic modes contributed to more equal power relations for the students by speaking back to hegemonic narratives and reconstructing their identities. The chapter exemplifies the contributions of multiple modes and media to the accomplishment of a critical perspective through interactivity and hypertextuality.

In Chapter 8, Alansari problematizes the act of localizing global English language teaching textbooks from a gender perspective in the context of Saudi Arabia. The author compares the multimodal representations of human participants in the global, regional (Middle East) and local editions of one specific textbook series. Through a multimodal analysis, the author discusses what it means to be a woman and a man in different settings and according to specific values and cultural expectations.

In Chapter 9, Richards discusses the role that teaching resources play in language education. The chapter reports on a small-scale study into representations of gender and sexuality in a sample of materials and interviews conducted with teachers. It addresses the question of where educational materials are now in relation to issues of gender and sexual identity in English language education.

In Chapter 10, Gerlach draws on his experience as a teacher educator in Germany to explore his role in the training of future English language teachers and how his agency may challenge norms and structures. By means of a reanalysis of an empirical, reconstructive study on practices of language teacher educators, the chapter shows how fit or non-fit trainee teachers enable or prevent the addressing of critical perspectives.

In Chapter 11, Rahman and Haque investigate gender diversity and online English language teaching during the Covid-19 pandemic in Bangladesh. The study employs an interview-based qualitative research method to address a twofold aim: (1) to investigate the gender issues in the way male and female teachers use digital space for the purpose of teaching English where they have access to the same technology, and (2) to illustrate gender issues in online English teaching practices.

In Chapter 12, Pawelczyk brings together the three parts in which the volume is divided. The author discusses the main takeaways from each chapter and puts forward insightful ideas about the possible ways in which (a)gender and (a)sexual diversity in English language education can move forward.

On behalf of the contributors and ourselves as editors, we hope that the research-informed practices and practice-oriented studies included in this volume trigger further developments and initiatives at the levels of curriculum, policy, pedagogy and research. The volume, we believe, illustrates different trajectories as we wish to represent how educators around the world have embraced/started to approach gender and sexuality in English language education. We would like to take this opportunity to thank Maria Brauzzi from Bloomsbury and the reviewers who provided helpful feedback as we worked on the volume proposal and the book itself.

1

Queer Critical Literacies and Initial Teacher Education: Transnational Moments

Grant Andrews and Navan Govender

Introduction

Gender and sexuality diversity are still considered controversial topics in many places. Education, particularly, has been a site of heated debate about the 'appropriateness' of curricula and classroom discussions that include critical reflections on gender and sexuality. Schools and higher education institutions in many countries are characterized by heterosexist pedagogical approaches that erase, devalue or actively oppress the experiences and lived realities of queer people (see, for instance, LGBT Youth Scotland 2018 and OUT LGBT Wellbeing 2016). A queer critical literacies (QCL) approach (Govender & Andrews 2021) challenges heterosexism by promoting critical analysis and reflection on discourses and representations of gender and sexuality. QCL brings diverse representations into classrooms where these were predominantly (actively or unconsciously) excluded before, enables readings of texts that recognize and validate (a)gender and (a)sexual diversity, and critically confronts the heterosexism inherent in dominant discourses in societies that inform the production and reception of texts. QCL, like critical literacies more broadly, has a social justice agenda that seeks to transform societies through pedagogical approaches that build consciousness of systems of domination, access, diversity and design (Janks 2010).

However, coherent frameworks for QCL are still emerging (Govender & Andrews 2021). Educators are still grappling with how to approach (a)gender and (a)sexuality diversity in meaningful and transformative ways, especially in societies with widespread homophobia. The authors of this chapter work in initial teacher education (ITE) at universities in Johannesburg, South Africa, and Glasgow, Scotland, and we have both incorporated QCL in different ways in our courses. Our approaches to QCL have been influenced by sociopolitical factors including the histories of queer rights in our respective contexts. In this chapter, we use autoethnographic research methods (Adams & Holman Jones 2011) to reflect on courses and lessons where we incorporate QCL into ITE. This, in many ways, is reflected in the queer border crossings we make from reflecting on processes of teaching and learning, to personal and cultural experiences, to emotional tensions tied to ways of doing QCL in teacher education. First, we present brief comments about our positionality as educators and discuss policies and historical factors that influence the teaching of QCL in Johannesburg and Glasgow. Second, we unpack the QCL approach, explain its utility in diverse contexts and describe the autoethnographic method employed in this chapter. We then discuss key moments in our teaching and how we incorporated QCL in our classrooms. We conclude the chapter by reflecting on these transnational approaches and how they reflect the context-specific ways that QCL might be brought into ITE. We argue that QCL is important in ITE in diverse global contexts because teachers can play a role in transforming school contexts and challenging heterosexism and queerphobia, if they are empowered to teach in ways that interrupt heteronormativity (Martino & Cumming-Potvin 2016).

Letters to Our Readers

Greetings from Johannesburg, South Africa (Grant Andrews)

I work as a lecturer at a school of education at a major university in South Africa. Many of my courses focus on topics of gender and sexuality, and I teach in ways that encourage critical thought around these topics and on the role that my students will play in challenging harmful and oppressive ideologies when they become teachers.

South Africa was the first country in the world to explicitly enshrine protections for gender and sexual minority groups in its constitution in 1996. LGBTQ rights activists were actively involved with national politics during the transition from apartheid, advocating for greater legal protections (Carolin & Frenkel 2019) that eventually led the country to legalize same-sex marriage in 2006, only the fifth country to do so worldwide (Vincent & Howell 2014). South Africa is still one of the very few countries in Africa where protections exist for LGBTQ people, whereas the majority of African countries still criminalize same-sex sexualities or acts, with some nations punishing homosexuality with life in prison or even death (Msibi 2011). Thus, South Africa is often praised as a leader in LGBTQ rights on the continent.

However, even as social and political gains have been made after the end of apartheid, attitudes are still largely conservative and queerphobic among various groups, and there is 'an enormous gulf between constitutional protections on the one hand, and the violence and discrimination experienced by many South African gay and lesbian citizens on a day-to-day basis' (Vincent & Howell 2014: 473). South Africa is a country with rampant violence. For queer people, violence and 'corrective rape' – where queer people are raped in the belief that this will 'cure' them of their same-sex attraction or non-normative gender expression – are common occurrences, particularly affecting Black lesbian women in rural or township areas (Koraan & Geduld 2015). In addition, homophobic discourses in the country are common, framing same-sex sexualities as '"[u]nnatural", "unAfrican" and "unGodly"' (Vincent & Howell 2014: 475).

In educational spaces, attitudes towards sexuality are similarly conservative. In 2019, the Department of Basic Education announced that the country would expand comprehensive sexuality education (CSE) in schools, beginning at grade 4. This announcement was met with a moral furore by religious and civic groups, as well as by many parents and teachers. Chaskalson et al. (2019: n.p.) explain that initiatives like the expansion of CSE sought to 'provide adolescents and young people with knowledge, skills and efficacies to make informed decisions and positive lifestyle choices regarding sex and sexuality'. However, the furore that followed demonstrated how South African society is largely still conservative around issues of sex and sexuality despite progressive policies. One of the political parties in South Africa, the African Christian Democratic Party (ACDP), staged marches to government offices as they claimed the curriculum 'encourages children to engage in oral, anal, homo and heterosexual practices, among other horrific sexual teachings' (quoted in Chaskalson et al. 2019: n.p.). The discourses surrounding the anti-CSE protests were similar to those found in anti-LGBT rights circles in South Africa, including accusations that the curriculum is a Western import and erases 'African culture', and blatant homophobia and transphobia in anti-CSE online groups (Chaskalson et al. 2019).

Studies in South African schools demonstrate widespread homophobic violence and discrimination on the part of students, teachers and community members. Dennis Francis, in his review of literature on school experiences of LGBT youth (2017), notes that multiple studies across provinces demonstrated that 'schools perpetuated and reinforced social prejudices and discrimination toward LGBT learners' and 'LGBT youth are victimized and harassed and yet lack the protection and support of teachers and school leaders' (6). A national survey conducted by OUT LGBT Well-being (2016) showed that among other harms, young people reported the following forms of discrimination and violence while they were at school:

1. 55 per cent of LGBT youth experienced verbal insults in schools;
2. 35 per cent were threatened with physical violence;
3. 18 per cent experienced physical violence such as being 'punched, hit, kicked or beaten';
4. 11 per cent had been sexually abused or raped while at school.

The research indicates that schools in South Africa are generally unsafe spaces for queer people. A QCL approach can equip teachers and learners to consider the ways that ideologies might be reproduced through school curricula, and offers a framework for critically engaging with questions of gender and sexuality in language and texts. The QCL approach also challenges dominant discourses around gender and sexuality diversity in South Africa.

Greetings from Glasgow, Scotland (Navan Govender)

As an early career academic in the field of applied language, literacy and literature education, and with a particular interest in critical literacies, I am drawn to the ways in which both communication and ways of communicating are intrinsically connected to power, identity and ideology. As a queer cisman of South Asian heritage, having grown up in South Africa, and now living and working in Scotland, the politics of queer identities and cultures has come to affect my work in research and teaching. Living and working across national, continental and cultural boundaries also revealed the broad range of politics, identities, cultures and possibilities in (a)gender and (a)sexual diversity.

Recent policy developments in Scotland have sought to position the country as a progressive nation, despite the increasing conservatism in Westminster, and the UK more broadly, and current rule of the Conservative Party in parliament. This is particularly relevant for issues related to (a)gender and (a)sexual diversity. For instance, in 2018 the Scottish Government announced that it would implement LGBT-inclusion in its national curriculum for all state schools (Stone & Farrar 2021). Started in 2015 by the Scottish Government's LGBTI Inclusive Education Working Group, and then taken on at the end of 2018 by the LGBTI Inclusive Education Implementation Group, the new educational policy shift sits within a wider policy context of health and wellbeing in the Curriculum for Excellence, which includes Getting It Right For Every Child (GIRFEC), the Early Years Framework, children's rights and the Building Safer Communities programme which collectively contribute towards the Government's aim of making Scotland the best place in the world to grow up. (Scottish Government 2019)

Such a move to situate (a)gender and (a)sexual diversity in mainstream, state schooling also builds on a recent history of inclusive policy shifts in Scotland and the UK more broadly: from the legalization of same-gender marriage across England, Wales and Scotland, and the passing of the Equality Act 2010; to the LGBT Action Plan initiated in 2018, and growing pots of educational resources for doing LGBT-inclusive education by Scotland's Time for Inclusive Education (TIE) campaign and LGBT Youth Scotland.

Despite these big-P Political (Janks 2010) changes in legislature, the experiences of (a)gender and (a)sexually diverse folx in Scotland demonstrate a lack of material and cultural change. Consider the following statistics from LGBT Youth Scotland's (2018: 5) survey, *Life in Scotland for LGBT Young People*:

1. 46 per cent of LGBT young people and half (53 per cent) of transgender young people rated their school experience as 'bad'.
2. 71 per cent of LGBT young people experienced bullying in school on the grounds of being LGBT. This is a rise from 69 per cent in 2012 and 60 per cent in 2007.
3. 82 per cent of transgender young people experienced bullying in school on the grounds of their gender identity. This has risen from 77 per cent in 2012.
4. Transgender young people are now more likely than they were in 2012 to rate their university experience as 'good', with an increase from 37 per cent to 60 per cent.
5. 9 per cent of LGBT young people and 27 per cent of transgender young people left education as a result of homophobia, biphobia and transphobia in the learning environment.

Schools, it would seem, continue to be sites of symbolic, emotional and physical violence.

While policy shifts have sought to include (a)gender and (a)sexual diversity in the curriculum, the resources predominantly place queer issues, identities, cultures and so on outside of the main disciplinary subjects in schools. That is, the available resources do not necessarily support teachers and learners to embed (a)gender and (a)sexual diversity into their curricula and pedagogies, but instead act as springboards for *discussing* queer politics and people or making them visible through posters. While discussion may bring queer issues into the classroom, moves towards action and transformation are vital for ensuring that inclusivity is not just superficial (Govender & Andrews 2021; Kumashiro 2002). Therefore,

> The extent to which the LGBT Action Plan [and other related policies in Scotland] represents shifts beyond policy status quo is questionable, with some areas – such as the experiences of LGBTQI+ people seeking asylum, LGBTQI+ rights post-Brexit, and pressing equality issues in devolved UK states – completely excluded, thus arguably reproducing existing absences, silences and enduring 'sticking points' in policy and politics. (Lawrence & Taylor 2020: 3)

A Framework for QCL

The QCL approach draws from the fields of queer studies and critical literacies (Govender & Andrews 2021). It provides a framework for a teaching approach that challenges dominant norms and discourses of gender and sexuality, and allows for students and educators to question how these discourses affect ways of knowing and engaging with their worlds and themselves. A QCL approach recognizes that texts and bodies are situated within matrices of power that favour dominant groups, particularly through enforcing ideologies of heterosexism, cisgenderism and patriarchy. These ideologies give legitimacy to particular expressions and experiences of gender and sexuality, and disparage, invisibilize or delegitimize diverse (a)gender and (a)sexual identities and epistemologies; for example, heterosexism sees heterosexuality as the ideal and only legitimate form of sexuality, and cisgenderism sees only cisgender identities as valid or 'normal'. Thus, the experiences of straight, cisgender people (particularly males) are often overrepresented in everyday texts, and these experiences are naturalized in ways that marginalize gay, bi, trans, asexual, nonbinary and/or queer people, among other forms of gender and sexuality diversity.

For example, very few classroom texts, including prescribed literature or textbooks in formal school curricula, represent LGBTQI+ identities, and even when these identities are represented, they are often shown in ways that might favour binary definitions of gender or represent diverse sexuality as 'abnormal' (DePalma 2016). QCL can challenge these representations and the discourses that inform them, as well as questioning how existing representations and discourses of (a)gender and (a)sexuality might influence the way we see ourselves and others.

The term *queer* in the concept QCL has two interconnected meanings: first, *queer* is used as an adjective to describe people with non-normative gender and sexual identities and/or those who identify with a label under the LGBTQI+ umbrella (Andrews 2019); and second, *queer* is used as a verb to describe the process of 'interrupting heteronormativity' (Martino & Cumming-Potvin 2016) and cisnormativity. This process includes challenging dominant epistemologies and ideologies that exclude those from gender and sexual minority groups from recognition, representation and legitimacy in spaces like schools, everyday texts and political discourse. A part of this process is to 'denaturalize' heterosexuality and cisgender identities, to demonstrate how these sexual and gender identities are constructed in systems of power, and to show how gender expression, bodies and intimacies are policed and regulated; in other words, 'the criteria defining recognizability and respectability are examined and questioned' (DePalma 2016: 836). QCL thus focuses on the normative discourses around gender and sexuality in order to challenge the assumption that particular bodies are linked to particular genders and sexualities.

This process of queering is appropriate for the field of critical literacies, and indeed has been an important part of how critical literacies operate in many settings. If critical literacies invite teachers and learners to 'analyze power and inequality in human relationships for the purpose of creating a more just world' (McClung 2018: 403), then settings that are queerphobic and that reproduce normative discourses of gender and sexuality call for greater inclusion of QCL. Schools and universities are important spaces to introduce approaches and materials that foster QCL as these spaces are seen as sites of legitimate knowledge making and are primary sites of formal learning. Engaging meaningfully with gender and sexuality, and situating these topics as legitimate and important in educational settings, can 'expose how the suppression and marginalization of diverse voices lead to significant epistemological shortcomings, impositions and the devaluing of certain types of knowledges including experiential knowledges of gender and love' (Govender & Andrews 2021).

Strategies for implementing QCL are still emerging, and we reflect on some of the moments in our practice of QCL to demonstrate the tensions and opportunities that can arise in this approach. In our framework for QCL (Govender & Andrews 2021), we blend four moves of critical literacies (identification, deconstruction, disruption and transformation) with forms of questioning that allow students

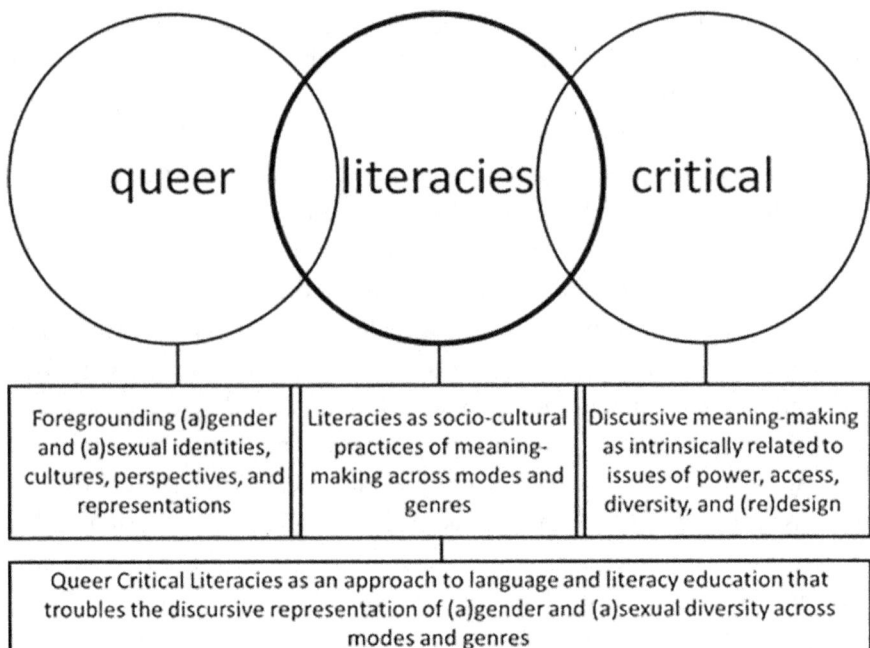

Figure 1.1 A framework for QCL (Govender & Andrews 2021).

to queer knowledges, texts and discourses. Students are able to see literacies (practices of meaning-making) as socio-culturally defined, and can begin to recognize how their ways of knowing, being and doing are impacted by systems of power within which they operate. Students build dispositions that are critical towards the norms, assumptions and knowledges of gender and sexuality that they might bring with them to the classroom. We work with multiple modes and genres to demonstrate the various ways discourses of gender and sexuality operate. Figure 1.1 illustrates how the QCL approach integrates the various theoretical and methodological approaches outlined.

Capturing Moments: Autoethnography and Teacher Education

> You tell these stories because you believe they do something in the world to create a little knowledge, a little humanity, a little room to live and move in and around the constraints and heartbreaks of culture and categories, identities and ideologies. (Adams & Holman Jones 2011: 109)

Adams and Holman Jones explore the interconnections between reflexivity, queer theory and autoethnography by telling the stories of their identities and classroom practice in higher education. Weaving narrative with theoretical and research-based enquiry, their work demonstrates the possibilities for navigating storied lives with academic rigour – and that the lines between these two are not always so clear-cut.

Autoethnography has been described as 'an approach to research and writing that seeks to describe and systematically analyze (graphy) personal experience (auto) in order to understand cultural experience (ethno)' (Ellis, Adams & Bochner 2011: 273). It is a methodological approach to doing research in the social sciences that bridges big-P and little-p politics (Janks 2010), revealing the nuanced connections between the personal or communal and the socio-cultural. Where big-P Politics refers to the larger (global) relations of power such as homophobic and transphobic policy-making, heterosexism or even racism in and out of LGBTQI+ communities, little-p politics refers to the power relations embedded in everyday interactions between folx, the words spoken in conversation and the ways in which lives play out day-to-day. By looking and relooking at everyday events, texts and interactions (what we call here, collectively, *moments*) through a critical lens, autoethnography enables us to critically reflect on, address and potentially transform dominant, often oppressive, ideologies of gender and sexual normativity.

Recent literature provides useful illustrations of the possibilities of queer and critical autoethnography. Javaid's (2020) exploration of their own experiences with the stigmatization of sexual violence in both their personal and professional (research) life is one example. Javaid considers how their own experiences with sexual violence had resulted in them 'becom[ing] invested in researching the topic of sexual violence against men to understand more about this neglected phenomenon' (2020: 1200), and how this in turn resulted in further experiences with the stigma. Taking up an autoethnographic approach thus enabled Javiad to capture those experiences with colleagues, research participants and others, and to 'transform [their] experiences of pain into knowledge' (2020: 1200).

Similarly, Govender (2017) and Hibbard (2020) draw on their own classroom experiences in higher education institutions as a means to grapple with their non-normative identities. In both cases, their stories of coming out to students, in curriculum content and in professional spaces, were intrinsic to their personal identities as queer and Trans* folx, respectively. While autoethnography provided a methodological tool for capturing these experiences, it was the critical lens through which they (re)evaluated those experiences that turned the everyday into knowledge for understanding identity, power, education, culture and ideology in context. Therefore,

> by looking at critical incidents and experiences (as texts) in relation to issues of power, teachers and students might interrogate the ways in which social and political power influence the everyday construction of individual identities, how individuals take up or resist hegemonic orders, and the ways in which individuals occupy positions of privilege and subordination at different times and in different spaces. (Govender 2017: 353)

Finally, Andrews's (2020) publication demonstrates the insight that a critical autoethnographic study provided in understanding the shifting forms and uses of disruption in higher education. In his study, Andrews captures moments of teaching and learning in ITE to trace and evaluate how

> disruptions that had once been coloured by unflinching homophobia and assertions of restrictive gender norms now became much more tentative, and other students were less apprehensive about engaging in conversations after these disruptions took place, even challenging the students who sought to silence critical conversations of gender and sexual identities and norms. (2020: 11)

This is paired with a deep consideration of the changing power dynamics taking place at the time in relation to ongoing student movements in South Africa and the call for decolonizing higher education.

Therefore, drawing on this notion of a critical and queer autoethnography, we present and analyse two moments from our careers in ITE. We describe each moment before drawing on a QCL framework to unpack how these moments relate to issues of power, ideology and meaning-making.

Johannesburg: Teaching Texts with African Queer Characters (Andrews)

In presenting courses at undergraduate and postgraduate levels to students, I include topics of gender and sexuality in multiple ways, ranging from text selection to examples used during classroom discussions. I incorporate these discussions due to my positionality as a gay man who has experienced discrimination and marginalization due to my sexuality and gender presentation. In addition, I present this material to preservice teachers because I recognize how stigma is reproduced in schools due to heterosexist curricula, social structures and attitudes of teachers and school leaders (Francis 2017), and thus the school environment can be important in addressing the widespread homophobia and transphobia in South Africa. I am purposeful in developing QCL in addition to the other competencies that my students require in order to be successful English teachers.

One of the courses where I introduce a variety of texts with queer themes is a fourth-year English course on marginalized stories. As this course usually is presented in the final year of study for students, they already have a wealth of knowledge from previous courses that dealt with identity, as well as a great deal of school-based teaching experience to draw on when analyzing the texts in my course. Many of these students have developed a strong sense of empathy for their learners' contexts, as they often have completed teaching experience in urban, township and rural schools and worked with diverse learners. This experience can contribute to classroom discussions, since many students bring examples of their own understandings of gender and sexuality diversity to the classroom or share experiences that they have had while teaching.

The fourth-year English group is usually around 80–120 students. In the course, I present a number of short stories and films, and I alternate texts from year to year as I find new relevant materials to present to students. While these texts discuss various types of marginalization based on race, culture and class in different societies, I purposely include texts that focus on gender and sexuality diversity each year. This is because many students are reluctant to discuss this topic openly in South African universities (Andrews 2020), and the texts offer me a way to challenge students' preconceptions while developing QCL. In previous years, I have included the film *The World Unseen* (2007) by British filmmaker Shamim Sarif, which represents two Indian–South African women in 1950s South Africa who develop a romantic relationship despite their oppressive surroundings. I have also used the short stories *How to Carry On* by South African author Sally-Ann Murray, focalizing a white middle-class mother who reflects on the experiences of her child who is presented as a trans male in the text, and *Jambula Tree* by Ugandan author Monica Arac de Nyeko, which explores two Black girls in a small Ugandan town who are surveilled and marginalized because of their same-sex relationship. In addition, I include a number of academic articles that speak about issues of gender and sexuality diversity in South African society and schooling.

My aim with presenting these texts to students and using a QCL approach is to develop their critical capacity around questions of diverse identities, particularly in contexts that they are familiar with. As these texts represent the realities of discrimination which gender and sexual minorities face in Africa, students usually reflect on culture and religion when we discuss these texts in class, and the topic of race is often raised, especially in confronting notions of homosexuality being 'unAfrican' (Vincent & Howell 2014: 475). Students have often felt comfortable to discuss their teaching experience at schools, such as explaining how they discussed sexuality in their classrooms and how they dealt with bullying of queer or gender nonconforming learners. Some students have even shared how they have personally experienced discrimination due to being queer, and have challenged students who expressed homophobic views in our class discussions. These interactions demonstrate how students related the topics to their own lives and to their social contexts. Students were able to reflect on how language, perspectives and ideologies influenced the ways they reacted to the texts under discussion. For example, some students were able to voice their challenges in finding the language to describe the gender-expansive child in Murray's short story, and in their essays at the end of the course, many students used more inclusive and affirming language. Many students also began to recognize that texts are not only produced in contexts but are also read differently in different contexts (Janks 2010).

Presenting these texts is a deliberate attempt to challenge the silence around queer people and their experiences in South Africa, and to 'interrupt' heteronormativity and cisnormativity by asserting the existence and validity of non-normative experiences (Martino & Cumming-Potvin 2016). I ask students to reflect on why some of them become so uncomfortable when working with texts with queer themes and characters, such as the tendency of many students to laugh when the two female-presenting protagonists of Sarif's film share a kiss. I also ask them to explore why texts like these are rarely taught in South African schools, and what this says about dominant ideologies in formal learning environments.

The final assignment for the course is an essay where students are asked to analyze and compare forms of marginalization in two of the texts, and also to consider how they would teach these texts or similar texts to learners in schools. This approach, and the use of critically reflective writing, could lead to 'identification (locating oneself in the content of the classroom) [… as well as] application (using the content of the classroom to reconsider one's own experiences)' (Govender 2019: 356). Due to common discourses of gender and sexuality diversity being '"[u]nnatural", "unAfrican" and "unGodly"' (Vincent & Howell 2014: 475), there is often discomfort around discussing these texts, and even some of the essays that students have submitted contained the sentiments that as teachers, they would 'set learners straight' (in other words, enforce hetero- and cisnormativity) if learners presented as queer. The work of QCL thus can lead to critical reflection about gender and sexuality, both within the individual and in relation to their societies, but is not necessarily transformative for every student.

Glasgow: Gender Constructions in Advertising (Govender)

In the English specialism for the Professional Graduate Diploma in Education (PGDE) at my university, I have incorporated the QCL framework as a means to engage students with critical literacies as an approach to deconstructing texts that represent (and conflate) gender and sexuality. To do this, the student teachers and I analyse a series of short advertisements, and then turn to the QCL pedagogical framework to reflect on the ways in which the texts were selected, sequenced and deconstructed, and the potential (re)design activities that might be imagined to get secondary learners to transform their thinking and practice. Due to the limited time that PGDE English students have to engage with English language, literacy and literature content and methodology in their diploma, it has become necessary to ensure that queer and other significant perspectives are embedded into the fabric of their teacher education provisions. The texts we use include (presented in order of use in class):

Text 1: Lynx (2006) *Billions*

https://www.youtube.com/watch?v=KWvs94CcYgo

As a normative text, this advertisement represents both gender confirming actors and heteronormativity. Female bodies are objectified and dehumanized while placing a single male body at the centre of the narrative.

Text 2: Old Spice (2010) *The Man Your Man Could Smell Like*

https://www.youtube.com/watch?v=owGykVbfgUE

This text represents another version of the normative but excludes women and gender-variant men entirely. The advertisement centres on a single, hypermasculine, heteronormative male body and narrative.

Text 3: Lynx (2017) *Find Your Magic*

https://www.youtube.com/watch?v=LZ4KNrCkDH0

This final text represents a relatively subversive representation of male bodies and masculinities by including a broader range of gender and sexual identities. However, as a mainstream advertisement, there are certain exclusions and (mis)representations that persist.

We view each advert in turn, pausing after each to discuss the main features of the text and the social issues they represent: from visual metaphors and innuendo, to frame position and word choice. We typically map these ideas on a whiteboard to track various students' contributions when unpacking the text. That is, we move from discussing the whole text (and first impressions) into identifying and discussing particular moments and film techniques in the text, and then trying to pull the threads together by returning to a discussion about the whole text and the discourses they contribute to. It is at the final stage that we begin to attend to the overarching critical question: Whose interests are served? Moving across the categories of questions from the QCL framework (namely: identification, deconstruction, disruption and transformation), we do multimodal critical discourse analysis (CDA) through conversation.

We follow this process for each of the texts. It is important to note that students invariably refer to the previous adverts. Comparison becomes vital for revealing the design choices employed, with each new advert revealing something about the previous one. Students' discussions begin to mix and intermingle which is represented by the criss-crossing lines on our mind maps on the whiteboard – the separate mind maps constructed for each advert become visibly interconnected, and intertextual, repeating and undoing ideas as we move through the lesson asking critical questions: What is the difference between how men and masculinities have been represented in each text? Where are women, and (how) are they included? What kinds of femininities make it into the texts, who does them and why does this matter? How have LGBTQI+ identities been represented, if at all, and how do we know?

Admittedly, these are relatively 'safe' texts (Govender 2015) that do not include queer intimacies or visibly subversive queer bodies. However, this is important to note as the students and I find that we have to look very carefully to spot the non-normative identities which are only represented in Text 3. On the one hand, this raises the question about my own (in)securities in presenting and using texts with queer intimacies. On the other hand, in using everyday texts that the students and I recognize and that reflect the Western society we inhabit, the process of having to search for non-normative gender and sexualities echoes our daily experiences and invisibilities (Govender 2019). When students do spot queer identities, such as the male dancer in heels or the same-sex/gender attraction hinted at in the record store, Text 3's seemingly inclusive approach to representation can then be troubled. Over and above this, issues of race/ethnicity, age, bodies and body-types, consumerism and language variety arise depending on what and who the students notice.

Turning from analysis to critical reflection, the students and I then consider the pedagogical significance of the lesson. Three main ideas have emerged over the years: (1) the role of critical text selection as a critical literacy practice, (2) sequencing as a practice of positioning and (3) CDA as a method of questioning for secondary English classrooms. The dimensions of description, interpretation and explanation provided by CDA (Fairclough 2001) therefore help to frame teachers' pedagogical decisions and question-making in critical ways.

We use the QCL pedagogical framework to help us think through these particular practices and issues. That is, we reflect on the selection, sequencing and processes of analysing the texts by considering whether and how these actions relate to QCL's processes of identification, deconstruction, disruption and transformation. We therefore also consider how teaching is a kind of design whereby we construct environments and (im)possibilities for engaging with difference and diversity – in this case, (a)gender and (a)sexual diversity.

While 'decisions about texts can have far-reaching consequences for skill development and even for secondary students' attitudes toward reading' (Watkins & Ostenson 2015: 246), critical text selection also sees those decisions as positioned and positioning (Janks 2010). That is, teachers inevitably play a gatekeeping function by making decisions about what content, whose stories, whose identities and what value systems (do not) make it into the classroom space. The questions we ask of the series of texts are the same questions we ask about the ways in which those texts have been used to do teaching and learning.

Similarly, the sequencing of texts does not happen by mistake. I have thought about what ideas and identities to reveal, and in what order. This has its affordances and limitations: I wanted to trouble how masculinities have been represented as well as our own assumptions about gender and sexuality when reading texts, but this reproduces practices of backgrounding women, Trans* identities, race/ethnicity and so on. By moving from Text 1 to Text 3, we begin to notice how patterns of representation have shifted in some ways and remained the same in other ways. We move from more normative representations of gender and sexuality towards more disruptive representations, all the while considering whether or not these changes have been disruptive enough. Sequencing, then, is vital because

> heteronormativity is pervasive, and maintains its ascendant position through the taken-for-granted repetition of norms in multiple texts [and therefore] teachers and students will need regular opportunities to critically analyse gender and sexuality norms across a range of texts and contexts. (Sandretto 2018: 8)

By embedding critical analysis in everyday practice and curriculum content, and using this model to inform questions (and their responses) we are able to move from text, to (intended) meaning, to social context (Fairclough 2001; Govender 2018; Janks 2010; Rogers & Mosley Wetzel 2014). This, then, puts us in a position to (re)imagine more socially just futures.

Transnational Approaches to QCL

The framework we present calls for adaptive approaches that consider processes of production and reception of texts in educators' specific sociopolitical contexts, and that are sensitive to the particular backgrounds and experiences of students. Based on our different contexts, we approached QCL in ways that would tap into the affordances of our unique student bodies and social settings. These approaches demonstrate the ways that QCL can be incorporated into ITE to engage with the unique backgrounds, perspectives and experiential knowledge that students bring to classrooms in order to participate in critical discussions of representations and identities. As the goal of QCL is to 'trouble the discursive representation of (a)gender and (a)sexual diversity across modes and genres' (Govender & Andrews 2021) in ways that are accessible to a range of educational levels, both authors included texts that represent diverse gender and sexual identities. We taught these texts in ways that could create consciousness in students about how heterosexism and cisgenderism not only inform the production of everyday texts and how texts are selected in educational spaces, but also impact on the way students engage with texts that they encounter. This diversity elicited critical conversations about which identities are represented in various modes, from advertising to short stories and films about African queer characters. This allowed 'the criteria defining recognizability and respectability [to be] examined and questioned' (DePalma 2016: 836).

The most significant factor informing how we approach our different courses is the socio-cultural settings we teach in. As the course in the first example is taught in Johannesburg, with common discourses of homosexuality being unAfrican (even from public figures and politicians) and widespread homophobic and transphobic violence, there was an imperative to present the realities of violence and discrimination in the QCL classroom. As these forms of violence are also widely experienced in schools (see OUT LGBT Well-being 2016), the students' roles as future teachers were troubled through the inclusion of critical readings on heterosexism in school environments (including Francis 2017). The author is also deliberate about choosing texts that represent queer people of diverse *racial* identities, especially in light of discourses that homosexuality is a Western 'import' into Africa. The discussions were often heated, with deeply personal reflections from some students, and others showing resistance to discussing the topics.

For the course taught in Glasgow, the students' contexts and experiences are very different, and more nuanced conversations on representations become possible. Social attitudes and public discourses can be seemingly more accepting of queer people in Glasgow, and thus students might be more familiar with representations of diverse identities. However, what is termed as LGBT-inclusive education in Scotland risks being situated outside of specific subject areas, being relegated to renewed policies and practices in Relationships, Sexual Health and Parenthood (RSHP) (Education Scotland 2019) that are implemented as separate health and well-being initiatives at schools under the guise of cross-curricular work. Teacher education and continuous professional development programmes therefore need to consider how LGBT-inclusive education, and wider (a)gender and (a)sexual diversity, fit into the everyday practices of curriculum design and praxis of teachers (Stone & Farrar 2021).

The QCL approach in this course therefore attempted to situate QCL in the English subject area by focusing on critical analysis of specific textual elements that reflected limiting discourses of gender and sexuality. The selection and sequencing of texts scaffolded a gradual recognition of how gender is constructed through different modes and how it is implicated in dominant understandings of sexuality, and allowed students to recognize disruptive representations in order to challenge dominant ideologies. The representations of men and masculinities in the various advertisements demonstrate how concepts of gender are socially constructed, and how pervasive and normalized heterosexism and cisgenderism are.

This example therefore also illustrates how the work of critical and inclusive pedagogies is not yet completed, despite increasing rhetoric and public discourses of hyperinclusivity (Govender 2019; Güthenke & Holmes 2018). Glasgow, and Scotland at large, is still a context where queer inclusion is met with public vitriol. For example, the TIE campaign continues to receive backlash for their LGBT-inclusive education progress, where the 'reoccurring theme among the responses was to conflate homosexuality with paedophilia and child abuse, and to compare the teaching of gay, bisexual, lesbian and transgender issues in schools to child-grooming and the promotion of pornography' (The Glasgow Guardian 2020: n.p.). QCL can provide a framework for transforming this.

These approaches to QCL are important in ITE because queer or gender nonconforming learners are often victimized within school spaces in contexts in the West and in Africa. Our transnational approaches to QCL demonstrate that students in these very different spaces can become more conscious of how texts interact with dominant discourses in context, and how this might shape social relations. This chapter has demonstrated how different approaches can be taken in contextually relevant ways in order to reach the aims of QCL. Our autoethnographic reflections on these approaches show how the educator's positionality is also an important factor in the QCL teaching environment.

Questions for Change

Consider a course or unit of work that you teach:

1. To what extent do the texts you use represent normative gender and sexual identities and experiences?
2. How might a QCL pedagogical framework enable you and your students to trouble these normative representations by
   a. identifying and deconstructing how normativity has been constructed in those texts (i.e. the grammar of power);
   b. disrupting normative representations by exploring subversive texts and alternative representations from queer and nonconforming perspectives (i.e. the grammar of subversion); and
   c. transforming representation and language/literacy practice by engaging students in the production of texts from critical, inclusive and queer perspectives?

2

An Intercultural Experience with a Gender Perspective between Post-secondary Students from Argentina and Canada

Antonella Romiti and Jessie Smith

Introduction

In July 2019, faculty members Antonella Romiti, instructor of Academic Reading Comprehension in English (ARCE) at the Universidad Nacional de General Sarmiento (UNGS), Buenos Aires, Argentina, and Jessie Smith, coordinator of the Latin American Studies programme at Langara College, Vancouver, Canada, met and decided to incorporate a Collaborative Online International Learning (COIL) project[1] into their courses. The central idea of COIL is for post-secondary students in two different institutions to collaborate (in small groups with members from both institutions) on a course assignment that allows them to practise intercultural competencies in an online environment.

Framed in exploratory practice, the innovation described in this chapter emerged from our attempt to (a) include a gender perspective in the Argentine English as a foreign language (EFL) class, and (b) enable students from Langara to have first-hand experience with Latin America. This served to boost motivation and genuine interaction among our post-secondary learners. We agreed to the inclusion of gender topics following a content-and-language-integrated learning (CLIL) approach for a period of six weeks.

Theoretical Framework

CLIL is often defined as a dual-focus approach through which curriculum content is taught through an additional language so that learners gain both content and language learning at the same time (Coyle, Hood & Marsh 2010). CLIL practitioners and research support the position that CLIL enhances motivation (Doiz, Lasagabaster & Sierra 2014), language learning, critical thinking skills and content learning (Coyle, Hood & Marsh 2010) and it benefits the development of cross-curricular aims. Due to the focus on integration, CLIL is usually configured as (a) a content-driven approach or (b) a language-driven approach. The first approach implies teaching a subject through an additional language, for example, teaching science or history (e.g. Lara Herrera 2015) in English. The second approach is adopted in EFL lessons in which English learning is contextualized in curriculum to increase authenticity of purpose and topics (Banegas 2013). In view of this, CLIL may improve the teaching of English through gender issues, and in so doing learners develop their proficiency in English to discuss matters that are critical and present in their daily lives, inside and outside their post-secondary environments.

In the case of our COIL project, the Canadian instructor adopted a content-driven approach because her main objective was to show how Latin Americans may use art as a powerful force for social change, using gender issues as a case study. The Argentine instructor adopted a language-driven CLIL approach since the subject was still English, yet it is mandatory to include a cross-curricular gender perspective in Argentine university education. This chapter describes our experience using CLIL to engage with feminism and its intersection with other gender-based theories.

In the field of English language education, Norton (2005) suggests that gender is not as an individual variable but rather as a 'complex system of social relations and discursive practices, constructed in local contexts' which include important facets of social identity as they interact with race, class, sexuality, (dis)ability, age and social status. Most importantly, Norton argues that it is crucial to understand that gender corresponds with learning environments, and should therefore be addressed properly in curricula as part of cross-curricular comprehensive sexuality education (CSE). Moreover, as defined by UNESCO (2019a), CSE should not be limited to sexuality as a biological trait; it should sit at the intersection of gender and identity and the effects that these have on all human activities such as personal rights, relationships, and work-related aspirations and practices.

Even though the twenty-first-century political and cultural agenda across the Americas has welcomed the rise of feminism, LGBTIQ+ and other key gender discussions, these may not be wholly reflected in post-secondary education curricula, where such topics are often invisibilized unless the students are taking specific courses related to gender. We noted how certain kinds of diversity sit within and without the mainstream and compulsory courses of post-secondary education. For example, students taking history degrees are often not taught the specifics of women's history, or when dealing with the history of First Nations peoples, students are not taught that such peoples comprehended sexuality and gender in more diverse ways than traditionally assigned by European societies. The concept of Two-Spirits, which is an indigenous umbrella term for naming a transgender person, is often blatantly invisibilized. This reinforces Western values that we are now living in more open societies due to the twenty-first-century understanding of gender and sexuality.

Darvin and Norton (2014) define investment in L2 learning as a critique of the monolithic notion of motivation, by which they understand that identities are fluid and changing and that 'a student may be a highly motivated learner, but may not be invested in the language practices of a given classroom if the practices are racist, sexist, or homophobic' (Darvin & Norton 2013). This provides strong evidence and a theoretical framing for discussing how, when and for what reasons language learners (including adult learners) become invested in their learning or not.

The role of motivation and engagement for successful learning has been widely discussed in L2 academic literature (Ashwin & McVitty 2015; Lawson & Lawson 2015; Mehdinezhad 2011). The concept of engagement includes effort, time on task and use of resources from a student point of view (Mehdinezhad 2011), or on socio-cultural factors, including a perceived sense of belonging, or lack thereof (Tinto 1973, 2012). Furthermore, Litwin (2016) discusses the role of spaces or activities free from evaluation in boosting students' learning. In this sense, it must be noted that the students in Canada were graded for participating in the project, and the final photo gallery was one of the required assignments for passing the course (further details on the courses below). Both instances together constituted an external type of learning motivation. The project was optional for the students in Argentina; therefore they were not graded. We can assume that their participation was more connected with an intrinsic and integrative motivation to learn more about the topic that was chosen, and to work with people from other countries in English.

Context of This Study

The UNGS is a fully state-run university located in Los Polvorines, a northwest suburb of Buenos Aires. In February of 2020 over 2,500 students were enrolled at UNGS; the majority were domestic students (95 per cent), though there were also students from other Latin American countries. All UNGS students are required to take at least two English courses as part of their degree. This project was carried out with a group of ARCE students from diverse undergraduate degrees ranging from information and technology, chemistry and history. Students taking ARCE courses show low proficiency in English at entry level, but gradually by levels two and three, most students manage to read 800–1,500 word academic texts successfully. Moreover, ARCE students often expect some level of practising other skills such as listening, speaking or writing, which made Romiti confident that students would be able to engage in different types of interaction with their Langaran counterparts.

Langara College is a community college located in South Vancouver. Langara is located on unceded Musqueam (First Nations) territory; the Musqueam honoured Langara with the name snəw̓eyəɬ leləm̓ (*sno-way-ith lay-lum*), the house of teachings. In the Spring of 2020 over 16,000 students were enrolled at Langara College. The majority (68 per cent) were domestic students and 31 per cent were international students. Langara is partially funded by the province of British Columbia – less than 40 per cent of the cost of running the College now, but decades ago the province covered 80 per cent. Today the College is primarily funded by tuition, especially international tuition, which is approximately six times higher than domestic tuition.

This COIL programme at Langara is embedded in the course Latin American Studies 1101: Latin American Cultural Perspectives. The 'Canadian' classroom was deeply diverse: there were only a handful of native English speakers in the class. The majority of the students were either native Spanish speakers (born in Canada or Latin America), or international students from (primarily) India, Bangladesh, Japan and the Netherlands. As such, in this chapter we do not refer to 'Canadian' students but 'Langaran' students because many of the students were not actually Canadian.[2]

After years of working in post-secondary institutions, we have gained a sense of the local institutional and student cultures. Langaran students tend to have career-oriented views of their time at college, as higher tuition and a higher cost of living suggest that they now face more pressures while studying than their counterparts one or two decades ago. Many international students in Canada are uniquely motivated to pass courses as they need two successful years of post-secondary education in order to apply for permanent residency, and therefore increasingly, students tend to focus more on grades and passing subjects rather than the intercultural learning experiences that the institution might offer. On the other hand, 80 per cent of UNGS students are first-generation university students, and most of them are full-time workers. Furthermore, some students become parents by age twenty-two to twenty-four, therefore study time is usually viewed as a paced learning process. In our identity as instructor-researchers, we needed to be very aware of the substantial differences presented within each group in order to carry out our project in a sensible, realistic way.

Collaborative Project Building

Since 2019, Law 27.499, usually called the Micaela Law,[3] is mandatory at university in Argentina. The law establishes compulsory training on gender rights and violence for all people who work in public service at all levels and hierarchies in Argentina. Given that Romiti's course is on English for academic purposes, with a CLIL approach to L2 education, and her course's materials are embedded with a gender perspective due to the implementation of this law, she taught English through indigenous people's history in Argentina and Canada, and indigenous women's history, in particular. For example, Romiti explored North American Indigenous views on sexuality that include Two-Spirit people, and the struggle they face to have other people acknowledge their particular gender points of view. Smith was impressed by the fact that professors at UNGS get credits for including a gender analysis in their courses; this is unheard of in Canadian academia.

Smith's course, on the other hand, is on how Latin Americans may use the arts for social change. The topic of gender and sexual orientation and art for social change was the space where our two courses met. Once we landed on this commonality, we built the COIL assignments together, keeping in mind the needs of both classes to muster their way through communication across time zones, cultures and languages.

We both started by working with our individual classes, introducing gender and sexual education issues in the Americas. Our main objectives were threefold:

1. that the students engage in the topic of arts for social change with a gender perspective;
2. that the students participate in an enriching and interesting intercultural experience mediated by technology;

3. that the students acquire skills to use digital tools to collaborate internationally and carry out a metacognitive reflection about the learning of foreign languages in each context.

The UNGS students worked on a survey with questions regarding their experience (or lack thereof) with CSE during their primary and high school years. The Langara students began to engage in these issues by reading, discussing and analysing the gender and LGBTIQ+ chapters in *Voices of Latin America: Social Movements and the New Activism* (Gatehouse 2019). We then created five groups of about nine students per group (four/five students per country, split relatively equally by gender identity). In forming the groups we considered linguistic, academic and technical skills in order to enhance the chances of strong communication and rich interaction in each group.

Communication and Engagement

Tuition, enrolment, retention and dropout rates are important factors to consider when analysing motivation in post-secondary systems, and when creating viable projects for students. While the national dropout rates in Canadian post-secondary institutions are average compared with the rest of world (30 per cent), Argentinian universities have a very high national dropout rate (65–70 per cent) even when most universities are fully state funded (Ezcurra 2011). Tinto (2012) warns about the *revolving door effect* by which students begin post-secondary education but cannot continue due to a series of convergent factors, such as unequal high school access, among others.[4]

As engagement theory suggests, engagement and working with authentic materials and for an authentic audience can help create a sense of belonging (Gilmore 2007). Unlike the lack of interest language learners often show when learning from a textbook, or producing written assignments for their teachers, our project with real people and deadlines gave a unique incentive. There is nothing like *needing to communicate* to force the issue. In this instance, *everyone* involved was in the same boat to some degree. The CLIL approach and the international nature of the project provided a genuine motivation for learning. This was reported by a UNGS student who was retaking the English course:

> With this project I was able to realize that maybe it wasn't that I was 'getting along poorly' with English, but that I hadn't had a real motivation to learn

before. In this case, I was very interested in the topic and learning about another culture, too. (Diego, UNGS)

Regarding communication, teachers can model and help students feel more at ease while communicating in a foreign language. Smith chose to occasionally communicate in Spanish with the Argentine students and tell them funny anecdotes about the mistakes she made while learning Spanish. This put her in the position of being the one feeling embarrassed about making a mistake and sounding foolish. While Smith has spent decades being the non-native Spanish speaker who makes mistakes, it was a different story to have to speak to students, from both a place of 'I am the teacher' and 'I too feel my heart pounding as I make this WhatsApp recording in another language.' It proved to be a powerful reminder of the bravery it takes to communicate for real in a second language. Smith felt the support of the Argentine students when they sent her emojis of hands clapping. Building an environment that might enable students to feel comfortable by engaging explicitly with their (and our) vulnerabilities to communicate made us wonder in what ways might one's vulnerabilities in language use help students 'get into' addressing possible vulnerabilities in gender (re)presentation, if at all. Argentine students (the ones who were actually taking an EFL class) seemed to lack confidence when speaking in English, but they expressed very clearly their views on gender issues in L1, so it seemed their difficulty was speaking in L2.

Moreover, as translingual theory suggests (Canagarajah 2013), the English spoken by multilingual speakers is not deficient, and English can be taken as a contact language where communicative success is not predicated on monolithic native speaker norms. In this sense, multilingual students often display an ample range of hybrid strategies to communicate. This might explain why the South Asian students from Langara encouraged some shy Argentine students to communicate in English; the South Asians were also communicating in L2, but have more experience doing so, and they could offer motivational words along the way.

The Langara students often reminded the Argentine students that in Canada everyone is used to communicating with multilingual speakers on a daily basis, as Canada receives thousands of migrants from non-English-speaking countries every year. The hope was that this knowledge would encourage the Argentines, who live in a relatively monolingual context, to overcome their fears of speaking English.

Group Work in a Cross-Cultural Environment

Our COIL project began in March 2020, days before the institutional shutdowns due to Covid-19. This was both a blessing and a curse. In some ways it made it more difficult to facilitate communication, and students and teachers alike struggled with academic and non-academic challenges and a unique level of stress. On the other hand, being thrown into a virtual environment with an opportunity to have meaningful collaboration with people across the globe who were dealing with the same issues arguably enriched our project. We had students reflect on what each group knew about the other country, and what aspects of their lives they had in common now that the pandemic had started.

We anticipated that it could be challenging for students to swoop in and understand complex issues in a national context and pull out key themes of such intimate, nationally specific issues without the full historical, social context. How can a student in Argentina understand indigenous women in Canada without understanding the broader historical context and concepts of unceded territory, the legacy of trauma brought on by residential schools, the Truth and Reconciliation Commission and the national conversations it has sparked? How can students in Canada fully grasp issues of femicide and Ni Una Menos in Argentina without understanding the role of the Catholic Church and *machismo*? How can students in Canada even begin to understand the nuances of the white elephant of the dictatorship (1976–83)?

On the first day the students interacted, we had each group reflect on different gender-based quotes that we used as the profile image for each WhatsApp group:

> When men are oppressed, it is a tragedy, when women are oppressed, it's tradition. (Letty Cottin Pogrebin)

> I'm not free while any woman is unfree even when her shackles are very different from my own. (Audre Lorde)

> The most common way people give up their power is by thinking they don't have any. (Alice Walker)

This discussion gave the students an engaging but gentle introduction to the course material and a chance for thoughtful reflection. It set the stage for future analysis by placing a foregrounded feminist take as a given. While students reported finding other courses boring and cumbersome as they flipped to online learning, this project was lit with energy and infused with enthusiasm, as we embarked on an analysis of gender issues that are part of national and international agendas.

First Step: Autobiographies and Portfolios

The first COIL assignment was a short autobiography of three hundred to four hundred words that was shared on a Padlet mural, a virtual platform, so that everyone could read and comment on each other's autobiographies. The second was a portfolio, in which the students shared their reflections, advances and difficulties when interacting with their international partners (which provided opportunities for metacultural and metacognitive reflection), as well as their reflections on gender issues in the Americas.

The choice of these assignments was based on a series of discursive genres that circulate at the academic level. From a didactic perspective, it is thought that the autobiography favours the acquisition of tools that provide opportunities for reading comprehension in English for UNGS students, adding the challenge of writing about one's own life. This assignment proved to be a powerful way to exemplify commonality across all of these mostly twenty-something students.

In a similar vein, a portfolio is a familiar pedagogical tool for many UNGS students, who use it in different university courses to reflect on their own learning and that of their classmates, and consider ways in which they could get their group back on track if they had gone astray. In the portfolio, the students were asked to reflect on diverse problems such as language barriers, and other cultural differences they faced when interacting as international groups, and the possible ways to overcome them. The portfolio also served as a travel companion to the moments of anxiety that can be caused by interaction with people from other latitudes and languages, especially when engaging in potentially uncomfortable topics that we do not often talk about, such as gender and LGBTIQ+ issues.

Norton and Pavlenko (2004) hold that autobiographies and portfolios can be 'transformative practices, which include but are not limited to reading and reflection, personal storytelling, journal writing, and discussions of scenarios'. These pieces also incorporate students' lived experiences and then 'locate their experiences and beliefs within larger social contexts'. Portfolios also helped us see how the project was landing for the students. As evidenced by these words from one portfolio, it also gave us a sense of what was working well:

> This experience has been absolutely mesmerizing and new to me. I feel so privileged to be able to be a part of such an innovative learning process where

multiple cultures have the opportunity to mesh into one virtual dimension of academic nurturing and creative collaboration. (Soledad, Langara)

Second Step: Choosing Project Topics for the Photo Galleries

Given the fact that we had less than six weeks to roll out this project, we gave students specific project topics from which to choose. The following is the list of topics the students chose:

- Compare and contrast LGBTIQ+ Rights in Argentina and Canada
- Femicide in the Americas
- Abortion Rights Compared: Argentina and Canada
- *Me Too* and *Ni una Menos* from Canada to Argentina
- Indigenous Women of the Americas Under Attack

The groups then engaged in a six-week process of creating their photo gallery. They started by choosing twelve to fifteen photos, which were later accompanied by student analysis of how each photo served to bolster and illuminate, in a visual way, the key arguments the students wanted to make regarding their selected topic. This part was the bulk of our project and research as it required a great amount of asynchronous work, exchanges, messages and online meetings where communication and discussion around gender took place.

Third Step: Real-Life Learning through Current Topics

As mentioned earlier, the connection between authentic materials, authenticity, the use of real life for learning and motivation in L2 learning has been thoroughly studied (Gilmore 2007; Litwin 2016; Tinto 1992) since working with current topics can empower group work. In the project, the students engaged in a rich debate over the definition of the term 'femicide' regarding the situation of Argentine actress Luisana Lopilato and her Canadian husband Michael Bublé. While our project was in progress, videos circulated of the singer elbowing his wife and other forms of aggression.[5] The debate focused on whether it could be taken as violent treatment (domestic violence) or as a type of 'couple's code', which implies physical contact in a playful manner in public.

Using a violence-o-meter (a traffic light scheme that measures the different ways in which violence can escalate from harsh words, to lying, to hitting and eventually up to murder), the students engaged in a debate over how to identify different patterns of violence. Though some students still found it hard to identify some of Bublé's behaviours as violent, they realized that gender violence is often (or used to be) associated with full femicide, as if there was nothing before or in between. Moreover, the students discovered how little coverage the controversy over Bublé and Lopilato received in Canadian media relative to how much it received in Argentina. While in Argentina the six major printed newspapers quickly published articles echoing Lopilato's followers' complaints and exposing the domestic violence, the Canadian major newspapers published short articles stating that Lopilato stood up to her husband, and these few articles were published almost a week after the Argentine press had covered the situation. Was this because the issue of femicide is less understood in Canada than in Argentina? Was it because Bublé is a beloved, white man of privilege that the press was unwilling to expose? Was it because Lopilato is a woman and a migrant in Canadian society? Or was it a combination of many factors?

Discussions also included thinking about how to help victims of violence, particularly those who are migrants and live far away from their family and friends (such as the case with Lopilato, who currently lives in Vancouver with Bublé). By using the violence-o-meter, students finally agreed that it was abuse, and even made a collage with the different moments where Bublé's aggression seemed to escalate. Also, some Argentinian students suggested that had the couple been living in Buenos Aires, most probably *escraches*, exposure protests, would have taken place in front of their house to expose Bublé's aggression, as often happens in Argentina.[6]

In terms of literacy and interculturality, this is perhaps an example of how 'new' genres for making meaning emerge through intercultural exchange. Intercultural learning of this nature enhances understanding of gender issues. Only the Argentine or the Canadian perspectives on the five topics chosen would have limited the depth of understanding, but by combining the collective experiences, students learned more.

Learning Core Gender Concepts

As the groups worked together, we realized that different students had different ideas about core concepts regarding gender issues, such as the meaning of femicide and the definition of the LGBTIQ+ community. For example, a student from Argentina found a 2017 newspaper that portrayed a femicide in Argentina and a van attack in Canada on the front page. The student immediately noticed:

> The news item about an 'accident' in Canada on the front page and on the side, very small, the news about a femicide at Nordelta. I was outraged that a femicide was presented in a box on the side almost as if it didn't matter, but I also found it interesting to show the place it occupied in the cover. (Nadia, UNGS)

One dictionary defines femicide as 'the gender-based murder of a woman or girl by a man' (Merriam-Webster 2021). However, the UNGS and Langara students evidenced different conceptions of the term 'femicide' and different understandings emerged. From the same newspaper cover another unexpected controversy appeared regarding the 'accident' or 'van attack'. The Argentinian newspaper reported it as an accident with a truck. However, a Canadian newspaper presented the news as an attack attributed to the INCEL movement, which is a terrorist group made up of men who claim they are 'involuntarily celibate' and for that reason they carry out attacks against women. A debate then arose among the students as to whether this was an accident, an attack or a collective femicide. The group realized that, on the one hand, Argentinians tend to understand a femicide as an individual act, whereas in Canada a femicide can be understood as an act of an individual towards a woman or a whole group of women.

It was also interesting as the experience was further enriched by the perspectives on gender norms in the countries from which the international students came. The Indian Langara students noted that Indian legislation on LGBTIQ+ and abortion is not aligned with current international standards of human rights and gender policies promoted by UNESCO, among other international organizations.

Fourth Step: Finalizing the Photo Galleries

Educators are often faced with the conundrum of how much to leave open for discovery versus how much to guide students. For example, when it comes to violence against women in Canada it could be considered remiss not to include the fourteen female engineering students who were murdered in a femicide in Montreal in 1989. None of the photo galleries included this important element of women's history in Canada. We chose not to insist on its inclusion but rather to simply point out this important historical event.

Regarding the choice of photos, we realized that there could be potentially controversial situations (e.g. there was one Argentinian student who shared many anti-abortion photos). As instructors, we wondered how to be progressive, and yet respect differing views on sensitive topics. While we cannot reduce grades for being anti-abortionist or homophobic, it is our responsibility as educators to show the connection between gender rights and human rights. We can use these in-the-moment opportunities to challenge students to provide evidence to support their views. We also did our best to remind students that when looking at gender and sexual orientation, Black, Indigenous and women of colour and LGBTIQ+ identities face deeper marginality than white, cisgendered women. Imposing seemingly universal ideas of heteronormativity or mainstream values constitute a double violence on them. The same goes for class and inequality; rich women tend to face less discrimination than their poor counterparts. It was imperative that we helped students understand intersectionality. Though some groups listened more to our recommendations and intersectional suggestions, all the groups managed to finish their photo galleries successfully (appendix). As instructors, we decided that the cross-cultural learning process was more crucial than achieving high standards in terms of language accuracy, academic research and gender perspective.

Flexibility in Technology, Communication and L2 Learning

L2 learning does not take place in a vacuum; it is intimately linked to the learning of new cultures as well. Learning about Argentina and Canada was part of the mix. This layered learning also included learning the language of so many new forms of technology as well as the language of new concepts concerning gender, sexual orientation and art for social change. These multiple levels of language learning created an exponential and explosive learning environment; the combination created more learning than would have been possible if each element was engaged in isolation.

While the students in Argentina were officially learning a foreign language and the students in Canada were not, in an intercultural experience such as this, L2 learning is happening in many diverse ways. It was fascinating to watch students become creative in their eagerness to communicate. Some chose to use Google translate or u-dictionary, or to make videos, which seemed to create a strong sense of community. Likewise, the asynchronous language learning of the project gave students ample time to think clearly before communicating. Even over the fast pace of WhatsApp, it is easier to *write* than it is to *speak* (and it is less intimidating).

In relation to writing in English, students from both institutions did better at writing the autobiography as they were provided with a model by their teachers. However, the photo gallery blurbs were long and inconsistent, which required editing support from us. The Padlets were empty at first and the lack of samples seemed to result in weak photo descriptions as well. Students may need to be guided into realizing that composing texts involves a sequenced process from the generation of initial ideas to the final product. Approaches such as the genre approach (genre pedagogy) can be useful along the teaching and learning cycle. We need to make students aware that in the composition of pieces of writing that we intend others to read, this writing process usually includes the steps of planning, drafting, editing and proofreading.

While we encouraged the students to communicate in English, we allowed them to revert to Spanish when a quick clarification was needed. In one instance, a Canadian-born student called on her Peruvian father to help her communicate with one of the students from Argentina. We allowed all of these communication streams to flourish; it reflected how real people in the real world find creative ways to make meaning.

Conclusion

With each step of the project, we both learned many pedagogical lessons about what works and does not work well in terms of running virtual international courses of this nature. The purpose of this chapter is to disseminate the knowledge we gained, with the hopes that others may follow in our footsteps in including gender-related topics in their teaching.

All the exercises and debates, online or offline, were aimed at delving into the relevance of the debates on women's movements and dissidence, rights and gender perspectives for post-secondary students. We belatedly realized that it would have been useful to conduct a survey about what students knew about gender and LGBTIQ+ topics. It would have been more effective to start by sharing some basic concepts (such as the meaning of the term 'femicide') so that they could more easily dig deeply into the research on their topic rather than having to take the time up front to understand core concepts related to their project.

Throughout the experience, there was a creative tension between the idea that 'we have come a long way' and 'we have a very long way to go'. Activists in Argentina and Canada have pushed the envelope surrounding gender and LGBTIQ+ issues forward in ways previous generations could never have imagined, but we still have so much work to do to create equality and equity in Argentina, Canada and around the world. It is hoped that projects such as the one reported in this chapter can inspire students to think more critically and become involved in creative movements for change the world desperately needs. While we have taken steps forward, there are many more steps to go.

Questions for Change

1. How can educational projects negotiate the creative tension between 'We've come a long way' and 'There's still a long way to go' in terms of feminism, gender issues and LGBTIQ+ concerns?
2. How can post-secondary instructors raise awareness about gender equality and sexuality regardless of their field of study?
3. How can L2 instructors infuse their teaching with both gender agendas and intercultural competencies?
4. What lessons learned from our COIL project can inspire pedagogical possibilities in your own teaching?

Appendix

Photo Galleries

Femicides in the Americas:
https://padlet.com/cmalvino571/av1np3eeq9e6

Abortion in Canada and Argentina:
https://padlet.com/lucasmbatt/g5gjc5x6f55d

Indigenous Women's Rights:
https://padlet.com/eleizaldemar/IndigenousWomenUnderAttack

LGBTIQ Rights:
https://padlet.com/amninder3009/pmcnb8byq21lsg8g

Me too/Ni una Menos:
https://padlet.com/gomezchristabel/coil_group5

Notes

1 COIL programmes were born at the State University of New York (SUNY) in 2006. The aim was to create online courses with an international dimension as a tool to promote cooperation and internationalization of learning among post-secondary students and faculty from different countries around the world. Over time it has grown, and now COIL (or Virtual Exchange) programmes are found in post-secondary institutions around the world. We felt that COIL gave us both the theoretical and practical tools to carry out our plan of interaction among our students, since it promotes communication and creativity of all agents in their educational contexts.
2 According to *Education at a Glance* (2019) students from Asia constitute the largest group of international students in tertiary education (58 per cent), and about three out of four international students are Asian. Argentina presents the world's lowest share of national students enrolled in foreign universities (*Education at a Glance*, 2019). *Education at a Glance* collects data from the thirty-one OECD member countries and it incorporates information from many others.
3 Law 27,499 (known as 'Micaela Law') was passed in Argentina in 2018. It arose from the femicide of Micaela García in 2017, a young woman who was raped and murdered in Entre Ríos by a man with a criminal record who was on probation. Micaela was a university student and an activist for women's rights, and she participated in the 'Ni una Menos' movement. National universities in Argentina were regional pioneers in applying this law to their courses of study and making it compulsory for the students to obtain credits on gender perspectives before finishing their degrees. The Micaela Law is one of the gender-related laws that have been passed in Congress in Argentina. Other laws include: Law 26.150 (2006) to create a national programme for Comprehensive Sex Education; Law 26,485 (2009) to eradicate violence and harassment against women; Law 26,618 (2010) to make same-sex marriages legal; and Law 26,743 (2012) to exercise the right to choose gender identity.
4 A study by the IMF reports that the main factors of high drop-out rates are: (a) the scarce funding for tertiary education students who cannot afford tuition or materials; (b) unequal high school access; (c) lack of information about higher education's requirements and rules; and (d) low expectations of low-income youth regarding the possibility of really pursuing post-secondary education. The battle against dropout makes for social justice on a global scale (Ezcurra, 2011).
5 One of the videos where Bublé shushes and elbows Lopilato: https://www.youtube.com/watch?v=ON_fy-Hmwtg&ab_channel=LucasM%C3%A1rquez.
6 See these articles for a detailed explanation of *escraches* history and evolution: https://abladeofgrass.org/articles/concepts-and-practices-of-justice-experiences-from-the-mesa-de-escrache/ and https://www.eldiario.es/sociedad/escrache-escrachar-argentina-hijos-represion_1_5601866.html.

3

Visually Significant Spaces: Mediating Queer Picturebooks for Deep Reading in Primary ELT

David Valente

Introduction

This chapter aims to offer classroom practitioners, teacher educators and curriculum developers in the primary English language teaching (hereafter PELT) field fresh thinking for mainstreaming a focus on gender-queerness through the pedagogical use of picturebooks. PELT is an umbrella term encompassing the multiple global contexts in which teachers of English as another language work, including English as a foreign language (EFL), English as a second language (ESL), English as an additional language (EAL), and content and language integrated learning (CLIL). As the term *primary* is variously applied in school systems and out-of-school English programmes, it refers here to children between six and twelve years old learning English, which is sufficiently broad to offer scope for adapting the focus in ways that are both contextually congruent and age-relevant. The chapter's theoretical underpinnings weave interdisciplinary insights from queer theory, children's literature scholarship, critical visual literacy and the dynamic discipline of children's literature in English language teaching, introducing a varied set of terminology which will be operationalized below.

The terms *transgender* and *gender-queerness* reflect the plethora of non-binary identities which resist social constructions of gender and societally attributed labels. These identities are regarded as being inherently fluid and shapeshifting. When applying this view, it is useful to consider Armstrong's (2021) definition, which highlights how

> genderqueer, gender non conforming, and non binary individuals embody gender in many different ways, often blurring the boundaries between masculine and feminine in specific and purposeful ways. There is no one way to be transgender. (740)

Gender-queerness will be specifically considered in relation to school education by referring to queer literacy scholars such as Miller (2015), who in advocating for teachers to develop greater understanding of the plurality and socially constructed nature of gender posits,

> Educators who engage with queer literacy are mindful about how specific discourse(s) can reinforce gender and sexuality norms, and they purposefully demonstrate how gender and sexuality are fluid, or exist on a continuum, shifting over time and in different contexts. (42)

When identifying the affordances of *picturebooks* for addressing the neglected, under-researched focus on gender-queerness in PELT, Bader's (1976) seminal definition is valuable. She highlights,

> As an art form, a picturebook hinges on the interdependence of pictures and words, on the simultaneous display of two facing pages, and on the drama of turning the page. On its own terms its possibilities are limitless. (1)

The picturebook is therefore an example of a multimodal text (Kress 2003), resulting from the dynamic fusion of its visual and verbal elements and, in the case of well-selected titles, striking ability to both show and tell, sometimes in significant, divergent ways, as Magnet and Dunnington (2020: 3) maintain, 'the space between the words (what is said) and the pictures (what we see) offers a particular imaginative and multimodal space'. This chapter intends to demonstrate how it is partly such imaginative hybridity that affords picturebooks catalytic potential (Hope 2017) when used as pedagogical vehicles by PELT practitioners aiming to create spaces for gender-queerness. The visual potency of picturebooks has multiple affordances for primary learners of English, as the often evocative images can help make challenging and complex topics age accessible (Madalena & Ramos 2022), thereby helping teachers to foster the development of children's English as well as wider educational goals by igniting their imaginations, enabling them to exercise agency and encouraging social action-taking (Morgado 2019; Whitelaw 2017; Wissman 2019). From this perspective then, picturebooks featuring protagonists with gender-queer identities whose roles are central to a book's plot (Brown et al. 2019) can contribute to counterbalancing the persistent erasure of gender-queerness in ELT coursebooks (Gray 2021; Ruiz-Cecilia, Guijarro-Ojeda & Marín-Macías 2021).

Regardless of these laudable sentiments, this chapter does not claim that the catalytic potential of picturebooks will be automatically realized as a result of teachers including gender-queer characters, their stories and related themes in PELT. On the contrary, fostering dialogic engagement in the lived realities of gender-queer characters as represented in picturebooks requires practitioners, teacher educators and curriculum developers to fully (re)turn to Bader's 'drama of turning the page'. Essentially, this foregrounds empowering practitioners to become skilful mediators of – and, in so doing, creates classroom spaces for – children's responses to (Mourão 2016) and embodied experiences with (Habegger-Conti 2021; Lähdesmäki & Koistinen 2021; Magnet & Dunnington 2020) picturebooks for illuminating gender-queer perspectives and experiences. *Mediation* refers here to the read-aloud strategies, scaffolding techniques and learning tasks and activities which PELT practitioners can implement when exploring gender-queerness through the picturebook vehicle. Ellis and Mourão (2021: 23) maintain how picturebook mediation in a PELT context

> begins with the picturebook selection, continues during the read-aloud itself and extends into the follow-up activities. Mediation is dependent upon the teacher using a combination of competences effectively to plan and manage an inclusive and effective read-aloud experience where the children interact in a language-rich environment and share their personal responses to the picturebook.

When shining a light on the mediation of picturebooks with gender-queer characters, the goal is to provide alternatives to the ubiquitous pre-while-post reading/listening/viewing PELT lesson frameworks, which arguably lead to the superficial use of multimodal texts. This can be achieved by adopting an approach to children's literature in PELT known as 'deep reading for deep learning' (Bland 2018: 6–8). Deep reading necessitates children's active participation in English language tasks and activities based on picturebooks, which, through mediation, enables them to delve into the realities, feelings and perspectives of characters who are gender-queer. Thus, deep reading can help to create pedagogical spaces which are dialogic, nuanced and vibrant (Wissman 2019) while remaining accessible in terms of learners' ages, stages of conceptual development and, importantly, their English language proficiency. In order to concretely demonstrate this, it is necessary to unpack *visually significant spaces* in the context of picturebooks for deep reading in PELT.

Conceptualizing Visually Significant Spaces in PELT

Space is a multifaceted, temporal concept used in various ways in PELT, and by embracing an expanded notion of PELT teachers' roles as *educators* (Byram & Wagner 2018; Ellis & Ibrahim 2021), visually significant spaces for gender-queerness through picturebooks in PELT can be framed. Furthermore, with their focus on transgender and gender non-conforming learners in mainstream education, Wozolek and Mitchell (2018) maintain that the nuanced, fluid and hybrid nature of gender itself, as reflected by Armstrong's (2021) definition, has 'spaces of possibilities where gender-queer understandings thrive' (318). In this chapter, creating such spaces of possibilities in PELT is regarded as requiring:

1. opportunities for gender-creative engagement in safe classroom contexts (Wozolek & Mitchell 2018);
2. use of picturebooks which foreground children's diverse identities (Dervin & Gross 2016) and amplify their voices (Ellis 2019; Ibrahim 2020);
3. enrichment of English language lesson frameworks with moments for booktalk where learners can ponder, imagine and respond personally (Mourão 2016) to picturebooks with challenging themes (Madalena & Ramos 2022; Magnet & Dunnington 2020; Whitelaw 2017);
4. critical exploration of social justice issues through picturebooks (Bland 2022; Whitelaw 2017; Wissman 2019) functioning as age-relevant, relatable vehicles;
5. taking action beyond the classroom in support of children and their family members with gender-queer identities (Vasquez, Janks & Comber 2019; Vasquez, Tate & Harste 2013).

These will be explored in an interrelated manner to conceptualize *visually significant spaces* for PELT and five areas of space creation will be considered with the affordances and challenges highlighted. These comprise spaces for: (1) safe engagement with gender-queerness; (2) usualizing and actualizing gender-queerness; (3) diverse diversities in the classroom; (4) mediation of deep reading of picturebooks; and (5) taking action in the community.

Creating Spaces for Safe Engagement with Gender-Queerness

During pre-service and in-service primary teacher education programmes, there is an increasing focus on child protection and safeguarding to ensure a safe classroom environment (e.g. Bourke & Maunsell 2016; Treacy & Nohilly

2020). However, the requirement to protect and safeguard children who are gender-queer seems continually overlooked at both the policy and practice levels in numerous countries. As ELT has a global presence, one of the most fundamental drivers for safe spaces in PELT relates to addressing the rise in violent acts committed against learners who identify as transgender and gender non-conforming (Wozolek & Mitchell 2018). In an effort to evidence this, the United Nations has recently developed tools for monitoring and reporting school-based violence, with a particular focus on violence towards learners with diverse sexual orientations, gender identities and gender expressions or SOGIE (UNESCO 2019a).

Identifying and tackling SOGIE-based violence and bullying in schools relates to United Nations Sustainable Development Goal 4, which aims to 'ensure inclusive and equitable quality education' by 2030, and while this specific type of bullying is often hidden or ignored, statistics from all global regions indicates that learners who are gender-queer are at significantly higher risk than their peers who do not identify as gender-queer (UNESCO 2019b). It is noteworthy how these findings apply to several countries ranking highly in annual International Lesbian, Gay, Bisexual, Trans and Intersex Association (ILGA) reports for their LGBTQIA+ rights, including New Zealand and Norway, for example, underscoring how widespread this serious issue is.

Tackling SOGIE violence requires well-planned whole-school, cross-curricular approaches which lay the foundations for safe space creation, and within this context PELT also has a significant role. Seen through the lens of safe classroom spaces, picturebooks which are purposefully selected by teachers to supplement or replace coursebook materials in PELT (Ellis & Brewster 2014), with protagonists who are gender-queer being visually represented in agentic roles (Miller 2019), help to counter criticisms regarding the erasure of gender-queer identities in published ELT materials. As empirical research suggests, rather than being largely conveyed through the plot in children's literature – as is commonly assumed – stories are first and foremost about the experiences of *characters*, than episodic sequences or actions (Brown et al. 2019), giving PELT an opportunity for centring characters (Sindland & Birketveit 2020) who are gender-queer by including picturebooks where they are protagonists in English language lessons.

Principled picturebook selection for PELT lessons contributes to 'disrupting the common place' (Vasquez, Tate & Harste 2013: 8), which helps address the prevailing situation characterized by the invisibility of queer identities in ELT coursebook visual representations (Gray 2021). This in turn could further offer *mirrors* (Sims Bishop 1990) for children and their family members who identify as gender-queer to see themselves represented in materials used in PELT. However, where the goal is to establish safe classroom spaces, any simplistic or tokenistic identification (Nikolajeva 2014) with gender-queer picturebook characters should not be the main target for PELT practitioners. Instead, the aim is to ignite learners' empathy (Lähdesmäki & Koistinen 2021) with gender creativity and gender-queer expressions by providing eye-opening windows on to characters' lived realities and experiences (Ellis 2018a; Mpike 2019; Sims Bishop 1990), which can deeply resonate with all of the classroom community, whether identifying as gender-queer or otherwise. In this way, classroom spaces can therefore be perceived as emotionally safe by those who use them and picturebooks can help create a welcoming space for diverse groups of readers (Hirsu, Arizpe & McAdam 2020).

Creating Spaces for Usualizing and Actualizing

By disrupting the commonplace using picturebooks in PELT, practitioners can help to visually normalize the presence of gender-queer characters during lessons so they start to become familiar and non-essentialized people in the eyes of children (Bland 2020). This approach to mainstreaming gender-queerness in school contexts is what Sanders conceptualizes as a psychological construct referred to as 'usualizing' (Bollas 2021: 137), which can be applied to the strategic mediation of picturebooks in PELT. One of the earliest examples of a picturebook representing a child who is gender non-conforming is *My Princess Boy*, first published in 2009, written by Cheryl Kilodavis and illustrated by Suzanne DeSimone. This non-fiction story is a tale of affirmation and acceptance centred on the protagonist, Kilodavis's son, who enjoys wearing dresses and tiaras, which leads to bullying at school, and all the while, his mother's love remains steadfast. A compelling example of usualizing which helped usher in safe spaces in PELT was when *My Princess Boy* was included in out-of-school intensive English language courses in France in 2011 based around picturebooks for children aged nine to ten. The creative activities linked to the picturebook had linguistic and wider educational goals, namely, to focus on questioning gender stereotypes, and the week's lessons culminated with a storytelling performance for parents and caregivers, where children could optionally wear clothes considered gender non-conforming (Francis, personal correspondence, 20 May 2021). Interestingly, the use of *My Princess Boy* in this out-of-school PELT context coincided with a controversial, short-lived period in France's educational history which attempted to embed gender theory in mainstream schools. This pilot programme known as *ABCD de l'égalité* faced strong criticism from conservative parents and caregivers and was subsequently scaled back to focus instead on gender equality in accordance with a binary notion of gender (Massei 2014).

The out-of-school example above illustrates early and valiant adoption of picturebooks with gender-queer themes in PELT; however, as previously mentioned, the inclusion of gender-creative and non-conforming characters in English language lessons should be considered as an initial step rather than the final goal. Moreover, when a pre-while-post receptive skills framework informs and shapes the planning of children's encounters with multimodal texts in PELT, there is also a risk of the explicit focus on diversity being partially eclipsed or completely omitted. This is based on a misconception that primary-aged children are too young to engage with gender-queer themes. This necessitates Sanders's second concept which extends beyond usualizing towards actualizing, requiring a purposeful and, therefore, explicit focus on queerness and gender fluidity. A noteworthy example of actualizing was at a teacher education college in Argentina in 2016 where like the earlier example in France, the teacher educators on this pre-service PELT programme adopted picturebooks with queer themes, to enable exploration of gender and sexual orientation, resulting partly from the selected picturebook titles themselves. One of these is also an early example of a book which centres same-sex marriage – *King & King* by Linda de Haan and Stern Nijland, first published in English in 2002. The student teachers focused on the visual and verbal narrative by considering how they might use this picturebook about a prince whose mother pushes him to marry a variety of potential brides, whereas he falls in love with another prince whom he finally marries – reflecting further celebratory affirmation of queer identities and lifestyles. Furthermore, this pedagogical move aligns with wider educational policy developments in Argentina, including the introduction of a law mandating that teachers focus on comprehensive sexuality education (CSE) during compulsory schooling (Beacon 2019).

Creating Spaces for Diverse Diversities

The practical applications of usualizing and actualizing in the two examples above clearly have value for PELT practitioners and teacher educators alike. To make the deep reading of picturebooks related to gender-queer themes a PELT classroom reality however, this chapter posits that these concepts would benefit from reimagining to be sufficiently relevant and resonant in PELT. It is useful to consider the critique of usualizing and actualizing by Bollas (2021), who advocates for an enhanced focus on *diversity approaches* in ELT, which more genuinely foreground the nuanced plurality of sexual orientations and gender identities, reflecting the complexity conveyed in *diverse diversities* (Dervin & Gross 2016). Applying these criticisms to the use of both *My Princess Boy* and *King & King* in PELT, these titles can be considered as belonging to the inclusive category of children's literature (Davison in Ellis 2019: 64–5). Despite being created by well-intentioned authors and illustrators, these titles are classically didactic with deliberate aims to teach children about gender non-confirming expression and/or marriage equality.

Focusing on PELT specifically, Ellis (2019: 64–5) cites examples of picturebooks with disability themes to argue for a less didactic, more *mainstreaming* approach to diversity, which she refers to as 'immersive' children's literature, based on Davison's original categorization. In the context of gender-queerness, a more *incidental focus* on inclusion (Antony 2019) in line with this immersive approach favours picturebooks with characters whose gender-queerness is one aspect of their complex, intersectional identities, and while important, it is neither their only nor their defining characteristic as a person. However, this is not to imply that authors and illustrators of immersive picturebooks do not make conscious decisions about their characters, but instead that they are cognizant of the dangers of Othering and the vital importance of intersectional representation. Moreover, based on Miller's (2019: 1645) detailed analysis of what she terms 'queer children's literature', it is valuable for PELT practitioners when selecting picturebooks for usualizing to distinguish between what she refers to as 'old and new queer children's literature', which aligns with inclusive and immersive literature categories. From this perspective, *My Princess Boy* and *King & King* are examples of the older, inclusive queer children's literature category, whereas, for example, two picturebooks created by author-illustrator Jessica Love, *Julián Is a Mermaid* (2018) and *Julián at the Wedding* (2020), are exemplars of newer, immersive queer children's literature.

New queer children's picturebooks which are immersive, rather than inclusive, help to create visually significant spaces for children learning English to embrace diverse perspectives and consider multiple interpretations about gender-queer characters. This occurs when such interpretations are skilfully mediated through personalized, creative and possibly divergent responses to the book's themes (Mourão 2016). This category of picturebooks can therefore enable PELT practitioners to transcend a narrow focus on author intention which inclusive literature and its didactic messages inevitably lead to in the English language classroom (Delanoy 2018). Furthermore, applying usualizing and actualizing in a way which facilitates multiple interpretations is congruent with PELT approaches which prioritize discovery learning (Ellis & Brewster 2014). This is as opposed to situations in which children have English language lessons on or about difference, which inadvertently lead to Othering (Bland 2020).

For actualizing to create a space where discovery learning approaches flourish, there is an additional need to reconsider the default positioning of picturebooks with gender-queer themes as windows (Sims Bishop 1990), particularly when encountered by learners who do not themselves identify as gender-queer. As the development of empathic responses (Lähdesmäki & Koistinen 2021; Nikolejva 2014) to gender-queer experiences is the goal, windows can obstruct the development of empathy and the genuine 'standing with characters in picturebooks' (Habegger-Conti 2021: 54) and could lead to positioning the characters as objects of curiosity, thus further reinforcing Othering (Mpike 2019). To address this, Habegger-Conti (2021: 59) advocates the creation of classroom spaces for what she calls 'sliding door moments' actualized by learners' taking agentic roles. In this particular context, this is in order to demonstrate support of children who are gender-queer and potentially engaging in social justice actions outside the classroom space. To elaborate on the creation of space in PELT, which foregrounds diverse diversities and multiple responses to the visually significant representations of gender-queerness, it is useful to apply the concept to a new queer picturebook.

Reflecting an Immersive Orientation to Diversity

Jessica Love's debut picturebook, *Julián Is a Mermaid* (2018), centres on the eponymous character, Julián, and opens with a boy riding the subway accompanied by his abuela (grandmother) one day in New York City. He starts to dream about becoming a mermaid after seeing three women also dressed as mermaids on their way to the annual Coney Island Mermaid Parade – an artistic celebration to mark the arrival of summer. During an interview at the Edinburgh International Book Festival (23 August 2020), Love explained how Julián's character was inspired in part by the lived experiences of a former partner's gender-queer relative. She also shared her motivations for creating the picturebook, with the goal of authentically representing children who are gender non-conforming and their intersectional worlds. When usualizing Julián's character in PELT through the lens of diverse diversities, it is particularly important for teachers to invite children's personalized interpretations of each visually significant opening. For example, the prologue illustration and the opening where the main character is dreaming about becoming a mermaid have the potential to trigger character-based predictions and invite contemplations in English, when sensitively mediated in PELT.

In pairs, learners could brainstorm what they notice about Julián's reflection in the prologue illustration and the similarities and differences between his actual appearance as he stands in front of the mirror. This could be creatively extended to a guided visualization where the children picture themselves in their mind's eye looking in the mirror. They then could contemplate whether their reflection differs from what their classmates see on the outside. Opening their eyes, they could use their thoughts to recreate their own versions of the mirror image with themselves and their reflections, being as creative as they like, and finally, they could display their mirror reflections as a classroom gallery walk to affirm everyone's personal interpretations. In groups, the children could use the opening which illustrates Julián's imaginary transformation into a mermaid to describe changes they notice about the character's physical appearance and clothing in each of the five images. They could also describe changes in the setting from the subway train to the ocean and suggest what this represents. For some children, this character could perhaps be a child who loves to dream, for some it could be a child who enjoys pretend play and dressing up, and other children may interpret the visuals as representing the character's gender-creative expression or, possibly, gender transformation. For example, when using this picturebook with primary children from six to nine years old in Portugal in research conducted by Madalena and Ramos (2022: 153–4), they found,

> When the children were asked about the possibility of a boy's desire to be a mermaid, the majority expressed their agreement and viewed his dream as acceptable ... The final surprise, with the participation of the grandmother and Julián in the mermaid parade, was immediately identified as a moment of celebration and happiness shared by the protagonists.

The personalized response activities suggested above could progress to actualizing gender identities in the classroom space and to ensure a diverse diversities lens can be maintained, Delanoy (2018: 152) proposes tackling the dangers of a 'single story' by supplementing the focus on the picturebook character with space for the stories and voices of real children, in this case, those who are transgender. Farrar, Arizpe and McAdam (2022: 51) highlight how 'exploring a challenging theme in a fictional context cannot guarantee a safe transfer of compassion and understanding in a real-life context' and to mediate this, Delanoy suggests incorporating text ensembles, which given the multimodal focus of this chapter could be readily extended to text and image ensembles (Serafini 2014) curated by the teacher and/or the learners. With the support of parents and caregivers, children in upper primary could research on child-safe search engines and share their discoveries as class multimodal ensembles. This curation process helps prompt the involvement of parents and caregivers who as very influential adults in primary-aged children's lives also have a significant role (Ellis 2018b) in affirming and encouraging empathy with children who identify as transgender or gender-queer. Multimodal ensembles and related tasks for upper primary could also include viewing clips from documentaries, for example, *Transhood* (HBO 2020) and *Gender Revolution* (National Geographic 2017).

With sufficient mediation including translanguaging, older primary children (aged eleven to twelve) could work collaboratively with visual representations of gender diversity such as *The Genderbread Person* (hues 2017) and *The Gender Unicorn* (Trans Student Educational Resources n.d.) shown in Figures 3.1 and

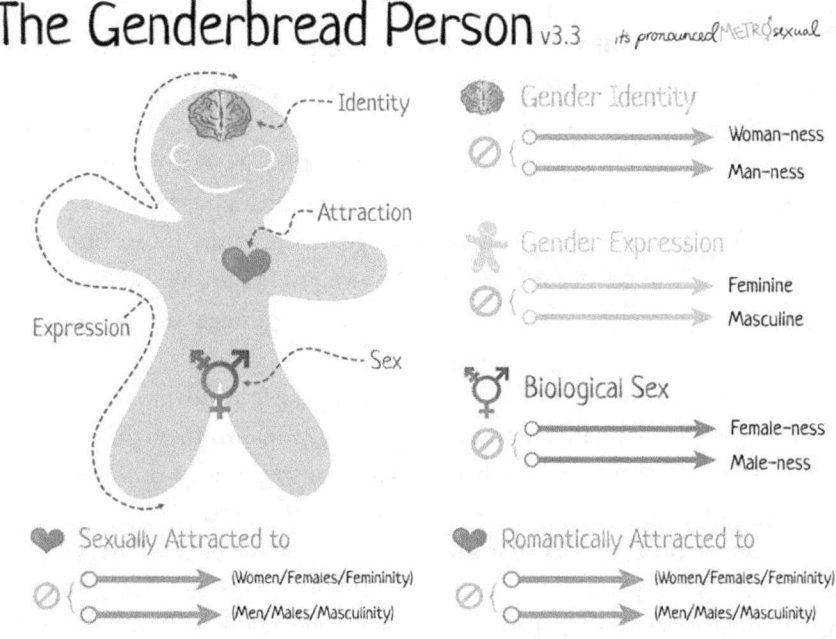

Figure 3.1 *The Genderbread Person.*

Figure 3.2 *The Gender Unicorn.*

3.2 and make links to the picturebook character and the lives of children outside the classroom.

Based on an adaptation of Ibrahim (2020), this could also be actualized by both younger and older primary children as a class jigsaw where each child has two puzzle piece templates: one for Julián and one for them, and they then draw and/or write their own individual interpretations of identity-related aspects for the character (see the example in Figure 3.3) and themselves. Brought together as a classroom display, this jigsaw then visually represents and gives physical classroom space to diverse identity expressions. Finally, the infographics mentioned above could act as springboards for children's artistic representations (Whitelaw 2019) of gender diversity by enabling them to create their own gender infographics in groups. This would further help to illuminate the socially constructed nature of gender in age- and linguistically accessible ways.

These pedagogical suggestions for *Julián Is a Mermaid* have reimagined Sander's concepts of usualizing and actualizing by refracting them through a lens which affords PELT the space to help overcome a single story and foregrounds diversity approaches. However, the shortcomings associated with picturebooks as *windows* on diversity persist unless there is a widening of PELT lesson spaces for mediating deep reading opportunities, with empathetic *standing with* characters and possibilities for *sliding door moments* (Habegger-Conti 2021). This approach to visually significant mediation and space creation through

Figure 3.3 Character identities jigsaw piece.

picturebooks can be explored through *critical visual literacy* lens fusing visual semiotics (e.g. Serafini 2014) and critical literacy (e.g. Vasquez, Janks & Comber 2019; Vasquez, Tate, & Harste 2013).

Creating Wider Spaces for Mediation of Deep Reading

When identifying entry points for teachers to mediate the deep reading of picturebooks with gender-queer themes, it is necessary to revisit the notion that this *aesthetic object* (Sipe 2002) has important affordances as a pedagogical vehicle while also returning to Bader's (1976) reference to the child as a beholder (1976: 1). This helps conceptualize the way children in PELT may first encounter a picturebook with gender-queer characters and shines a light on possibilities for teachers to aesthetically mediate the book using talk during a picturebook read-aloud event in the English language classroom (Ellis & Mourão 2021). Linked to this, research on read-aloud events in schools has raised several criticisms regarding a lack of space for divergent responses as well as teachers' limited – and limiting – use of questions which may reinforce what Holt referred to as a 'culture of right answerism' (Meighan 2014: 21). This can result in low tolerance of ambiguity as well as little opportunity for nuanced interpretations (Magnet & Dunnington 2020; Whitelaw 2017). These findings are a cautionary tale for PELT practitioners given that tolerance of ambiguity is one of the characteristics necessary for success as an English language learner (e.g. Little, Dam & Legenhausen 2017).

Positioning the picturebook as an aesthetic object by enveloping children in its total design and enabling them to become text and image beholders requires moving convincingly beyond the pre-while-post PELT teaching framework. Also, when attempting to identify the *sliding door moments* Habegger-Conti calls for, picturebook read-alouds in PELT need to provide genuine opportunities for children to deeply explore the *peritextual features*. Peritext can be considered as *the* defining characteristic of a picturebook as an aesthetic object and to overlook this in PELT denies children essential possibilities to develop their critical visual literacy (Mourão 2016). Features of peritext well-worth engaging children with and talking around include, but are not limited to, the covers, the endpapers, the blurb, the dedication and title page, and exploration of these provides space for children to make crucial character- and setting-related predictions, triggered by the visual aspects as they behold the picturebook in its entirety. Thereby, on encountering the characters in the openings during the read-aloud, children have invested opportunities to connect their predictions and crucially for exploration of gender-queerness, to have their beliefs about the diverse world expanded. Such peritextual ponderings extend to the personal significance children may attach to the colours and layout of the openings and illustrations and how involved in (Habegger-Conti 2021) and how empathic they are with characters who are gender-queer.

Mediating the Peritextual Ponderings

Jessica Love's picturebook, *Julián at the Wedding* (2020), can be used to demonstrate how teachers could mediate the peritextual ponderings in PELT classroom practice. Julián and Abuela return in this sequel, which is a richly visual, almost wordless picturebook representing diverse intersections. Starting with a focus on the front cover, children can ponder in pairs how the title and the two characters (Julián and Marisol) might be connected, leading to who they predict is getting married, then sharing their own experiences of weddings in groups, followed by the teacher collating these as a class. While sharing the picturebook, the children encounter the brides and the powerful definition of *A Wedding* and depending on their variously lived experiences of weddings, this could enable the learners to re-examine their beliefs regarding who can marry. Unlike the didactic focus of earlier queer picturebooks such as *King & King*, the story centres on the two main characters (i.e. the children) on the front cover, rather than the brides. The definition of a wedding as 'a party for love' on the back cover is highly significant, as it is not limited to genders, sexual orientations or religious beliefs. In this way, the brides' kiss visually represents incidental inclusion as neither the same-sex wedding nor the characters' Afro-Latinx ethnicities are focused on didactically. During the read-aloud, the teacher can also highlight features which celebrate diversities such as the picturebook's brown paper which sensitively represents the characters' ethnicities.

To illustrate the affordances of widening the classroom space in PELT for deep reading approaches to become commonplace, Bland (forthcoming) has developed a four-stage pedagogical model for use with children's literature formats, including picturebooks. This clearly aligns with a critical visual literacy theoretical framework and enables PELT practitioners to develop wider educational goals, including the exploration of gender-queerness. The main stages are organized sequentially as: (1) Unpuzzle and explore; (2) Activate and investigate; (3) Critically engage; and (4) Experiment with creative response. An adapted version of Bland's model is applied to *Julián at the Wedding* as shown in Table 3.1.

Creating Space for Community Action-Taking

Providing the space in PELT for children to encounter gender-queer picturebooks using a deep reading framework such as the one above has considerable potential to open the classroom space for sliding door moments as well as to opportunities for standing with characters, and thereby fostering empathy through in-depth learning. However, as Vasquez, Tate and Harste (2013: 18) argue,

> Critical literacy is not just a subject we want added to the curriculum. It involves action, starting with one's self. We see critical literacy as fundamentally a call to action; a call to position oneself differently in the world. (18)

In PELT, this emphasis on taking action is arguably the dimension which risks being afforded least space, perhaps in part due to the misconception that the political realm lacks age-appropriacy, resulting in avoidance by practitioners. While there are considerations regarding ethical, permission and safety questions which arise when promoting activism outside of schools (and homes), such a cautious approach to taking action arguably relates to particular constructions of childhood that PELT contexts may be working within. Moreover, to ensure children's voices are heard and that their experiences with gender-queer picturebooks are not erased (Douglas & Poletti 2016), a more nuanced view of the child as activist is worth exploring, such as the role *individual versus collective* activism plays in school contexts, and as a result of the in-depth learning that deep reading of picturebooks can lead to, children may be inspired to engage in community initiatives outside of PELT.

Returning to Vasquez, Tate and Harste's (2013) emphasis on civic action as involving a shift in perspective, a key consideration arises regarding how to mediate this beyond the PELT classroom. Prioritizing a focus on the taking of collective action in the community rather than depending on potential individual actions would be worthwhile, and this can only be realistically achieved with parental and caregiver involvement, as alluded to earlier. By positioning parents and caregivers as partners (Ellis 2018b) in children's English language learning and collective action-taking, logistical and ethical challenges can be alleviated, thus providing additional positive role models for embracing gender-queerness outside of school. An example of community-based action using *Julián at the Wedding* as a catalyst could be for the children and their families to organize a neighbourhood street party to recreate the final double spread of the picturebook. The children could design party invitations in English creatively inspired by the diverse characters and picturebook themes. For example, a PELT student teacher on a pre-service teacher education programme in Norway created the model invitation in Figure 3.4 for her grade 4 practicum class to scaffold their creations. Her artistic interpretation uses vivid

Figure 3.4 Model street party invitation. Picture reprinted by permission of *Anonymous*.

colours for the characters' silhouettes, evoking the final picturebook opening and welcomes all (inter)sections of the community to join *Our Neighbourhood Party for Love*.

Conclusion

This chapter has operationalized the concept of visually significant spaces to illuminate the mediation of queer picturebooks as vehicles for deep reading in PELT contexts. This has drawn on interdisciplinary approaches enabling a fusion of queer literacy theory, children's literature scholarship, mainstream education pedagogies and the scholarly application of children's literature to ELT. Critical visual literacy has been argued to be a valuable theoretical and practical lens for supporting practitioners in their effective mediation of deep reading in PELT. Five dimensions have been proposed for space creation to visibly amplify gender-queerness through picturebooks in PELT. These are space for safe engagement with gender-queerness; usualizing and actualizing gender-queerness; diverse diversities in the classroom; mediation of deep reading of picturebooks; and community action-taking. Considering the rise of violence against people who are transgender and gender-queer around the world, it is hoped that this chapter offers some inspiration for PELT teachers, teacher educators and curriculum developers, so they can confidently approach the valuing of gender diversity in primary English language education.

Questions for Change

1. How can a focus on gender-queerness using picturebooks in PELT be embedded in national and/or institutional ELT curricula and syllabi?
2. What changes can PELT practitioners make to collaborate with parents and caregivers as equal partners for exploring gender-queerness with children learning English?
3. What kinds of innovations are required in PELT teacher education programmes to provide an in-depth focus on diverse gender identities through picturebooks?

4. What community action initiatives can primary schools engage with to better support children and their family members who identify as gender-queer?
5. How can PELT practitioners focus on gender-queer perspectives through picturebooks in contexts where legislation prohibits this?

4

Breaking the Heteronormative Prosody: What a Family Tree Tells Us about Gender and Sexuality in the EFL Classroom

Germán Canale

Introduction

The English as a foreign language (EFL) classroom is a potentially rich space for addressing gender, sexuality and heteronormativity (Norton & Pavlenko 2004). However, research demonstrates that language education – and to some extent instruction – still shows considerable resistance (Coda, Cahnmann-Taylor & Jiang 2020; Evripidou 2020; Nelson 2010). There are many reasons for this, including the long-ingrained view of (some forms of) heterosexuality as the default identity in educational syllabuses, materials and instruction (Evripidou 2020). Heteronormative ideology has naturalized (some forms of) heterosexuality to the extent that it usually is not perceived as a form of sexuality (Morrish 2002 drawing on Sedgwick 1994). In other words, heterosexuality is the *unmarked* (Hall 2003) or ideologically assumed identity in language education while other ways of identifying oneself and others are either excluded or marginalized. Another reason is that English language teaching (ELT) is a massive and global business targeting markets with substantial differences in terms of how gender and sexuality are legally, politically and culturally addressed. This translates into different motivations for (not) promoting gender and sexuality in language syllabuses and materials. Strategically, ELT materials often opt for *safe contents* (Gray 2010a, b) or seemingly unproblematic topics (which, among other things, reproduce, reinforce and perpetuate heteronormativity) in order for textbooks to be widely approved and adopted (Moore 2020).

These problems are reinforced by some mainstream views of language education, which tend to limit language learning to either language skills or to issues of (idealized) *global communication*, failing to see language learning in terms of power and identity (Coda, Cahnmann-Taylor & Jiang 2020). As a result, instructors may feel that *there is no gender* in the language materials they use, they may assume gender and sexuality are *not relevant* to all learners (Evripidou 2018, 2020), or they may view gender and sexuality as *private matters* outside the social world of learners (Nelson 2010). In other words, instructors might – willingly or unwillingly – operate within the logic of heteronormativity.

The issues outlined above respond to a broader problem in language education, namely that it usually (re)presents itself as *neutral* or *apolitical* (Byram 2008; Pennycook 2001). This devoids teaching and learning of their inherently political nature, contributing to an implicitly established agenda that – among other things – perpetuates heteronormativity by making matters of gender and sexuality invisible or, when visible, unspeakable. My point of departure in this chapter[1] is that (language) education is, by definition, *political* in the sense that it is a form of civic engagement (Freire 1994) and a form of action (Byram 2008). Gender and sexuality are part of education. Denying this is politically and rhetorically strategic in reproducing hegemonic discourses and practices.

In this chapter, I present data of an ethnographic research study to show how – during three consecutive school years – a teacher engages in reflexive work by (re)designing the visual representation of a family tree in the opening task of a classroom unit of work entitled *My Family*. In doing this, the teacher iteratively attempts to deconstruct some aspects of heteronormativity by problematizing the very notion of family provided by the ELT syllabuses and materials. While at first sight choosing a visual for an opening task might seem a trivial activity, it actually shows how the teacher *grows into* addressing gender, sexuality and heteronormativity in the classroom. In order to choose what she considers to be the most appropriate visual of a family tree, she evaluates what social meanings about the family are made by each visual, what topics they can trigger for classroom discussion and how learners might respond to them. This process shows how the teacher comes to envision the deconstruction of some aspects of heteronormativity as key to the political aims of language teaching. As a result, her lessons do not reproduce the content presented in the classroom materials; instead they reflexively contest such content and representations. To be sure, my aim in this chapter is not to evaluate the task or the visuals the teacher designs. My aim is to show how seemingly trivial small-scale classroom practices and decisions such as choosing an image help to raise the teacher's awareness of heteronormativity in her own EFL lesson, giving way to reflexive and critical work.

Heteronormativity in the EFL Classroom

My views on heteronormativity are informed by Queer Theory/Queer Linguistics in second/foreign language studies (Nelson 1999, 2010), as well as Critical Discourse Analysis and Gender Studies (Caldas-Coulthard 2020; Sunderland & Litosseliti 2002; Sunderland 2004). Along these lines, I see heteronormativity as a hegemonic regime of discourses and practices that normalize particular forms of heterosexuality (Nelson 2010). This normalizing work is based upon traditional discourses of identity as binary (male/female) and complementary gender roles, among others (Cameron 2005). Through heteronormativity, particular forms of heterosexuality become perceived as natural or normal (Evripidou 2020), therefore excluding individuals who do not conform with them (Coda, Cahnmann-Taylor & Jiang 2020) and imposing on both non-heterosexual and heterosexual identities an *ideal norm* that cannot be reached (Motschenbacher 2011). Ideas of superior and inferior, natural and unnatural forms of gender and sexual identity derive from this ideology and permeate our everyday practices by means of a heterosexual hegemony (Butler 2011).

Research in EFL has shown that heteronormativity permeates classroom practices, syllabuses and materials by excluding, avoiding, silencing or rejecting alternative discourses and ideologies (see Liddicoat 2009b). This constructs a sort of *heteronormative prosody*, that is, a chain of evaluative multimodal meanings that accumulate in time and space and which dominate classroom discourses, practices and artefacts. I assume that such prosody can manifest higher or lower degrees of heteronormativity (see, for instance, Pakula, Pawelczyk & Sunderland 2015) in terms of the array of meanings, valuations and interpretations it allows for. While higher degrees result in the delegitimization or downright neglect of non-conforming discourses and identities, lower degrees can mitigate or modalize its regulatory strength, thus allowing for counter-discourses or even entertaining potential contestations.

Along these lines, language education has drawn on heteronormativity to promote particular forms of dominant heterosexuality (Coda, Cahnmann-Taylor & Jiang 2020). In fact, a common denominator in critical research is the observation that it is hard to open spaces to defy such prosody in the classroom: heterosexuality is usually left unquestioned (Sauntson 2020) in language classrooms and is even reproduced in the most mundane interactions, such as asking male learners 'What is your girlfriend like?' (Evripidou 2020: 1023).

Heteronormativity and EFL in Uruguay: A Brief Contextualization

In the past decades, public official discourses and policies in Uruguay have started to address gender, sexuality and heteronormativity more explicitly. Long-standing activist groups and fifteen years of left-wing governments (2005–19) played a key role in making these matters more visible. This needs to be interpreted in light of a broader political agenda which has thematized (social, cultural, ethnic, linguistic) diversity to shift from a self-representation of a monolithic nation/culture to one of a heterogeneous and diverse country (Barrios 2011; Furtado 2018).

Some of the political actions that have taken place to address gender, sexuality and heteronormativity include: decriminalizing abortion (Law 18.987, 2012[2]), legalizing same-sex marriage and adoption (Law 19.075 and Amendment 19119, 2013[3]), granting legal identity rights to transgender people (Law 19.684, 2018[4]), the design of several educational guides and materials for sexual education in preschool and primary school, and implementing publishing policies for local textbooks in mainstream education to avoid gender stereotyping and promoting non-sexist language (Furtado 2018).

However, EFL education does not seem to fit into this picture: matters of gender, sexuality and heteronormativity have been excluded in top-down policies and discourses (including learning materials). English has been promoted by drawing on discourses of *instrumentality* (English for a profitable future), *personal growth* (English to understand other peoples and cultures) and *globalization* (English for success in the world) (Canale 2015), thus reinforcing views of the language as a non-ideological and apolitical tool for natural, symmetric communication (Rajagopalan 2003).

However, in the past decade some critical issues have been foregrounded in EFL policy discourse, such as the need to *democratize* and *universalize* access to the language across the country (Canale 2015, 2019). These have been interpreted through the lenses of class (or economic status) and geographical distribution (urban/rural), but not necessarily in terms of other dimensions of identity. A few isolated actions have begun to take place to introduce gender in EFL instruction, such as the design of a workbook on gender matters and foreign language learning (Fernández & Frade 2019), the introduction of the notion of gender identities in the first year official high school syllabus in 2018 – which is to date the only EFL syllabus addressing gender explicitly– and, more recently, the design of a series of local textbooks (*#livingUruguay*) that entertains a wider range of identity options represented if compared to previous textbooks. However, at the moment of writing this chapter (2021) most EFL materials and syllabuses still draw heavily on heteronormative ideologies. Whether and how gender and sexuality are addressed in the classroom mostly depends on teachers' and schools' efforts.

Methodological Considerations

In this chapter, I present ethnographic data to show how, throughout three consecutive school years, an EFL teacher redesigns the visual representation of a family tree in the opening task of a classroom unit of work entitled *My Family*. The research site is a small private school in a working middle-class neighbourhood in Montevideo, Uruguay. Vera (pseudonym) is an experienced and certified EFL instructor who teaches a beginner EFL class in the first year of secondary school (learners aged eleven to twelve).

The idea to follow a teacher's work and lesson design through three consecutive years was inspired by the original ethnographic study (reported in Canale 2019) which was sought out to investigate the enactment of a national policy in Vera's classroom. Later reviewing of the data and interviews with her shaped my interest in examining how she was reflecting on issues of heteronormativity in her lessons. Thus, I decided to track how Vera revised her own lessons and practices when teaching the same course to different students in three consecutive years.

Due to this reorientation of the original study, issues of design and access had to be negotiated with participants and with the school. As a result, in Year 1, I conducted classroom observations and interviews with the teacher, learners and other social actors at the school. I also collected students' work, the teacher's lesson plans and looked at learners' interaction with the textbook (*Uruguay in Focus*, Longman, 2006). In Years 2 and 3, I continued to interview Vera, collect teaching records, lesson plans and students' work, but no classroom observations were conducted. Consent forms were obtained from the school, the teacher, learners and parents.

The illustrative examples and events I present throughout the chapter point to teacher's reflexivity and growing awareness of how aspects of heteronormativity, gender and sexuality permeate the EFL classroom and materials and how the notion of family is highly influenced by heteronormative and traditional gender discourses. Examples and events presented are to be taken as a *telling case* (Mitchell 1984 in Sunderland 2004), which do not attempt to be generalizable.

Analysis

Much of the socializing and moralizing work of many societies is carried out through a traditional understanding of the family as a nuclear unit of cultural norms and social mandates. In fact, the struggle over the notion of family is key to the ideological tensions between forms of conservative and progressive education in the West. Conservative views fight for the notion of family as the *building block of society* and as a *source of moral authority* (Apple & Oliver 2003: 32). Any variation to the *traditional* family in syllabuses, learning materials or classroom tasks is a potential source of dispute. If, for conservative views, (public) education is in itself a dangerous site (Apple 2000), it becomes even more dangerous when it attempts to openly discuss sexuality, gender and heteronormativity through a deconstruction of what a family is or ought to be.

This makes simple, everyday classroom tasks about families a rich site for exploring heteronormativity since the tensions between textual representations (what families are represented to be in language materials) and the social reality of learners (what their families are) can be made evident. For instance, ELT materials for beginners usually introduce family vocabulary and descriptions portraying traditional families. Their heteronormative conforming identities and practices are taken for granted as the only possible form of identification (high degree of heteronormativity). When materials include tasks in which learners need to disclose information about their own families (Menard-Warick 2004 in Nelson 2010) the fact that learners' families are likely to differ from what is depicted in learning materials is overlooked (Koster & Litosseliti 2021).

Table 4.1 summarizes key aspects of Vera's enactment of the introductory task (and visual representation of a family tree) for the classroom unit *My Family* in three consecutive years.

As shall be discussed next, this sequence shows her critical reflections on how a simple image can open or close spaces for addressing gender, sexuality and heteronormativity in the classroom.

Year 1: Identifying Heteronormativity in the Family Tree

In Year 1, the main goal of the unit was for learners to be able to ask questions about the family of others and to describe their own. Vera initiated the lesson by introducing a family tree in the textbook *Uruguay in Focus* 1 (a similar image is found in Figure 4.1).

As in most ELT materials, the family tree found in *Uruguay in Focus* only portrays traditional families (verbally, visually and graphically), representing 'conventional, middle-class, age-appropriate, and heteronormative constructions of family' (Govender 2018: 137). The only occurrences of a *non-traditional*

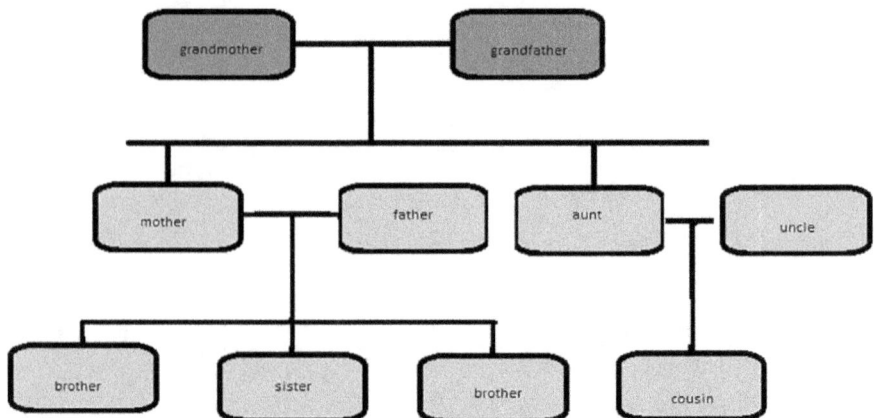

Figure 4.1 Illustration of family tree similar to the one used in Year 1.

family throughout the textbook are the words *stepmother* and *stepfather* followed by the definition 'when your mother or your father are remarried'. Thus, nonconformity in the textbook is represented exclusively in writing (not visually in the family tree) and it is constructed within heteronormativity. No space is open for questioning heterosexual and gender binary identities.

Since most learners had claimed they watched *The Simpsons*, Vera also provided a photocopy of *The Simpsons*' family tree. Learners were asked to describe and compare both family trees and its members through guiding questions (see Figure 4.2).

Both family trees share the same graphic structure of Figure 4.1: only *traditional* families (heterosexual, binary, married couples with their children) are represented, expressing a high degree of heteronormativity in that nuclear families with heterosexual parents and siblings are exclusively represented (Pakula, Pawelczyk & Sunderland 2015: 10). A lower degree of heteronormativity here would require, for instance, images and surrounding tasks with other potential readings of the family, but they are not present in the textbook or in other materials used throughout the unit.

Like family trees in numerous ELT textbooks, Figure 4.1 multimodally constructs a highly heteronormative prosody in two main ways. Horizontally, lines connect either heterosexual couples (husband and wife) or blood relatives (such as siblings). Vertically, lines connect couples with their children, representing the traditional family as a heterosexual nuclear social unit. Social continuity is hinted at if the family tree is read top-down and heterosexual normativity is hinted at if read from left to right. Each member of the family seems to identify as binary sex/sexuality/gender conforming as assumed by their given names and their visual representation.

However banal a family tree might seem, it actually does a lot of ideological work. It hints at how family members supposedly (should) behave and at the sexual desires they (ought to) have. Narratives and tasks surrounding these family trees in ELT textbooks also reinforce such heteronormative prosody by offering heteronormative contexts and scenarios (first dates, love letters, daily couple routines among heterosexual individuals).

The two family trees used in class did not cause any explicit debate in the enactment of the lesson: the learners and Vera seemed to assume heteronormativity or at least they did not defy the family trees at hand. However, by the end of the unit learners were required to use the school laptops to design their own family tree. One learner made a noticeable transformation in her family tree: she decided to include a half-sister which did not conform to the original structure of blood relations.

While the representation of the family tree in Figure 4.3 rejects a traditional notion of (blood) family, it does not reject heteronormativity. However, this small change to the family tree made Vera reflect on how problematic the representations she was using were. While discussing about culture in EFL materials during an interview, she mentioned:

V: I wonder why I used those two family trees. Is it because of culture?
G: What do you mean?
V: I mean, I did not put a family tree with two fathers, for instance.
G: And why do you think that happened?
V: Why did that happen? Honestly, I don't know. Maybe because it was just in the textbook … and the other one I picked (*The Simpsons*) is a very well-known TV family so it's easy for them to engage … so they can learn the names and family relations based on something they already know. I think if I were to use a non-tradition al family, I would need to explain other things first.
G: Like what?

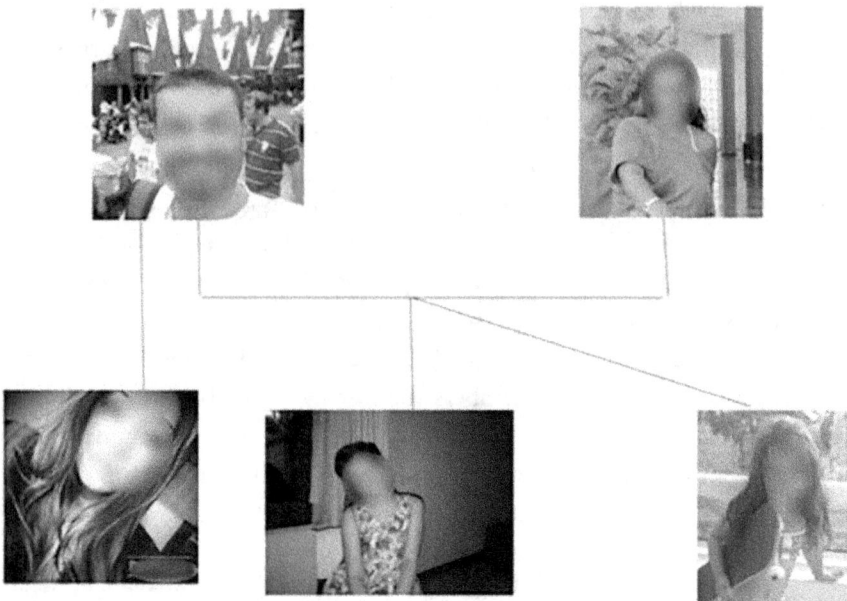

Figure 4.3 Family tree designed by a learner, originally published in Canale, G. (2019).

V: Well, you know. The textbook doesn't show other types of families. I hadn't thought of that. So, if I were to use a non-traditional family maybe I should explain many other things first.

G: Yes, well, I mean, textbooks don't show many other things either.

V: Yes, for instance, when they show things about culture they show cultural symbols, like Queen Elizabeth, Shakespeare, but not other things …
You know, it can happen in the classroom … this, I mean, this about the family. In a couple of years it will happen. You will have students with two mothers or two fathers, or just one parent. Well, it actually happens already.

G: Has it happened to you?

V: No. But, I need to think how I would address it. I want to teach things that they can relate to … that they can see in their own lives.

Extract 1: Interview with Vera There are three interesting points to be raised about Vera's reflections. First, she acknowledges that some ways of representing the social world in the ELT textbook pass unnoticed while others become *marked*. This observation seems to trigger her reflection about the need to expand the underlying notion of family represented in the textbook by going beyond the strictly heteronormative ('I mean, I did not put a family tree with two fathers, for instance'). This is particularly interesting because the learner's transformation in the representation of her own family tree triggered Vera's interest in introducing matters of gender/sexuality even when this was not the object of the transformation of the learner's family tree.

Second, her justifications as for why she used traditional representations of the family point to how effective heteronormativity is in naturalizing particular assumptions to the point that any representation that defies it requires an explanation ('I think if I were to use a non-traditional family I would need to explain other things first').

Last, she acknowledges that matters of gender and sexuality are changing in society and thus the classroom needs to be better prepared for this ('You know, it can happen in the classroom ... this, I mean, this about the family. In a couple of years it will happen. You will have students with two mothers or two fathers, or just one parent. Well, it actually happens already'). In fact, Vera's incrementum in epistemic modality ('it can happen', 'it will happen', 'it actually happens already') points to a recognition that a social change is indeed taking place and that the EFL classroom needs to accompany it.

These reflections resulted in Vera choosing a different family tree representation in the following year.

Year 2: Breaking Heteronormativity in the Family Tree

In the second school year, Vera decided to introduce the unit by showing learners *The Simpsons'* family tree, but not the one she had used before. This time she was not focusing on the main five characters, which compose a traditional family structure. Instead, she expanded the family tree to consider Patty and Selma, Marge's sisters. Throughout the series, Patty comes out as lesbian, Selma becomes a single mother by international adoption. While Vera did not know much about the series – and actually in some of the tasks and interactions reproduced in this chapter she confuses both characters and merges their stories into only one – she took this opportunity for introducing a new goal into the unit (see Table 4.1): presenting and discussing different types of families (e.g. single and divorced parents, blood, step and half-siblings, same-sex marriages). This allowed her to articulate critical goals and linguistic goals in the lesson.

As shown in Figure 4.4, this family tree resembles the ones used in the previous year since it provides a similar organization of the family. However, the main difference is the monoparental link between Selma and her daughter.

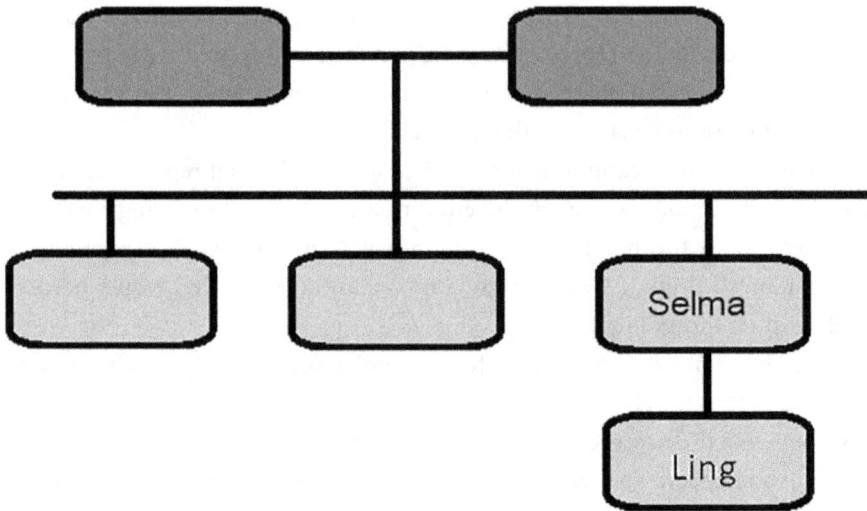

Figure 4.4 Illustration of family tree similar to the one used in Year 2.

Despite her initial fears that introducing a non-traditional family would require a justification (see Extract 1), Vera did not do so: she decided to present it and wait for learners to react (see Extract 2).

G: What made you use this family tree?
V: I wanted to show a different family. ... They know who The Simpsons are. Selma is a single mother and a lesbian *[N.B. Patty is the character that comes out as lesbian]*. She has adopted a daughter ... she is different from what students see in the classroom and in the (text)book.
G: Did you have any hesitations or doubts when selecting this (family tree)?
V: At first, but not now. Students are younger than we are. I realized that for them these things are more natural. They are not scared of two women or two men together. It is important that they feel it is ok to talk about these things in the classroom but you cannot do that with the English materials we have. I don't think it changes everything, but at least they talk about these things in class. That's important.

Extract 2: Interview with VeraIn order for learners to have a discussion, Vera prepared some questions which foregrounded different types of families, gender and sexual identities (Figure 4.5).

She did not plan a full lesson around gender, sexuality or heteronormativity. Her idea was to let learners voice their views and experiences by reacting to the family tree and the questions, and then to introduce different types of families they knew about. This, together with the introduction of Patty as lesbian and Selma as a single mother, contributed to lowering the degree of heteronormativity presented in the visual representation of the family and the questions around which the task was designed in Year 1.

Not having access to classroom observations for this school year, I was not able to capture learners' behaviours in class. According to Vera, learners felt comfortable discussing these matters and they were curious about different types of families in Uruguay and in other parts of the world. During an interview, she recalled one student who talked about his own gay uncle and his partner. Vera recalled this vividly because for her it was the first time a student had brought up the topic of gay couples in their own family life. This encouraged her to introduce these matters because she felt 'they are much more open than us', referring to learners' lower heteronormativity when talking about their families:

G: You mentioned some learners did not know in advance that in the series Patty came out as lesbian and Selma became a single mother. What happens once they learn that? What do you do?

V: You don't have to do much. You let them talk. They always have something to say. Sometimes they say silly things,[5] when they are not serious, but most of the times they ask questions and talk to each other. Some girls asked 'Can I adopt here in Uruguay if I don't get married?' or 'Is it too difficult to be a single mother?' 'Can lesbian couples adopt here in Uruguay?'

G: And what do you say?

V: They talk to each other, they share information and they teach each other. I mean, other students answer the questions usually. Some students even knew where you need to go if you want to adopt a child or if you need a fertilization treatment.

G: How did you feel about it?

V: I was surprised and happy!

Extract 3: Interview with VeraInstead of viewing these topics as contents to be *taught*, Vera adopted a non-traditional and non-authoritative stance. She allowed learners to introduce topics she did not know in advance or knew much about (such as legal regulations for fertilization or gay couple adoption in Uruguay). She took this opportunity to learn with students, allowing them to take the floor and voice their questions and experiences, going far beyond what the EFL syllabus dictates. While representations of heteronormative families present in the textbook and other language materials were not explicitly contested, Vera and the learners defied them implicitly by collaboratively opening spaces for breaking – at least momentarily – such heteronormative prosody while at the same time accomplishing the linguistic goals of the unit.

Year 3: Breaking Down the Notion of Family in the Family Tree

In Year 3, Vera opted for what she considers to be a *more open* family tree (see Figure 4.6), which would not force learners into one particular representation of a family: '(In this new tree) students decide who they consider to be their family. They can put what they like and you're not pushing them.'

Instead of explicitly attempting to deconstruct gender and sexuality roles within the family as she did the previous year, this time she attempted to deconstruct the very notion of family by adopting a different type of tree representation. She still used the example of *The Simpsons'* series to introduce matters of gender, sexuality and heteronormativity, thus securing that learners

Figure 4.6 Illustration of family tree similar to the one used in Year 3.

would get to talk about different types of families. However, she became more sensitive to learners' own social lives and experiences. She started to reflect that addressing visual representations of other families (even for breaking heteronormative prosody or to discuss the notion of family) differed greatly from addressing learners' own lives. So, she decided to introduce a new type of tree for learners to represent their families. This pedagogical choice is relevant in that she opted to initiate the lesson by centring on learners instead of representing the experiences and identities of others.

Several differences can be found if we compare Figure 4.6 to Figures 4.2 and 4.4. Firstly, Figure 4.6 does not represent a particular family; it requires learners to complete the tree by adding their own family members (each member represented by a leaf with an image or name they add to the tree). This requires more interaction between learners and the representation at hand: they show their family as they wish to construct it. While this pertains to a way of deconstructing the notion of family, it does not necessarily foreground gender, sexuality and heteronormativity. In other words, the tree has the potential to become less heteronormative as far as these matters are brought up by learners or in previous tasks (such as *The Simpsons*' example).

Secondly, the family tree representation is in itself more iconic in that the shape and form of the family tree resembles an actual tree. Far from trivial, this has implications in terms of visual/graphic representation: unlike more symbolic family trees used in the previous years, this tree has branches (not symmetric connecting lines) which are unequally distributed and thus they do not favour a clear hierarchical reading but instead a more rhizomatic understanding of family relations. As a non-standard family tree, it does not guide learners towards one particular reading of family hierarchy or towards an unequivocal interpretation of relations among family members. Learners can adopt a more communal notion of family in which traditional hierarchical and blood relations are defied.

As reported by Vera, she opted for this family tree in order to raise awareness of the concept of family in a non-traditional fashion (Figure 4.7). She still uses textbooks and other EFL materials, but such materials do not cope with her expectations in that they only represent traditional families in terms of structure but also in terms of gender and sexuality.

Upon reviewing the family trees students designed, I learned that these touched on several topics that attempt to break the heteronormative prosody of the classroom, including: same-sex (partners and married) couples, bisexual identities and single parenting. The fact that learners are able to articulate these matters in their own family trees is a form of legitimizing alternative discourses and identities in the classroom. A wider range of represented identity options become legitimate and available and, potentially, such identities become legitimate and available for learners to adopt as their own (Canale & Furtado 2021).

When discussing what she would do with this task in the future, Vera mentioned that she plans to work with biology and social studies teachers to design other tasks for students to get more information about topics they have shown interest in, such as: fertilization, legal aspects of single parenting, as well as surrogacy and gay adoption in Uruguay. She feels comfortable not placing herself as an authoritative voice in these topics and allowing other voices (learners and other content subjects) to become part of her class. Either by introducing other voices in her lesson or by redesigning teaching materials, she seems to be aware that she needs to find strategies to make sure she can accomplish one of the main points in the political agenda of (progressive) education: transforming heteronormative views of the family and of individuals.

Conclusions and Implications

It is certainly important to pay attention to how EFL teachers question their own pedagogical choices and are ready to learn from other teachers and from learners. While each classroom is heterogeneous and unique, some experiences – like Vera's – can sensibly migrate across classrooms.

What, how and *when* to incorporate socially relevant matters (such as gender, sexuality and heteronormativity) depend on both the social and situational context in which teaching and learning are taking place. For instance, the school and the parents play a key role in Vera's teaching: in several interviews she mentioned she had never had any parent criticizing her for her progressive views of gender and family, which probably encouraged her to become more engaged in this type of work. The growing visibility of matters of gender, sexuality and heteronormativity in the local context also favoured this. However, many other local schools and parents may have serious objections to this work which can prevent teachers from addressing such topics in the classroom.

In more general terms, Vera's reflexive work shows that critical classroom material and task design require an understanding of: (1) the ideological tension between the social world as represented by language materials and the social world of learners; (2) the ideological tension between *marked* pedagogical choices (addressing heteronormativity) and unmarked choices that contribute to the heteronormative prosody; and (3) the fact that meanings are made in many different ways and by different resources in the classroom and that even an apparently simple image (such as a family tree) requires close examination for pedagogical and curricular purposes.

Along these lines, Vera's classroom tells a very interesting tale about the ins and outs of *growing into* matters of gender, sexuality and heteronormativity as an EFL teacher. It also tells us about how teachers and learners can interactively open spaces in the classroom for defying the dominant heteronormative prosody. Her strategy, thus far, has been bottom-up in that she opens small spaces for learners to have access to and discuss these topics. She does not attempt to change the full curriculum, but instead draws on her situated agency to introduce certain topics and manage them with learners so as to share power (see Norton & Pavlenko 2004). In other words, while her overall teaching objectives and goals perhaps are not considered feminist or queer *stricto sensu*, the small changes and revisions Vera makes to tasks contribute to challenging the heteronormative prosody found in EFL materials and discourses.

The analysis and findings presented also point to a more general aspect of ELT material design and teacher agency in research. Material and lesson design entail interactive and reflexive processes which need to be further investigated because pedagogical choices can potentially impact learners (Govender 2018a). In narrating Vera's story, I do not attempt to claim that her pedagogic choices are *the right* ones. My claim is that her choices show the laborious task EFL teachers engage in when attempting to break dominant ideologies, such as heteronormativity. Telling cases such as Vera's are very productive for reflecting on small steps and actions that can be taken in our everyday teaching practices to break this heteronormative prosody, albeit momentarily. However, this does not background the need for structural changes in language education and language teacher education (see Banegas, Jacovkis & Romiti 2020) to adopt a more critical perspective. Critical EFL instructors do not only face the challenge of turning the classroom into a space for *reading the world* (Freire & Macedo 1987), but they also face the challenge of planning and redesigning situated strategies to do so.

Finally, this study hopes to contribute to the specialized literature by addressing gender and sexuality from the perspective of classroom-based research and by critically examining family relations in the language classroom and language classroom material, which – thus far – have not been explored in much detail. More importantly, the study addresses these issues by focusing on a *telling case* in South America (Uruguay), a still underrepresented area in EFL and ELT research.

Questions for Change

1. In your own context (school, district, country), are there any topics of gender and sexuality under discussion? How do these matters (directly or indirectly) refer to heteronormativity?
2. Has local education adopted a particular (implicit or explicit) stance about such topics?
3. To what extent do the language materials, curricula and syllabuses you use/design reflect such discussions?
4. In practice, what role do teachers, material developers, school administrators, parents or other stakeholders play in excluding/including these topics in the EFL classroom?
5. Based on your own experience, what could be the most important benefits and risks of addressing these matters in local EFL classrooms or materials?

Notes

1 This chapter is part of the research project *Negociando identidades de género en el aula: representaciones discursivas en el libro de texto de inglés como lengua extranjera* (I+D, 2021–3), which has been funded by Comisión Sectorial de Investigación Científica, Universidad de la República, Uruguay. I am thankful to Dietha Koster,

Victoria Furtado and Martina Fernández Fasciolo for providing feedback on an earlier version of this chapter. Any remaining mistake is my sole responsibility.

2 http://www.mysu.org.uy/wp-content/uploads/2014/11/Ley-de-Interrupci%C3%B3n-Voluntaria-del-Embarazo-18.987-promulgada-por-el-Poder-Ejecutivo-2012..pdf. Last accessed: 23 March 2021.

3 https://www.impo.com.uy/bases/leyes/19075-2013 and https://www.impo.com.uy/bases/leyes/19119-2013. Last accessed: 23 March 2021.

4 https://www.impo.com.uy/bases/leyes/19684-2018. Last accessed 8 March 2022.

5 During my classroom observations in Year 1, I witnessed only a few events on which learners would mock or make fun about matters pertaining to gender and sexuality, but only when referring to the textbook or other language materials (e.g. assuming the character was lesbian because of what she was wearing and because of her name, see Canale & Furtado 2021), but usually not when publicly talking about other learners.

5

Exploring the Effects of Stereotype Threat on Men's Foreign Language Listening Performance in a Sample of Turkish University Students

Gulsah Kutuk

Introduction

There has been a long-standing concern that women are underrepresented in certain academic domains such as science, technology, engineering and mathematics (STEM) due to traditional stereotypes that men are more competent in these domains (Barone 2011). Such gendered and problematic perceptions have been found to undermine women's achievement in STEM in many ways as well as restrict their access to STEM subjects and fields. Compared to their male peers, for example, women tend to show less interest and experience more anxiety in these fields (e.g. Stoet, Bailey, Moore & Geary 2016). It has also been consistently reported that women tend to have lower self-efficacy, and they are less likely to believe that they possess an innate ability in STEM (Beyer 2014). While these studies offer valuable insights, they are largely confined to the issues surrounding the gender stereotypes and women's disadvantage in male-dominated academic domains. Conversely, men and their beliefs and achievement in female-dominated fields such as foreign languages have not received considerable attention from researchers, educators and policy-makers.

Second language (L2) learning is predominantly stereotyped as a female domain by language learners and teachers alike. In one of the earliest studies, for example, Carr and Pauwels (2006) interviewed over two hundred twelve- to eighteen-year-old boys learning French (as well as teachers and girls who work alongside boys in language classrooms) in the major English-dominant communities in Australia and found that not only boys but also girls and language teachers perceived L2 learning as more suited to girls. The majority of the boys believed that they would not succeed in languages. They felt alienated from the language learning context due to the fact that their teachers were mostly women who tended to favour girls, and that teaching resources and activities did not appeal to them. They also indicated that languages did not offer various career options or enough cognitive challenges for them, revealing that the perceived value of L2 learning as an academic domain was also low among these boys. Indeed, these stereotypes still hold true for today's language learners and teachers (see Chaffee, Lou, Noels & Katz 2020; Li, McLellan & Forbes 2021). Notwithstanding such evidence of gender stereotypes in foreign languages, the following questions posed by Schmenk (2004) still have not been fully addressed to date:

> Does the phenomenon called *stereotype threat* in social psychology (Kray, Thompson, & Galinsky, 2001; Steele, 1997), the tendency to confirm gender stereotypes when they are explicitly activated, occur in language learning contexts as well? What role do stereotyping and so-called self-fulfilling prophecies play in sustaining the belief in language learning as a feminine domain? (521)

Yet, these questions warrant more attention from researchers, practitioners and policy-makers for at least three reasons. Firstly, with the advent of globalization in the twenty-first century, internationalism and multiculturalism have gained increasing momentum, so it is essential that individuals develop skills and competences (e.g. language competence including language awareness and intercultural competence including cultural awareness) to better engage with this fast-changing world. Secondly, L2 learning enhances individuals' cognitive abilities (e.g. better executive functioning) and promotes their academic achievement through improving other relevant skills (e.g. increased memory performance and creativity). It also opens up new career opportunities for them in the growing global job market (see Fox, Corretjer, Webb & Tian 2019). Thirdly, English, among other languages, is currently considered a global language and used as the main language for international communication in many areas such as science, technology and business. As such, it is important that all individuals have the equal right of access to English – the language of power – regardless of their gender. This demonstrates that those, especially men, who prefer not to engage with foreign language learning due to its being associated with women might be missing out on the benefits and opportunities afforded by L2 learning.

In light of these reasons, this chapter sets out to contribute to the limited body of knowledge in the field of second language acquisition (SLA) by examining the relationship between gender stereotypes and a group of male university students' performance in English as a foreign language (EFL) in Turkey. By doing so, the chapter aims not only to raise awareness about the potential negative impact of gender stereotypes on men's language performance but also to lead discussions as to how to provide fair and suitable opportunities for both genders in foreign languages as well as other academic fields that are mostly associated with females. The chapter itself is organized into four sections. The first section describes gender and gender roles in the context of Turkey and briefly discusses the role of gender in Turkish higher education. The second section provides a thorough review of stereotype threat (ST) and examines its potential impact on men's L2 achievement. In the third section, the focus is on an experimental study conducted with a group of men learning EFL at university level in Turkey with a special focus on their L2 listening performance. The final section highlights the implications of the research findings for future research and practice.

Gender and Gender Roles in Turkey

Exploring the phenomenon of ST in a Turkish context is particularly interesting due to the cultural and social factors underlying gender differences in Turkey. Before discussing these differences, it is important to elaborate on what is meant by gender in the current chapter. Gender is socially constructed and, therefore, variable and subject to change. The way individuals construct their gender identities varies due to the characteristics assigned to each gender by society. The differences across genders are generally used to explain the extent to which individuals are masculine and feminine, rather than male or female.

Since gender is socially constructed, the meaning of gender roles and expectations must be situated within a particular context. In Turkey, where the present study was based, femininities and masculinities are mainly constructed in line with the traditional understanding of gender roles and expectations which are often strict and clear-cut (Eslen-Ziya & Koc 2016). In a heteronormative family structure, for example, it is expected that males are the sole or main provider for their family. They also have the authority and power to make decisions concerning family matters. On the other hand, females are considered homemakers and caregivers. They are expected to be loyal and obedient and seen as in need of protection and care.

Given these gender roles and expectations, one can assume that Turkish men and women's education and career choices might be different from each other. This assumption is supported by recent statistics (2020–1) provided by the Council of Higher Education (2021) in Turkey. According to these statistics, the majority of the students who enrolled in an undergraduate programme in languages (i.e. Language Acquisition and Literature and Linguistics) were women. In STEM programmes (e.g. mechanical engineering), the number of male students was disproportionately higher than that of female students. These statistics suggest that gender stereotyping of academic domains is prevalent in Turkey. In the current research context, however, learning EFL, which is stereotyped as a female domain, was compulsory for men rather than optional (see Participants for further details). As such, it is pertinent to determine the extent to which the stereotype that women are better at foreign languages than men would affect Turkish men's EFL performance under these circumstances.

ST and Men's Foreign Language Performance

ST is defined as 'being at risk of confirming, as self-characteristic, a negative stereotype about one's group' (Steele & Aronson 1995: 797). In other words, if there is an over-generalized belief attributed to a specific group (e.g. race, ethnicity, gender, sexual orientation), individuals who belong to that group are at risk of acknowledging this belief as a true representation of themselves when it is made salient or applicable. In their pioneering research, Steele and Aronson (1995) tested this theory through a series of experiments. Their hypothesis was that whenever African American students perform an intellectual task, they are under the risk of fulfilling a negative racial stereotype about their ability or competence. The results showed that under the experimental conditions of ST (i.e. ability-diagnostic conditions), African American students' intellectual test performance was worse than that of the European-American students. However, when the same tests were taken in non-ST conditions (i.e. non-diagnostic conditions), no such differences were observed between the groups, which supported the hypothesis that stereotype activation impairs performance.

ST is not limited to social groups that are commonly and widely stigmatized in a society. Any individual who is a member of a group to which a negative stereotype can be applied is under the risk of being threatened by ST. More specifically, given the well-known stereotype that women are better in foreign languages than men, it can be hypothesized that men in foreign language studies might also be susceptible to ST. However, there is a general lack of research exploring this hypothesis directly. One exception is Chaffee, Lou and Noels's (2020) recent study which investigated whether explicit STs affected men's language-related performance and their sense of belonging to language-related domains in a series of four experiments. Contrary to expectations, this research did not report a significant effect of ST on men in language. However, as in some earlier studies, one limitation of this work was that ST was conceptualized and treated as a single construct which may partly account for non-significant or inconsistent results reported from previous studies and jeopardize the generalizability of published research.

As Shapiro (2011) emphasizes, there are multiple forms of STs, and it is essential to differentiate between these to be able to conclude the absence/presence of ST and subsequently reflect on the need for intervention. Accordingly, the author proposed a 2 × 3 multi-threat framework featuring six different types of ST which are grouped based on the source (the self, the in-group or the out-group) and the target of the threat (the self or the in-group). According to this framework, individuals might be more susceptible to one type of threat than others, and their performance might be influenced depending on which type of threat is made salient. The current chapter focuses on the target of the ST, namely self-as-target (i.e. self-concept threat) and group-as-target (i.e. group-concept threat), both of which are outlined in detail below (see Shapiro 2011, for the other four types of ST). Although promising, the multi-threat framework has not yet received enough empirical support revealing the distinct processes behind each of the distinct STs (Pennington 2016), especially in SLA. As such, one of the aims of this chapter is to determine whether self-as-target threat or group-as-target threat is more detrimental to Turkish men's L2 listening performance.

While acknowledging that each language skill (i.e. listening, speaking, reading and writing) is essential to L2 learning and that they all have their own challenges which could create circumstances conducive to ST, the present study focuses on a listening task for two main reasons. Firstly, listening has a crucial role in L2 learning. Not only does it have a role in communication, but it is also an essential source of language input and provides a number of opportunities for language development. As such, it is likely that the task value of listening is high among L2 learners. Secondly, compared to the other skills, listening is more challenging for some learners. In addition to comprehension problems such as failing to understand the intended message, there are also some other external factors influencing learners' listening achievement such as speech rate, unfamiliar accents or noise in the environment (Goh 2016). This demonstrates that a listening task would be potentially of high difficulty and demand, which may heighten any ST effects.

Self-Concept Threat and Group-Concept Threat

Self-concept threat (i.e. I am afraid that my behaviour will confirm, *in my own mind*, that the negative stereotypes which are held of my group are *true of me*) is a self-as-source, self-as-target ST (Shapiro 2011). It is the fear that occurs when individuals see themselves as having a negatively stereotyped characteristic which is normally attributed to their group. For example, Ahmet, a male L2 learner, might fear that a poor performance in a language test will substantiate the belief in his own mind that he is, by virtue of his gender, less competent than his female classmates. Individuals experience self-concept threat when they believe the negative stereotype is possibly true (i.e. stereotype endorsement). If Ahmet is not convinced that the negative stereotype might be true, he would not fear having the negatively stereotyped characteristic, and therefore, he would not experience self-concept threat.

Group-concept threat (i.e. I am afraid that my behaviour will confirm, *in my own mind*, that the negative stereotypes which are held of my group are *true of my group*) is a self-as-source, group-as-target threat (Shapiro 2011). It occurs when individuals are afraid of legitimatizing the negative stereotype about their own group in their own mind by having the negative stereotypic characteristic themselves (i.e. afraid of being a bad ambassador of their group). For example, Ahmet, a male L2 learner, might fear that a poor performance in a language test will substantiate the hypothesis in his own mind that men are, by virtue of their gender, less competent at L2 learning than women. To experience group-concept threat, however, individuals need to (a) believe that the negative stereotype is possibly true; (b) identify themselves with their stigmatized groups (i.e. seeing a stereotyped characteristic such as gender as central to one's self-concept). More specifically, if being a man is not central to Ahmet's self-concept, he would not be afraid of being a bad ambassador of the stigmatized group, and therefore, he would not experience group-concept threat.

Mediating and Moderating Variables of ST

There are various affective, cognitive and motivational processes through which ST determines individuals' performance (Pennington 2016). This chapter focuses on two of the affective mediators, namely *anxiety* (i.e. subjective feeling of nervousness, tension or worry) and *self-efficacy* (i.e. perceived capability to perform the target behaviour) (Bandura 1997). Previous research findings into these mediators have been inconsistent and contradictory. For example, in Steele and Aronson's (1995) original study, self-reported anxiety did not mediate the ST effect on African American's intellectual performance, whereas Chung et al. (2010) revealed that both anxiety and self-efficacy mediated the effects of ST on African American's exam performance. In some other studies, self-efficacy did not mediate the effects of self-as-target threat on African American's cognitive ability (Mayer & Hanges 2003) or group-as-target threat on women's mathematical performance (Spencer, Steele & Quinn 1999).

The existing mixed findings support the notion that the effects of ST on individuals' performance outcomes vary, and this can be attributed to numerous moderating factors. One of these moderators is stereotype endorsement. It is evidenced that individuals who endorse the negative stereotypes attributed to the group they belong to tend to be more susceptible to ST compared to those who do not endorse these stereotypes (Schmader, Johns & Barquissau 2004). In addition, ST effects tend to emerge on tasks of high difficulty and demand. In their study, Keller (2007) showed that ST had different effects on low and high domain identifiers' performance depending on the task difficulty. When the task was difficult, low identifiers showed higher performance, whereas high identifiers had lower performance under the ST condition. Such results were not observed when the task was easy.

The Study

Taking previous research and findings into account, this chapter aims to make a significant contribution to the limited ST literature in SLA with a special focus on the listening skill. To achieve these, a number of research questions were devised:

1. Does self-as-target and group-as-target threat influence men's English listening performance differently?
2. To what extent does anxiety mediate the effects of self-as-target and group-as-target threat on men's English listening performance?
3. To what extent does self-efficacy mediate the effects of self-as-target and group-as-target threat on men's English listening performance?

Participants

The present study was concerned with learning and teaching EFL in English preparatory programmes provided by universities in Turkey. These programmes are generally one full academic year (eight to nine months) long and are compulsory for students who are registered for an undergraduate course adopting English as a medium of instruction (EMI) or a combination of EMI and Turkish as a medium of instruction. Before students start their undergraduate studies at university, they must attend the English preparatory course at their university and pass the proficiency test at the end of the course. The participants of the present study were chosen from among EFL learners in these courses.

A total of 103 Turkish male EFL learners were recruited using the convenience sampling method (M_{age} = 19.23, SD = 1.17). At the time of the data collection, the participants had been learning EFL for about six months at university.

ST Manipulations

In line with Shapiro's (2011) multi-threat framework, participants were randomly assigned to self-as-target (n = 42), group-as-target (n = 33) or control conditions (n = 26) and primed accordingly. The priming (i.e. the process through which knowledge about the participant's group membership is activated) was carried out twice: before the questionnaires and before the performance measure (i.e. English listening test), and it was in Turkish. The stereotype manipulations implemented in each condition are described in detail below.

Participants in the self-as-target threat condition were primed with the following instructions to make the gender stereotype that L2 learning is a female domain salient. The instructions also sought to emphasize that the test was diagnostic of the participants' individual ability as a man, not that of their group's ability as a whole. The instructions they received were as follows:

> There is a negative stereotype that men have less ability in foreign language learning than women. Today, I would like you to take an English listening test. The score you will get from this test will help me establish *your personal ability in EFL learning as a man*.

Participants in the group-as-target threat condition were primed with the same instructions as above, but in this condition, they were informed that the test was diagnostic of their gender group, not that of their individual performance as a man. The below sentence in the instructions aimed to heighten the salience of gender stereotype and emphasize that it targeted the men's ability as a gender group:

> The score you will get from this test will help me establish *men's ability in EFL in general*.

Participants in the control group did not receive any information about the negative gender stereotype that was made salient in the treatment conditions. They were informed that the test was not diagnostic of their ability. They were primed with the instructions below:

> Today, I want to assess the reliability of an English listening test which I have prepared for foreign language learners. I would like to see how many correct and wrong answers each question will get. The test is not diagnostic of your language ability in EFL. Please listen to the audio recordings carefully and answer the questions accordingly.

Data Collection Instruments

A background questionnaire was used to obtain information about the participants' demographic information (e.g. age, home region) and their language learning experiences (e.g. duration of English study at university, languages learnt other than English). This was followed by the 'gendered perceptions of academic subjects questionnaire' in which the participants were asked to rate a series of sixteen academic subjects including foreign languages on a 5-point scale (1= women are always better, 5= men are always better). The test value of 3 (i.e. Both women and men are equally good) was defined as the neutral value. The questionnaire aimed to provide a wider picture of the participants' existing gender stereotypes about a series of academic subjects. To assess the participants' level of identification with their gender group, Cameron's (2004) 'three dimensional strength of group identification scale' was used. Internal consistency reliability of this scale was acceptable (Cronbach's alpha, $\alpha = .72$).

Participants' listening anxiety was measured using the listening activities anxiety sub-scale of the 'multidimensional language class anxiety scale' (Kutuk, Putwain, Kaye & Garrett 2020). The scale consisted of six items assessing affective, cognitive and physiological components of listening anxiety ($\alpha = .89$). Participants' listening self-efficacy was measured using L2 reception self-efficacy sub-scale of the 'questionnaire of self-efficacy beliefs in learning a foreign language' (Kutuk, Putwain, Kaye & Garrett 2020). There was a total of five items in this questionnaire (α =.85). The participants were asked to rate all the items on a 5-point scale (1 = strongly disagree, 5 = strongly agree).

Participants' English listening performance was assessed using the listening part of the Preliminary English Test (PET) (UCLES 2015). The PET was chosen because it is normally administered by a well-known institution, the University of Cambridge Local Examinations Syndicate (UCLES), and the results gained from their tests are officially recognized around the world as proof of ability to use English. As such, reliability and validity of these tests are considered as high. The PET is designed for learners at B1 level (independent user) of the Common European Framework of Reference (CEFR), so to avoid the ceiling effect on performance (i.e. that the test is either too easy or difficult resulting in similar scores in performance), it was ensured that the level of the test was just above the participants' actual English level. The participants' English level was double-checked with the language teachers of the chosen classrooms prior to each experiment, and a particular attention was given not to select any participants whose level of English was considerably below or above B1 level. The test consisted of four sections and it lasted twelve to thirteen minutes to complete all the sections. In the test, the participants listened to: seven short recordings and chose the best of three pictures for each recording (Part 1); a long recording and answered six multiple-choice questions accordingly (Part 2); a long monologue and completed the missing parts in text (Part 3); and a long recording and answered six True/False questions accordingly (Part 4).

To determine whether stereotype manipulation was effective, the participants were asked to rate five statements assessing their gender stereotypes about EFL learning using a 5-point scale (1= women are always better, 5= men are always better). The midpoint of 3 was neutral (α =.75).

Data Collection Procedure

Experiments conducted in labs confirm the hypothesis of ST with a high degree of internal validity. However, such studies do not have external validity since their results cannot readily be generalized to real-world settings such as school or university settings (Owens & Massey 2011). Therefore, to provide a more ecologically valid context, the experiments in the current research were conducted in the classrooms where the participants' language learning normally took place. Since the participants were tested in a real-world context to their learning, domain identification (i.e. learning L2 is important to me) was likely to be more controlled than in other lab-based ST research.

Permission to collect data was granted by the directors of the Foreign Languages Schools and the teachers responsible for the selected classes. The learners were also asked to give their individual consent on the first page of the questionnaires. Each experiment lasted forty to forty-five minutes in total. After giving information about the nature of the study and getting the participants' consent, the participants were asked to fill in the background questionnaire, gendered perceptions of academic subjects questionnaire and the three-dimensional strength of group identification scale. On completion of these questionnaires, the participants in each class were randomly assigned to one of the three conditions (self-concept threat, group-concept threat and control). Based on their condition, they received the relevant ST manipulations which were followed by the questionnaires of anxiety and self-efficacy. Once the questionnaires were completed, the participants were primed with the same instructions again and asked to complete the English listening task. The participants were informed that they would hear the listening text only once. Following the task, the participants were asked to complete the questionnaire of gender stereotypes about EFL learning. At the end of each experiment, the participants were thanked for their participation and were provided with a debrief which emphasized that the negative stereotypes mentioned at the beginning of the experiment were not a true reflection of their ability.

Results

Gender Stereotype Endorsement

All data were analysed using SPSS v.27. A series of one-sample t-tests were conducted to determine the extent to which the participants endorsed the gender-related stereotypes attributed to the given academic subjects. The results concerning six academic subjects (i.e. fine arts, educational sciences, medical sciences, dentistry, humanities and tourism) were non-significant (all $ps > .05$). Consistent with the literature and the expectations, the participants endorsed the gender stereotype that women are better at foreign languages than men: $t(100) = -2.70, p < .01$. Additionally, the participants believed that women are better than men at three other academic subjects: architecture and design: $t(100) = -4.73, p < .001$; health sciences: $t(100) = -13.15, p < .001$; and communication: $t(100) = -4.23, p < .001$. On the other hand, they endorsed that men are better than women in sports sciences: $t(91) = 4.86, p < .001$; aviation and space sciences: $t(91) = 4.86, p < .001$; economics: $t(91) = 4.86, p < .001$; life sciences: $t(91) = 4.86, p < .001$; engineering: $t(91) = 4.86, p < .001$; and agriculture: $t(91) = 4.86, p < .001$.

Following the initial analyses, a series of multivariate analysis of variance (MANOVA) were conducted to determine the extent to which participants in the three conditions differed from each other in terms of their stereotype endorsement level. The overall MANOVA analysis revealed that there were no significant differences between the conditions ($F(32,166) = 1.26, p = .175$, $\eta_p^2 = .196$), suggesting that the participants' pre-existing beliefs were controlled. That is, any differences in the results were due to the stereotype manipulation rather than the participants' existing beliefs.

Group Identification

The overall mean score for gender identification was 36.96 ($SD = 5.43$, $M_{range} = 16–56$), suggesting a moderate level of group identification. Thus, it was evident that men tended to view their gender identity as somewhat important to them. The results further examined for any differences in participants' gender identification level between the conditions. While the scores did not significantly differ between the control group ($M = 36.42; SD = 3.93$) and experimental conditions, a significant mean difference between the two experimental groups was observed. The participants in the self-as-target condition had significantly higher levels of gender identification ($M = 38.88, SD = 5.64$) compared to the group-as-target condition ($M = 34.93, SD = 5.47$).

Stereotype Manipulation Check

To evaluate whether there were any differences in the level of stereotype endorsement across the three condition groups, another MANOVA was conducted. Unexpectedly, the analysis revealed that the stereotype manipulation used in the current study was not effective, $F(4,190) = .782, p = .538, \eta_p^2 = .016$. Even though the stereotype manipulation check was non-significant, it was decided that the analyses in the following sections were still conducted. It is possible that the threat manipulation was effective (i.e. it worked to influence gender stereotypes), but it was not sensitive enough in the current research. It can also be speculated that the participants were motivated to disconfirm the negative stereotype attributed to their gender group and completed the questionnaires accordingly. The mean scores of the questionnaires support this (i.e. self-as-target condition, $M = 14.36$, $SD = 2.52$; group-as-target, $M = 14.45$, $SD = 2.04$; and control, $M = 13.73$, $SD = 2.34$). As seen, the participants in the experimental conditions were less inclined to endorse the common stereotypes than the participants in the control condition. The non-significant MANOVA might also be due to stereotype manipulations not being task specific (i.e. it was not related to the listening skill specifically) whereby responses were about L2 learning more generally. Given these concerns, the below analyses should be treated with caution.

English Listening Test Performance

A series of one-way analysis of variance (ANOVA) (Figure 5.1) were performed to determine whether there were any statistically significant differences between the mean scores of the English listening test and its sub-sections across the three conditions. First, participants' overall scores were compared. To determine the effect size, Cohen's (1988) guidelines were followed (i.e. 0.01 = small,

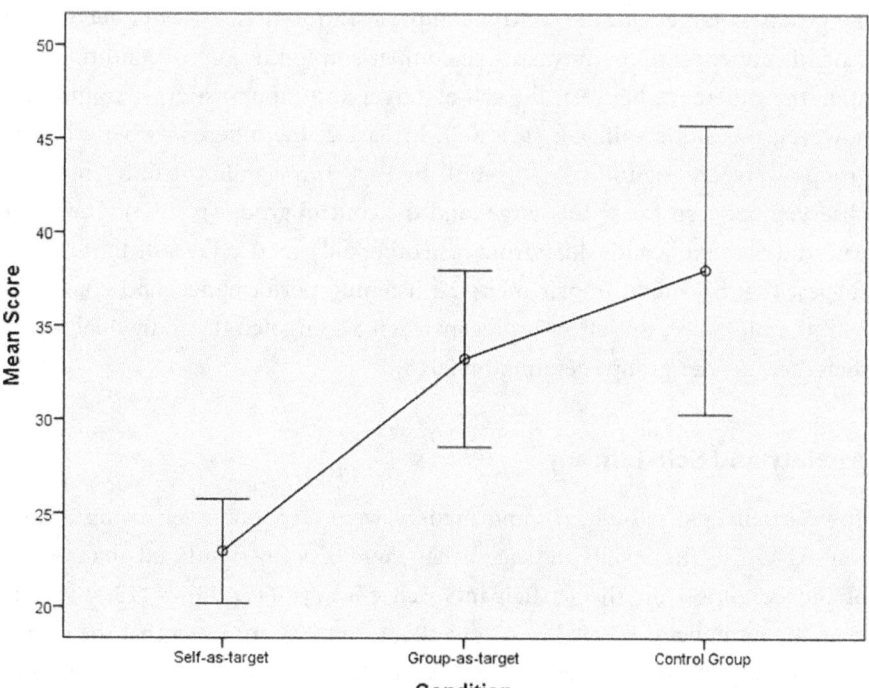

Figure 5.1 One-way ANOVA results for the English listening test scores across the groups.

0.06 = medium and 0.14 = large). Based on these guidelines, the results showed that there was a significant main effect of the condition on the performance: $F(2, 100) = 5.15$, $p < .01$, $n_p^2 = .17$. That is, the participants' performance were significantly different across the three conditions. The pairwise comparisons indicated that participants in the self-as-target condition had lower L2 listening scores ($M = 22.95$, $SD = 8.96$) relative to the group-as-target ($M = 33.26$, $SD = 13.74$) and the control conditions ($M = 38.00$, $SD = 19.10$). There was a significant difference between self-as-target condition and the two other conditions (i.e. group-as-target and control; $p < .05$). However, the difference between the group-as-target condition and the control group was not significant ($p > .05$).

As for the sub-sections of the English listening test, experimental condition did not have a significant effect on Part 4: $F(2, 100) = 1.92$, $p > .05$, $n_p^2 = .08$. However, there was a significant effect of the condition on Parts 1–3 (Part 1: $F(2, 100) = 4.06$, $p < .05$, $n_p^2 = .11$; Part 2: $F(2, 100) = 4.34$, $p < .05$, $n_p^2 = .06$; and Part 3: $F(2, 100) = 3.22$, $p < .05$, $n_p^2 = .07$). That is, the participants' performance in these sections were significantly different across the three conditions. In Parts 1–3, the participants in the self-as-target group had lower scores relative to the group-as-target and the control conditions. In Part 1, self-as-target ST had a significant effect on performance in comparison to the control condition ($p < .01$). The difference between the self-as-target and group-as-target conditions, however, was not significant ($p > .05$). In Part 2, the differences between the groups were not significant ($p > .05$). In Part 3, a significant difference was observed between the self-as-target and the control group ($p < .05$). The other pairs did not significantly differ from each other (all $ps > .05$). Overall, the findings suggest that ST might impair men's L2 listening performance, and consistent with the literature, this effect is greater when ST targeted the individual rather than their gender group (Pennington 2016).

Anxiety and Self-Efficacy

The participants' self-efficacy and anxiety were also examined using a one-way ANOVA. The results indicated that there was no significant main effect of the condition on the participants' self-efficacy: $F(2, 98) = .73$, $p > .05$, $n_p^2 = .03$ or anxiety: $F(2, 98) = .47$, $p > .05$, $n_p^2 = .006$, meaning that the results were not significantly different from each other across the three conditions. Such a non-significant result suggests that there is no need to provide any further tests. However, the following pairwise comparisons are presented in this chapter for exploratory purposes only. The pairwise comparisons showed that the participants in the self-as-target condition had the lowest self-efficacy ($M = 13.00$, $SD = 2.76$) compared to the control ($M = 14.04$, $SD = 3.16$) and the group-as-target conditions ($M = 14.24$, $SD = 2.84$). While the mean differences between the self-as-target and the control conditions were not significant ($p > .05$), they significantly differed between the self-as-target and the group-as-target conditions ($p < .05$).

Interestingly, the participants in the group-as-target condition had a higher level of self-efficacy relative to the control group, which suggests that the participants under this condition might be motivated to disconfirm the negative stereotype attributed to their gender group. However, the difference between the two groups was not statistically significant ($p > .05$). The anxiety results were also surprising in that the participants in the control group had the highest mean ($M = 14.69$, $SD = 4.76$) relative to the treatment conditions, self-as-target ($M = 14.14$, $SD = 4.15$) and group-as-target ($M = 13.85$, $SD = 4.33$). Consistent with the self-efficacy results, the participants in the group-as-target condition had the lowest anxiety mean, which might be due to their attempt to disconfirm the gender stereotype presented to them. However, the mean differences between the groups were not statistically significant ($p > .05$).

The Mediation Analysis

To explore whether the effects of ST on men's listening performance were mediated through their self-efficacy and anxiety, a parallel multi-mediation model was built and run using PROCESS macro 3.1v by Andrew F. Hayes (2013). Given that the independent variable (i.e. the ST condition) in the current study was categorical, $k - 1$ independent dummy variables ($k = 3$) were created. The self-as-target condition was selected as a reference group as it was the one with the numerically lowest value. Figure 5.2 presents the comparison results gained from the mediation analysis.

Based on 5,000 bootstrap samples, the self-as-target group was compared to the group-as-target and control groups. When it was compared to the group-as-target group, the total effect (c_1) of the ST conditions on the performance was significant. The path analysis demonstrated that both self-efficacy and anxiety predicted the performance as the confidence intervals did not cross zero. However, they were not significantly related to the ST condition, and therefore, the indirect paths from the stereotype conditions to the performance through

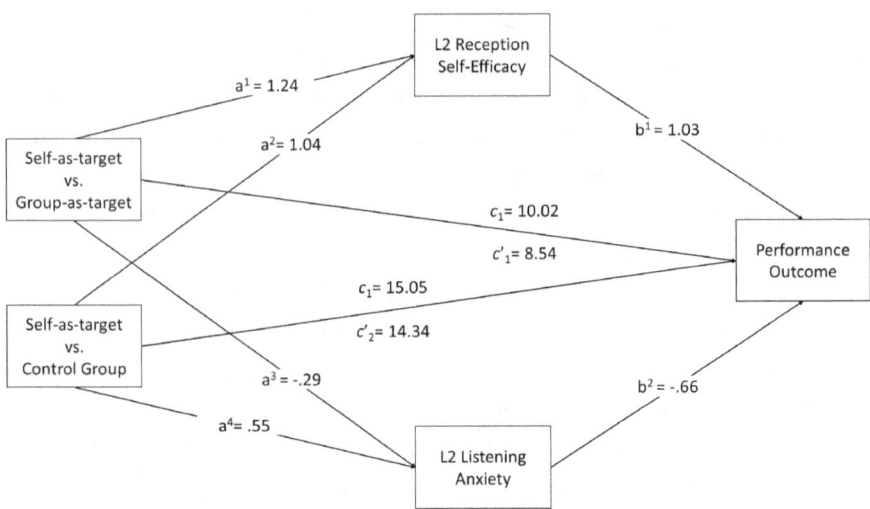

Figure 5.2 The Mediational Model – The difference between the self-as-target and group-as-target conditions.

these variables were not statistically significant. When the self-as-target group was compared to the control group, the same pattern was observed with regard to the direct and indirect paths. Overall, the results suggested that self-efficacy and anxiety did not mediate the link between the ST conditions and the listening performance. In other words, self-efficacy and anxiety were not the mechanisms through which ST caused performance decrements in the experiments.

Discussion

The findings demonstrated that the participants in the self-as-target threat condition had the lowest performance compared to the ones in the group-as-target and the control conditions. As expected, the highest performance was observed in the control condition. However, this performance was not significantly different from the group-as-target condition. These results should be evaluated considering the constellation of factors that yield each ST. Broadly speaking, individuals experience self-as-target threat when they care about the implications of their stereotype-relevant actions for the way they see themselves. Group-as-target threat is experienced when they care about the implications of their stereotype-relevant actions for the way they see the group. In the context of learning EFL at university level, which was the focus of the current chapter, it is likely that the participants cared more about their own performance than their group's performance since any failure would mean that the participants were not competent enough in English. Consequently, they would not be able to pass the English preparatory class which was the prerequisite for their further education at university.

Given that the consequence of the participants' poor performance would be more detrimental to themselves rather than the group, self-as-target threat might have been experienced more strongly than the group-as-target threat in the chosen context. It is also important to note that the gender identification level was higher in the self-as-target group than the group-as-target group, which might have heightened the effects of ST on the participants' performance. This corroborates well with previous research highlighting the moderating role of gender identity in the effects of negative stereotypes on performance (Wout, Danso, Jackson & Spencer 2008). Accordingly, it can be suggested that those who highly associate themselves with their gender may be more susceptible to ST effects.

It is important to note that in the present study, the focus was on the target of ST. However, the multi-threat framework has also another important dimension – the source of ST (i.e. whether individuals' performance will be judged by out-group members or in-group members). Although the participants in the experiments were not explicitly exposed to the source of ST, they might still have been concerned that their performance would be judged by in-group or out-group members such as their teachers. As such, their L2 listening performance may have been impacted by both the target and the source of ST. Further studies are, therefore, needed to determine whether the source of ST also plays a role in performance decrements.

With respect to the mediating factors tested in the current research, self-efficacy and anxiety did not mediate the effects of ST on L2 listening performance. This is somewhat in contrast with previous findings (Chung et al. 2010). However, the contradictory findings provide empirical support for the multi-threat framework which suggests that distinct experiences of ST may be mediated or moderated by different factors (Shapiro 2011). It is evident that more research is needed to better understand the association between the types of ST and the different mediating and moderating factors. For example, domain identification (i.e. learning L2 is important to me) is considered as a prerequisite of ST. That is, if being successful in foreign languages is not relevant to an individual's identity, they may not be susceptible to a ST concerning this domain. However, this was not tested in the current research. Future studies should take such factors into account and investigate different combinations of mediators and moderators to determine the ones that transmit the ST effects.

A possible explanation for the non-significant results gained from the mediation analyses may be that individuals under ST were motivated to disconfirm the stereotype attributed to themselves or their group (see Jamieson & Harkins 2007). In the current research, this trend was observed among the participants in the group-as-target condition. Contrary to expectations, they had a higher level of self-efficacy relative to the participants in the control group. Also, their anxiety was lower than the control group, suggesting that the participants in the group-as-target group were motivated to show that the given gender stereotype could not be applied to them. It may also be the case that they put extra effort in the English listening test to disconfirm the gender stereotype because their performance did not significantly differ from the control group. Such a result was not observed among the participants in the self-as-target condition, which again highlights the importance of differentiating between the distinct STs. An alternative explanation may be that the stereotype that women are better at L2 learning than men was not strong enough among the participants to create a significant ST effect on their performance via their anxiety and self-efficacy.

Conclusion

The findings of this study have a number of important implications for future language teaching and learning policy and practice. First, they raise EFL teachers' awareness of the potential negative effect of gender stereotypes on their students' L2 performance. Such awareness will be useful for teachers to pay close attention to their learners' gendered attitudes and beliefs in classrooms and ensure that none of them are at a disadvantage due to their gender identity. Second, it provides an opportunity for teachers to reflect on their own teaching practice and assess whether they sustain or legitimize any gender stereotypes either explicitly or implicitly in classrooms. They may, for example, realize that they have different expectations from their female and male students in terms of their attitudes or performance, which would affect their future achievement, and to address any inequalities in their classrooms, they may start seeking ways to provide equitable opportunities. Third, by examining how ST may limit men's language performance, the current research has shown that gender equality may also be a men's issue. It is therefore necessary to put the issue of men in a wider context and increase opportunities for collective action to achieve equality not only in language education but also in other areas of higher education that are largely associated with females.

Questions for Change

1. Is the stereotype that 'women are better at foreign languages than men' prevalent in your English language teaching (ELT) context? If yes, to what extent do you endorse this gender stereotype (wittingly or unwittingly)?
2. Do you think your students perceive foreign languages as a female domain? If yes, how do you address this issue in your classrooms?
3. Do you believe the phenomenon of ST might occur in your ELT context? If yes, what situations do you think might heighten the potential for ST?
4. Are there any other stereotypes that you observe in your ELT context? How do these reflect in EFL teaching and learning process?

6

Dating as an Alternative Educational Site: An Analysis of a Female Bisexual International Student's Access to English Learning in Canada

Liang Cao

Introduction

Drawing on a larger scale ethnography, this chapter explores a Chinese, cisgender female, bisexual, international student's (pseudonym: Xixi[1]) English learning experiences in her three dating relationships in Canada. The study aims to contribute to new directions in second language acquisition (SLA) research by introducing a non-schooling model of learning to expand the research site from traditional language classrooms to broader educational contexts. Informed by an intersectional perspective that examines how social structures interact with each other to produce systemic violence and further informs social action to address real-world issues (Collins 2019; Wong 2016), it provides an unconventional glimpse into how heteropatriarchy and the ideologies of linguistic nationalism and standard English crucially shaped the focal participant's access to English learning and identity construction. Analysis and findings underline the importance of investigating ethnolinguistic minority queer[2] migrants' English learning experiences in non-conventional educational settings and cautiously remind researchers and educators to be cognizant of gender, sexual, linguistic and racial inequalities that hinder marginalized students' access to learning and to promote effective tackling strategies in their practices.

In the paragraphs that follow, I first provide a brief review of sexuality-centred research in English language education, calling for the integration of a non-schooling model and an intersectional approach. This is followed by the illustration of the theoretical frameworks of legitimate peripheral participation (LPP) (Lave & Wenger 1991) and language ideology (Woolard & Schieffelin 1994). I then introduce the methodological approaches I adopted before delving into the detailed analysis of Xixi's English learning in her three dating relationships. The chapter ends with a discussion and questions for change for applied linguistic research and educational practices targeting adult migrants' English language education.

Sexuality in English Language Education

Historically, SLA research has undergone three developmental stages since its inauguration in the 1940s influenced by the scientific traditions of behaviourism, cognitivism and sociocultural theory (Johnson 2004). In line with the sociocultural turn in SLA (Block 2003, 2007), studies exploring second language (L2) learners' social identity and language learning experiences emanated and gradually developed since the mid-1990s (e.g. Darvin & Norton 2015; Norton 1997, 2000, 2001; Norton Peirce 1995; Norton & Toohey 2011). This socially and culturally sensitive approach to SLA highlights 'a comprehensive theory of social identity that integrates the language learner and the language learning context' (Norton Pierce 1995: 12) and, subsequently, sparked a growing body of scholarship examining L2 learners' social identity categories (race in Kubota & Lin (2009), gender in Norton & Pavlenko (2004), social class in Darvin & Norton (2014), sexuality in Nelson (2010) and the intersection between religion, socioeconomic status and race in Han (2014a), to name a few) in English language teaching and learning.

Early interests in studying sexuality in SLA can be traced back to Nelson's (1993) interrogation of heterosexism in ESL (English as a second language) classes and Vandrick's (1997) cautious reminder of investigating students' hidden identities (e.g. sexual orientation) in ESL classroom teaching. At the turn of the century, drawing upon Norton Pierce's (1995) identity approach and the emerging queer theory (Jagose 1996), Nelson (1999) challenged the long existing 'gay versus lesbian' binary view and reconceptualized sexual identities from a queer perspective in ESL teaching. Following Nelson's lead, a subfield exploring L2 learners' sexuality in English language education has been progressively developed in the past two decades (e.g. Coda, Cahnmann-Taylor & Jiang 2020; King 2008; Moore 2016; Nelson 2006, 2009, 2010; Nguyen & Yang 2015; Paiz 2019). Literature in this field has witnessed advancement of knowledge in three major areas: (1) queer-identified L2 learners' experiences in multiple EAL (English as an additional language) classroom contexts; (2) EAL teachers' knowledge, attitudes and pedagogical approaches in coping with sexuality-related issues in classroom teaching; and (3) the queering of sexuality-related topics and materials in EAL teaching curricula.

Notwithstanding the rising interests and ever-diversifying research topics, only a few studies investigated adult queer migrants' language learning in EAL classrooms in the United States (e.g. Nelson 2010; Nguyen & Yang 2015). Further, research targeting queer learners with intersectional marginalized identities (e.g. female, bisexual and racialized minority as in Xixi's case) or conducted outside traditional language classrooms is still very scarce (for an exception, see King 2008). To bridge these gaps, in this chapter, I will adopt an intersectional analytical lens to dissect Xixi's English learning experiences embedded in her three romantic dating relationships in Canada.

Learning English in Context: A Non-schooling Model

LPP is a social theory of learning developed by anthropologist Jean Lave and educationist Etienne Wenger (Lave 1988; Lave & Wenger 1991; Wenger 1998). In response to the traditional understanding of learning as a cognitive process of individuals internalizing knowledge, Lave and Wenger (1991) drew on Vygotsky's conceptualization of zone of proximal development and contended that the study of learning should go beyond the context of pedagogical structuring to consider 'the structure of social world' and 'the conflictual nature of social practice' (49). Learning in this model is understood as a situated practice that involves a dual process of learners' LPP and identity (re)construction in communities of practice (CoP) (Han 2009, 2014a, 2014b). The keywords *legitimate* and *peripheral* in LPP altogether entail a centripetal form of participation, in which learners are recognized as legitimate newcomers and gradually move from the periphery to the centre as full participants in the community. Key to LPP is newcomers' access to a wide range of activities, old-timers, information, resources and opportunities: when enabled, newcomers participate legitimately and peripherally; when cut off, participation becomes marginal, or centrifugal, which prevents newcomers from growing into full participants (Cao in press).

The construct of LPP suggests the decoupling of learning from schooling. Less a pedagogical strategy or teaching approach, LPP is an alternative educational form, which, in contrast to the instruction-centred tradition, foregrounds a learning curriculum. This attribute of LPP enables me to situate Xixi's English learning in a broader educational context than conventional language classrooms. In this chapter, I understand Xixi's dating as her participation in the local CoP where she engaged in a process of 'learning English in context' (Han 2014b). In this process, what matters the most were Xixi's access to learning resources (e.g. conversation opportunities) and old-timers (e.g. English-speaking dating partners) as well as her identity construction as a Chinese, female, bisexual dating partner. Combining LPP and the analytical framework of language ideology, I shall later discuss factors that have either opened up or shut down Xixi's access to aforementioned learning conditions and consequently shaped her experiences of learning English through dating.

Language Ideology

Borrowing Woolard and Schieffelin's (1994) classic mapping of ideologies of language, I understand the term 'language ideology' as 'a mediating link between social structures and forms of talk' (55). Under this framing, the ideological meanings of language can be better approached through scrutinizing the interplay between micro-level discursive practices and the macro-level social structures. In particular, drawing on critical sociolinguistic scholarship (e.g. Chun 2013; Goodwin & Alim 2010; Piller 2016), I see language, in its broader meaning encompassing both linguistic and multimodal (e.g. Kress & van Leeuwen 2001) ways of meaning-making, as a critical site for exposing, examining and interrogating the dominant ideologies about language users' hierarchically categorized social identities. Indeed, myriad studies have demonstrated that issues that are allegedly related to language are essentially ingrained in and governed by the dominant social structures of gender (e.g. Meyerhoff & Ehrlich 2019), sexuality (e.g. Wong 2016), race (e.g. Bucholtz 2011), nationality (e.g. Han 2013) and socioeconomic class (e.g. Piller 2016), among other constructs, in both local and global societies.

The two most relevant language ideologies in this chapter are linguistic nationalism (Han 2019) and standard language ideology (Lippi-Green 2012). Linguistic nationalism, as illustrated by Irvine and Gal (2000), assumes that 'ethnic groups were normally monolingual and there was some primordial relationship between language and a particular "spirit" of a nation' (51). In a more colloquial articulation, linguistic nationalism refers to the 'one nation, one language, one people' bundle (Han 2019). Standard language ideology defines 'standard English' as an abstracted, idealized, homogeneous spoken language drawn from the Whiter upper middle class (Lippi-Green 2012). It is therefore not only a linguistic ideology but an ideology of race and social class that marginalizes English speakers who are identified as 'non-White' and 'working class' in immigrant-receiving and postcolonial countries such as Canada.

To delve into the ideological interconnection between language-centred practices and social constructs of sexuality, gender and race in Xixi's dating, I will apply Irvine and Gal's (2000) approach comprising three semiotic processes of linguistic differentiation – iconization, fractal recursivity and erasure – as the major analytical framework. In brief, iconization involves a transformation of an indexical relationship (as in *indexicality*, see King 2017) between linguistic features and social images into an inherent, essential and thus iconic linkage (Han 2019). Fractal recursivity refers to 'the projection of an opposition, salient at some level of relationship, onto some other level' (Irvine & Gal 2000: 38). In this chapter, I focus on the recursive projection of heteropatriarchy, linguistic nationalism and standard language ideology between individuals' talk (micro-level) and the dominant social structures (macro-level) in North American society. Lastly, erasure, a semiotic process of reduction, implies that persons, activities and identities that are incompatible with a dominant ideology may be 'erased' from the ideological record (Bucholtz 2001). Among the three analytical lenses, fractal recursivity is the most germane to the present discussion and will be employed to dissect all three dates. Additionally, I will apply iconization and erasure wherever appropriate in my analysis.

Methodology

Data for this chapter was drawn from a larger scale ethnography exploring adult queer migrants' settlement and English learning experiences in the Greater Vancouver Area (GVA) in Western Canada. Xixi was the focal participant in the first phase (February to September 2019) of the study. Xixi was born and raised in the capital city of Sichuan province in the southwestern part of People's Republic of China (PRC). Growing up immersed in heteronormative familial and societal values, Xixi never disclosed her bisexuality to people in her family or social circles, except for a few queer-identified friends. At the age of twenty, Xixi moved to Hong Kong to pursue a bachelor's degree in Chinese linguistics and literature. Three years later, Xixi's life trajectory shifted again when she applied and was admitted to a master's programme in linguistics in a Canadian institution. Through studying, applying for work permit and then permanent residency, Xixi envisioned immigrating to Canada where she expected less oppression but broader sexual freedom and rights than in PRC and Hong Kong. In August 2017, Xixi landed in the GVA and embarked on a journey as an international student getting settled in Canada.

In my six-month ethnography, I first familiarized myself with Xixi's background through informal talks and interviews and then conducted home visits and observations in school and community events, classes and social gatherings, among other routines in her life. My fieldwork indicates that Xixi's learning of English mostly happened in three types of CoP: social, as in her social gathering in different groups or with friends; professional, as in her work at two university linguistic labs; educational, as in her participation in university- and community-based classes. Later into the research, I conducted a series of focused interviews with Xixi and two informal interviews with two secondary participants on three key topics (dating, schooling, working) that emerged in my earlier observation. For this chapter, I choose to analyse Xixi's three (out of a total of six) dating experiences in her first two years of settlement in the GVA. Table 6.1 presents important information about Xixi's three dating partners, including their gender and sexual identities, ethnicity, immigrant status in Canada and languages spoken.

My data analysis follows a four-step, non-linear framework of mapping, tracing, connecting and claiming (Heller, Pietikäinen & Pujolar 2017). Data units are interview clips and fieldnote excerpts with greater analytical value based on the research topic (i.e. Xixi's English learning through dating). Drawing on critical discourse analysis (Cameron 2001; Talmy & Richards 2011) and the three semiotic processes of linguistic differentiation (Irvine & Gal 2000), I highlight how heteropatriarchy and the ideologies of linguistic nationalism and standard

English impacted Xixi's identity construction and simultaneously shaped her access to English learning in the three dating relationships.

Analysis: Xixi's Access to English Learning through Dating

My analysis of Xixi's English learning is twofold. In the first half, I focus on unveiling how the binary view of bisexuality and the heteropatriarchal gender orders uncritically 'opened up' Xixi's access to two heterosexual male partners and, subsequently, how the limited access was shut down by the linguistic nationalism that rendered Xixi a perpetuated Other in Canada. In the second half, through examining the shift of Xixi's dating with Luke from a 'legitimate peripheral' to a 'marginal' model, I demonstrate a process in which Xixi's initially wide-open access to English learning was completely cut off due to the projection of the standard language ideology onto their dating practices.

An Invisible Bisexual, a Perpetuated Outsider

OkCupid, a popular dating app in North America open to users of twenty-two gender identities and twenty sexual orientations,[3] was the platform Xixi used to build initial connections with her two heterosexual male dating partners, Carvin and Nicky. Carvin is a second-generation Chinese Canadian citizen who was born and raised in Canada and is English monolingual. Nicky, a 1.5-generation Hong Kong immigrant who migrated to Canada with his family at the age of six, speaks both English and Cantonese as his first languages. For Xixi, dating these two partners entails the possibility to access conversations, information and English-speaking old-timers in a non-schooling environment, a typical process of learning English in context. Notably, Xixi's dating with both partners started from online chats on OkCupid and then transitioned to in-person dates in local restaurants in the GVA, in which her access to English learning was shaped by multiple social factors, as shown in the interview excerpts[4] below:

> (1) L: ... So how did Carvin and Nicky think of you as a bisexual?

> (2) X: You know I am the most special, hahaha (laughing as if in a mocking tone). I am neither straight nor a pure lesbian. I am usually labelled as a straight girl when I am with straight people and considered as a les when I am with les.

> (3) L: Well, then, so they think of you as heterosexual instead of bisexual even it [the information of Xixi's bisexuality] is on your OkCupid profile?

(4) X: Yes. They just think of me as straight, or as they say, 'so you can choose'.

(Interview Excerpt 1, 14 June 2019)

In Excerpt 1, when responding to my inquiry about Carvin and Nicky's stance on her bisexuality (turn 1), Xixi self-mocked as 'the most special' one for she did not belong to neither 'straight' nor 'lesbian' groups but was often 'labelled' as one of them (turn 2). With my further prompt (turn 3), Xixi confirmed that she was considered a heterosexual instead of a bisexual as her dating partners believed she could 'choose [to be either straight or lesbian]' (turn 4). This exchange mirrors a common misunderstanding that bisexuality is a dichotomy between heterosexuality and homosexuality and bisexual-identified individuals can freely choose to be on either side (Dodge et al. 2016). This dichotomous view contradicts the poststructuralist understanding that sexual identities are fluid, dynamic and contingent (Hall 1996) and blatantly obscures bisexuality for its incompatibility with the dominant 'hetero/homo' binary (Cao in press). In this case, Xixi's access to Carvin and Nicky was only made possible due to the projection of heteronormativity and heteropatriarchy onto their dating practices, which imposed on Xixi a 'straight girl' image (turn 2) and simultaneously erased her bisexuality in this dating CoP. Here, I argue that the opening up of Xixi's access to learning was dependent on her compliance with the binary view of bisexuality and the heteropatriarchal gender orders in these relationships. Such 'open' access could only be momentary as Xixi's sexual and gender identities were both positioned unfavourably in this CoP, which further impede her potential positive identity construction in learning.

Moreover, two other incidents that happened during Xixi's in-person dating expediated the shutting down of her access to both partners.

(5) L: How is Carvin like?

(6) X: Just local, who was born and raised here and only speaks English. He is a very Westernized CBC [Canadian born Chinese] ... (several turns omitted) ... and it's hard to connect to him as he rejects that we share the same ethnicity. I feel like I'd be very nervous speaking English, thinking repeatedly whether I made any grammar mistakes ...

(7) L: What made you feel nervous? You've got any examples?

(8) X: ... I remember on our first date I said, 'I thought it is (falling) ...'. He did not hear me well and repeated, 'you thought that was (rising) ...'. I immediately recognized my mistake and corrected, 'sorry, I thought it was (falling)'.

(Interview Excerpt 2, 14 June 2019)

In Excerpt 2, Xixi recalled her experience with Carvin on their first date. When I asked Xixi to describe her dating partner (turn 5), she chose the word 'local', supported by the facts that he was 'born and raised' in Canada and is English monolingual (turn 6). What was unsaid but can be reasonably inferred is that by contrasting Carvin's Canadian background (i.e. citizenship, language, and upbringing experience as a 2nd generation CBC) to her own, Xixi also engaged in the construction of a 'non-local' identity for herself. Later, Xixi reflected on how difficult it was to connect with Carvin, a 'westernized CBC', as he 'rejects' that they share the same ethnicity (turn 6). While it is biologically apocryphal, Carvin's Canadian upbringing and linguistic repertoire set himself apart and fostered a recognition that, compared to Xixi, he was closer to Whiteness (i.e. the implied Canadianness) than Chineseness.

These two moments are characteristic ones in which linguistic nationalism was mapped onto Xixi and Carvin's dating practices. The semiotic processes of Xixi constructing a clearly articulated local identity and an implied non-local identity and Carvin erasing his Chinese ethnicity were both dictated by the ideological interconnection between language, nationhood, and race ingrained in Canada's colonial and White supremacist history (Han 2019). Stereotypically, a Canadian identity is materialized as a White settler who speaks English and/or French with European ancestry, which excludes all indigenous groups and people of colour regardless of their family history, relationship to the land, and the citizenship status. Despite that Carvin may still be seen as an 'immigrant' and 'outsider' due to his racial identity (see also, Han 2012), between the two, Carvin's standard English, Canadian upbringing and nationality moved him higher up in the 'language-nationhood-race' bounded hierarchy, whereas Xixi was relegated to a lower position as a perpetuated Other in Canadian society.

Moreover, the unequal power relations attached to the linguistic nationalism also incurred psychological burdens for Xixi to access Carvin as she felt 'very nervous' and had to 'think repeatedly' to avoid grammar mistakes in their conversation (turn 6). With my probing (turn 7), Xixi justified her nervousness with a linguistic exchange that quite resembles interaction happening in language classrooms where teachers give indirective feedback to prompt students' correction of a grammar error (turn 8). This instance, at first glance, may seem like a teaching moment where Xixi learned a new knowledge point about verb tense. Nonetheless, as a master's student in linguistics, this simple grammar rule should not be unfamiliar to her and, more importantly, the error itself did not impede the intelligibility (Munro 2003) of their communication. Carvin's action of repeating it with the correct form and Xixi's reaction of apologizing and immediately fixing the error, unconscious as both might be, reinforced the 'Canadian' and 'non-Canadian' contrast and put the two interlocutors in different positions in the hierarchy undergirded by the linguistic nationalism. Together with other moments in which Xixi was excluded from the Canadian habitus[5] (Bourdieu 1991), this incident led to her decision to withdraw from the relationship (i.e. the shutdown of access to Carvin), as Xixi reflected, 'I feel we're like two people living in different universes' (Interview data: 14 June 2019).

Similarly, another episode with Nicky incurred Xixi's non-participation in the dating CoP, as shown below:

(9) X: When we were ordering, I spoke with the waitress in English, so he (Nicky) could understand what we were talking about. Then he said, "You don't have to do that. I don't care." I was like, how dare you! Of course, I don't have to. I was just being considerate for you! ... (several turns omitted) ...

(10) L: So, he thinks you ...

(11) X: ... that since I'm Chinese then just don't pretend to be an English speaker.

(Interview Excerpt 3, 14 June 2019)

Excerpt 3 is the reminiscence of a moment that happened in Xixi's second and last date with Nicky in a Shanghainese restaurant. When ordering food, Xixi spoke with a Mandarin-speaking waitress in English so that Nicky, who barely understands any Mandarin, could follow their conversation. However, Xixi's consideration was interpreted by Nicky as unnecessary (i.e. 'You don't have to do that') and insignificant (i.e. 'I don't care'), which made her feel angry and frustrated (turn 9). Despite the fact that Nicky may not have malicious intentions in his comments, Xixi deciphered them as a challenge to her rights and legitimacy of using English as a Chinese person (turn 11). The exchange here is connected to the semiotic process of iconization, which suggests that language itself is an inherent nature of its users (Bucholtz 2001; Irvine & Gal 2000). In this scenario, governed by the ideology of linguistic nationalism, 'English speaking' is regarded as an iconic and inherent characteristic of the Canadian identity, an attribute that is incompatible with Xixi's linguistic dispositions (Bourdieu 1991) nurtured by her Chinese upbringing and the transnational life journey from PRC to Hong Kong. Once Xixi perceived that her legitimacy of speaking English was challenged, her access to learning resources and opportunities would soon shut down as she was denied chances to even use English in conversation.

In both dates, Xixi was seen as a 'straight girl' rather than a legitimate bisexual member for the shared heteropatriarchal ideology in the CoP, which relegated Xixi, a female and bisexual dating partner, to a hierarchically lower position and predetermined the impossibility for her to engage in positive identity construction in the potential learning process. Further, due to the projection of linguistic nationalism onto everyday dating practices, Xixi was rendered as a perpetuated Other as her linguistic repertoire, cultural upbringing and immigration status were incongruent with the default Canadian habitus. Subsequently, it caused her psychological burdens (with Carvin) and the denial of rights (with Nicky) to use English, which induced a marginal and eventually end of participation in these dating CoP. Discourses produced in Xixi's dates, recursively, function to reinforce, reproduce and sustain heteropatriarchy and the ideology of linguistic nationalism deep-rooted in Canada's socio-political history, a reciprocal process of structuration.

A Legitimate Bisexual, a Delegitimized English Speaker

Xixi became acquainted with Luke in a university's linguistic lab where both worked as research assistants. Due to the mutual acceptance of each other's queer identities and shared interests in modern literature, pop culture and feminist politics, their collegial relationship gradually evolved into an eight-month romantic date. Xixi's dating with Luke differs from the previous two in that she was no longer viewed as a 'straight girl' but a legitimate bisexual dating partner, which liberated her from symbolic violence tied to the binary view of bisexuality and heteropatriarchal gender orders in this CoP. The recognized legitimacy of Xixi's gender and sexual identities was crucial for her English learning as it fostered positive identity construction and, concomitantly, opened up access to a wide range of learning resources and activities, as shown in Excerpt 4:

(12) X: They [Luke] were the only one who understand me as a female bisexual as they are the same [both queer]. I felt more conformable not just dating but being with them.

(13) L: How did this impact your relationship?

(14) X: I think it made our relationship smoother, and I learned a lot from Luke. You know, they are local so they taught me a lot of things and norms that I did not know before coming here … (several turns omitted) … Last year, they

introduced me to their family, and we were planning to visit them in Texas but the trip was cancelled ...

(15) L: What did you do when you were in relationship?

(16) X: We often went to movies, dinner, or excursion ... once we played at our friends' place and made a spinach pie.

(Interview Excerpt 4, 23 July 2019)

This interview took place shortly after their breakup in Summer 2019. In retrospect, Xixi claimed that the relationship with Luke was the most 'comfortable' one as Luke, a non-binary and pansexual partner, could 'understand' her gender and sexual identities in their dating (turn 12). When responding to my further inquiries (turns 13 and 15), Xixi pointed out that the fact that she could be a legitimate female bisexual partner was of paramount significance for her participation in various dating activities such as 'movies, dinner, or excursion' (turn 16), in which she was taught by Luke, a veteran and 'local' queer, 'things and norms that [she] did not know before coming [to Canada]' (turn 14). Additionally, this relationship expanded Xixi's social circle by introducing her to Luke's family in Texas (turn 14) and friends with whom they made a spinach pie together (turn 16), a sign of Xixi's access to other English-speaking old-timers. Arguably, in this relationship, Xixi engaged in a legitimate and peripheral participation: 'legitimate' as in her gender and bisexuality being recognized as legitimate social capital (Bourdieu 1986) in this CoP; 'peripheral' as in her access to a wide range of information, activities and old-timers being wide open. Although Xixi's goal of dating Luke was not to learn English, the recognition of her gender and sexual identities provided her access to a variety of resources that stimulated a process of 'learning English in context'. That is, when Xixi was treated as a legitimate female bisexual member, her learning of English naturally happened as a by-product of the participation in this dating CoP.

Nonetheless, several incidents that happened at later stages of their relationship induced a marginal pattern of Xixi's participation by calling the legitimacy of her linguistic habitus into question and eventually adjourned her dating with Luke:

Episode 1: The first dispute between Xixi and Luke about her pronunciation happened in Xixi's first day of work at the linguistic lab. Xixi first said 'staff/ɑː/', which was immediately corrected by Luke to staff/æ/. She then argued back, it can also be pronounced as staff/ɑː/ in British English. Xixi believed that Luke's pronunciation was no more than an American variety, and that they were all linguists so there was no need to listen to them.

Episode 2: In their excursion to Victoria, a city near Vancouver, Luke and Xixi had a discussion on Canadian versus American phonological rules, triggered by Luke's correction of Xixi's pronunciation of a word, 'project'. At that time, Xixi thought of it as 'good' and 'educational' as those were things English teachers never taught her in China … However, she started to feel stressful as Luke constantly corrected her English pronunciation and eventually became a 'speechless person' facing them.

Episode 3: The last event happened in the lab's weekend beach party, during which Luke laughed (very hard) at Xixi's pronunciation of a Japanese loan word, ginkgo, and claimed that Xixi's pronunciation was very funny in front of all other lab members. Xixi felt extremely embarrassed and humiliated and did not feel like talking to anyone else in the remainder of the event.

(Fieldnote Excerpt 1, 3 September 2019)

Fieldnote Excerpt 1 is a summary and brief mapping of three episodes which happened at different stages in their relationship. Initially, Xixi conceived of herself as a legitimate English user as illustrated by her self-ascribed identity (Han 2014b) as 'linguist', a type of social capital implying one's academic qualification, reputation and prestige. When Luke corrected her pronunciation, Xixi decidedly argued back by mentioning a phonological point that staff/a/ was the correct form in British English, just as staff/æ/ in its 'American variety' (Episode 1). Later into the relationship, Luke's correction of Xixi's English pronunciation became a routine in their dating. Although these experiences were at first considered by Xixi as 'good' and 'educational', as time passed by, Xixi perceived unprecedented and burgeoning psychological pressure and gradually became 'a speechless person' facing Luke (Episode 2). At the ending stage of their relationship, Xixi had an unpleasant encounter in which her pronunciation of a Japanese loan word, ginkgo, was 'laughed at' and claimed as 'funny' by Luke in the presence of all other lab members at a beach party. This occasion caused Xixi's feelings of 'embarrassment' and 'humiliation' and almost silenced her in the whole event (Episode 3).

Locating the three episodes in Xixi's dating history with Luke, I argue that it was the standard language ideology that deemed Luke's linguistic habitus, associated with 'standard American English' (Lippi-Green 2012), as legitimate and simultaneously deprived Xixi's legitimacy as a non-White and non-standard English speaker in this dating CoP. Due to the projection of the standard language ideology onto their dating practices, Xixi's pronunciation was constantly challenged and corrected by Luke until her self-ascribed identity as linguist deconstructed. This was also accompanied by the ever-growing psychological burdens of using English to communicate with Luke and others in Xixi's social circle. Adopting a raciolinguistic lens (Rosa & Flores 2017), I contend that the delegitimization of Xixi's linguistic habitus is interconnected to the systemic power of racism in Canada, which ties Xixi's linguistic practices to her racial identity and relegates her as an illegitimate English user. Over time in her participation in this CoP, Xixi's legitimacy as a female bisexual dating partner was overturned by her illegitimacy as a 'deficient English user' and 'racialized Other', and her initially wide-open access to English learning was subsequently shut down.

Discussion

Dating as an Alternative Educational Site

In English language education, learning has been long considered the consequential outcome of schooling. In this chapter, I argue for an understanding that learning is LPP in CoP. Under this framework, learning is not dependent on instruction but learners' legitimacy in the communities and open access to learning resources. This non-schooling model is particularly important for the study of language learning of adult migrants who do not qualify for government- or institution-funded language programmes (e.g. temporary workers, refugee claimants and international students among all non-permanent residents in Canada) and those who are not able to effectively learn in traditional language classrooms. In fact, research in migrant settlement and SLA shows that the majority of adult migrants' language learning happens in non-schooling settings (e.g. Han 2009; Roberts, Davies & Jupp 1992). In Canada, alternative ways of learning English were found in ethnolinguistic minority church (e.g. Han 2014b) and volunteer-led social groups (e.g. Cao in press), among other non-conventional settings. Compared to communities that are more tangible and predominantly perceived as sites for real learning (e.g. schools), dating has been rarely studied in SLA literature. Nonetheless, looking through the lens of LPP, dating is not just a process of building a romantic relationship, through which one may also access a variety of learning resources to achieve the goal of 'learning English in context'. In my study with Xixi, I discovered that, among her engagement in three types of CoP, dating was a significant component in her settlement as she 'devoted more than half of spare time seeing others' (Interview data: 16 June 2019). The study of learning through dating, therefore, is of great educational value as it demonstrates how Xixi's English learning happens or is hindered in a different context.

Further, seeing dating as an alternative educational site also benefits classroom-based language teaching as research conducted outside classrooms may be transformed into formal language education. By introducing my study with Xixi, I tend to instigate a conversation on how structural forces and language ideologies shape female bisexual international students' access to English learning, which could be a complementary resource in EAL teacher training and curriculum development. Future research may also promote explorations of theoretical tools and pedagogical strategies that directly address issues of power for more queer-friendly and inclusive teaching in EAL classrooms.

Reconsidering Gender, Sexual, Linguistic and Racial Inequalities in Learning CoP

Positive identity construction and open access are two most crucial conditions for learning in LPP. In the three dates, Xixi's identity construction as a Chinese female bisexual dating partner and access to English learning were crucially shaped by heteropatriarchy and the ideologies of linguistic nationalism and standard English circulated in the CoP. Firstly, gender and sexual equalities were central to the inclusion or exclusion of Xixi's participation and learning. When dating Carvin and Nicky, the shared binary view of bisexuality and heteropatriarchal gender orders deprived Xixi's legitimacy as a female bisexual partner and exerted a centrifugal force towards her participation. Conversely, with Luke, when Xixi's bisexuality was no longer viewed from a heteropatriarchal lens, she was able to access a wide range of information, learning activities and English-speaking old-timers to engage in the process of 'learning English in context' at the early stage of the relationship.

Secondly, the ideologies of linguistic nationalism and standard English deemed Xixi's linguistic habitus and racial identity as 'non-standard' and 'incongruent' with the Canadian habitus and consequently cut off her access to learning in all three relationships. Among Xixi's three dating partners, Luke's Whiteness and standard American English made them the most legitimate English user, whereas for Carvin and Nicky, their cultural upbringing and standard English marked them closer to 'Whiteness', a stereotypical trait and integral component of Canadian identity. Xixi, on the other hand, experienced a double exclusion and the shutdown of access to learning due to the illegitimacy of her linguistic habitus and racial identity determined by ideologies of language and race in these CoP.

The dissection of Xixi's dates above also leads to a question of whether all CoP can be characterized as ideal learning sites. My analysis shows that in each CoP that Xixi entered, the rules of engagement either included or excluded her as a newcomer, which consequentially facilitated or prevented her access to English learning. In this sense, I argue that CoP cannot be seen as a taken-for-granted structure but sites that are constructed and constantly reshaped by the dominant ideologies that circulate therein. With this, EAL educators and policymakers need to be cognizant of the intersectional structural forces that hinder marginalized students' access to learning and promote effective tackling strategies in their practices.

Questions for Change

Based on my research of Xixi's English learning experiences, I ask the following four questions for applied linguistic researchers and educational practitioners to provoke further thoughts and potential future research directions in adult migrants' English education:

1. Viewing learning as LPP in CoP, do we have enough research conducted in non-conventional educational sites?
2. Seeing identity construction and access as important conditions for learning, how can EAL educators ensure that students, particularly those with intersectional marginalized social identities, have open access to information, activities and old-timers in language classrooms?
3. In the current literature, do we have enough studies adopting an intersectional perspective to reveal social structures and ideologies that hinder ethnolinguistic minority queer students' access to English learning?
4. How can applied linguistic researchers, educational practitioners and policymakers collaborate to transform research conducted outside language classrooms into formal language education and to address issues identified in both schooling and non-schooling contexts in pedagogy?

Notes

1 This pseudonym was chosen by Xixi herself. It is not only the Romanized spelling form of her Chinese name '西' but also means 'Western', implying her aspiration to live in a Western country like Canada. Pseudonyms are used for all individuals throughout this chapter.
2 In this chapter, *queer* as a category is used as an overarching term referring to gender and sexual minority individuals. I also use categories such as non-binary and bisexual in specific cases.
3 This statistical data was updated on 24 December 2020. A complete list of gender identities and sexual orientations available on OkCupid can be found through this link: https://help.okcupid.com/article/208-gender-and-orientation-on-okcupid.
4 All interviews with Xixi were conducted in Mandarin and then transcribed into English. In all interview excerpts, L refers to the interviewer and X refers to Xixi.
5 Habitus is defined by Bourdieu as a set of dispositions which incline agents to act and react in certain ways. A Canadian habitus is a taken-for-granted or so-called normal way of doing certain things in the Canadian culture and society. For example, speaking a 'non-accented' English could be classified as a subcategory of Canadian habitus.

7

Multimodal and Critical Representations of Gender and Sexuality

Shin-ying Huang

Introduction

Despite increasing recognition of its importance in English language teaching (ELT), issues of gender and sexuality still remain, for the most part, at the periphery of the field and in actual classroom work. Research on gender and sexuality pedagogies is still scarce in ELT publications (Banegas & Evripidou 2021), and lesbian, gay, bisexual, transgender, queer plus (LGBTQ+) characters remain largely invisible in ELT materials (Gray 2013, 2021), even though critical scholars have drawn attention to these issues since the 1990s (e.g. Thornbury 1999). As Nelson (1999) pointed out, 'sexual identity is already an integral part of ESL' (373). At the very basic level, many vocabulary words, such as *husband, wife, in-laws, boyfriend, girlfriend*, are inherently heteronormative. Thus, even when gender and sexuality are not the focus of discussion, they are still being 'read, produced, and regulated' (Nelson 1999: 388) as part and parcel of any classroom interaction. Nelson (2010) made the best case for why gender and sexuality need to be incorporated into the language classroom. She explained that gender and sexuality are fundamental to an individual's self-expression and interpersonal communication, which is also an overarching goal of ELT, and thus should occupy a central place in the language classroom.

Importantly, critical scholars caution against the frequent conflation of gender and sexuality (e.g. Govender 2019). This chapter makes the distinction following van Leent and Mills (2017), who based their definition on a queer framework:

> Sex refers to the biological, anatomical, and physiological differences among people, which may or may not be a match with one's gender identity. Gender refers to the performance of one's biological sex based on social expectations;

and gender identity refers to one's self-identification. Sexuality or sexual orientation is multivariable and can be defined by several criteria, such as attraction, behavior, or identity. (401–2)

Govender (2017) more specifically referred to sexual identity 'as being lesbian, gay or bisexual' and gender identity as including being 'intersexed or transgendered' (24). Others use the term *queer* to broadly include LGBTQ+ identities, such as O'Mochain (2006) who discussed the narratives of 'queer-identified people' (57).

Drawing from the critical framework, many literacy educators have considered ways to explore gender and sexuality in their lessons. Threlkeld (2014) suggested using literature with LGBTQ+ characters in the elementary classroom as a way to discuss with children how difference is socially constructed. Sandretto (2018) proposed critiquing with children heteronormativity in *any* text, not just texts that highlight gender and sexuality, as a way to 'deconstruct the implicit heterosexual norms' (204) in society. Hermann-Wilmarth, Lannen, R. and Ryan (2017) emphasized the importance of including transgender topics and discussed a child's inspiring poem as a counter-narrative to the hegemonic heterosexual social order. Miller (2015) further advocated for the inclusion of '(a)gendered and (a)sexuality' (37) identities in discussions surrounding LGBTQ+ on a continuum. Blaise (2009) discussed sex, gender and sexuality based on conversations that took place between kindergarten children, which exemplified heterosexual views of femininities and masculinities, particularly about girls wanting boyfriends and believing that they need to be pretty and sexy to be desirable to men. She explained the regulatory power of gender and sexuality through Butler's (1990) heterosexual matrix, that is, that as relational concepts, valued forms of femininity are produced in relation to particular forms of masculinity, and vice versa. Gender and sexuality are thus intertwined, as particular ways of being are related to particular types of sexuality. As such, to resist heteronormativity, it is necessary to deconstruct heterosexual norms of gender and sexuality in early childhood education.

As an effort to contribute to the conversation surrounding gender and sexuality education in the language classroom, this chapter reports on a classroom inquiry which incorporates these issues through a critical multimodal perspective (Huang 2015). One of the characteristics of a critically oriented education, as Norton and Toohey (2004) explain, is 'exploring diverse representations of knowledge' (13), recognizing the power relations inherent in hegemonic ways of being (such as gender binary and heterosexuality) and traditionally privileged ways of meaning-making (such as writing). Multimodality has a lot to offer in the effort to validate more diverse and equitable understanding of gender and sexuality, as multimodality has been found to be conducive to identity representation. Despite the exponential proliferation of research exploring how youth represent themselves through multimodal digital means (e.g. Kajee 2011; Pandya, Pagdilao & Kim 2015; Vasudevan, Schultz & Bateman 2010), very few of these studies discuss identities relating to gender and sexuality. One rare exception has been the work of Curwood and Gibbons (2010). From a counter-narrative perspective, they discussed a student's multimodal moves in terms of how he interpreted and appropriated two canonical poems about being American to showcase his own identity as an Asian and homosexual American in his digital story. This work is an example of critical multimodal literacy (Huang 2017), that is, multimodal literacy practices that highlight students' reading of and resistance to dominant and often oppressive discourses. The present study extends this effort to better understand students' transformation or *journeys* in relation to race/ethnicity, class, gender and/or sexuality. Specifically, this chapter foregrounds issues relating to gender and sexuality and examines how students, in their multimodal ensembles, reflect upon the forces shaping their identities and their effort to reconstruct their subject positions.

Methods

Research Context

This research was implemented in the second semester of a year-long general English course I taught in a university in Taiwan. Thirty-one students were enrolled in the course, majoring in social sciences and humanities, and included a roughly equal number of males and females. The teaching goals of this classroom inquiry were: (1) to consider with the students issues of race, class, gender and sexuality through the discussion of popular media texts, and (2) for the students to make use of multiple semiotic resources to express themselves. To achieve the first objective, three movies were viewed and discussed in the first half of the semester: *Mean Girls*, *Better Luck Tomorrow* and *Prayers for Bobby*. These movies were selected because they highlight, respectively, issues of gender, race and sexuality and allow for the focused discussion of these issues. For each movie, I posed different questions regarding race, gender, class and/or sexuality, depending on their respective content, but two questions were discussed with all three: (1) What type of transition/journey did the protagonist experience? (2) In what ways can you relate to it?

To accomplish the second goal, a multimodal report (along with an accompanying note) was assigned at the beginning of the semester but due as a final assignment. In the first few weeks of the semester, multimodal meaning-making was discussed, as mainly involving the combination of two or more modes from the five modes of communication: visual, aural, linguistic, gestural and spatial modes (New London Group 1996). Examples of print and digital multimodal works, including youth-produced multimodal compositions, were also viewed. The instruction for the multimodal report was as follows:

(1) Through this multimodal report, you will present a reflection of the transition you have been through or a journey you have gone on. Please make sure you think about the transition/journey in relation to (a) race, class, gender, sexuality as well as any other aspects, and (b) the global/local world in which we inhabit.
(2) The multimodal report should last between 5 and 10 minutes, and should auto run and be able to be viewed and understood without any additional verbal explanation.

The instructions for the accompanying note were: Please submit an accompanying note in Word file that addresses: (1) your choice in the format (e.g. video, PowerPoint, etc.) and your choice/use of the various modes; (2) citation of all sources, including words, images and sound, which you borrowed from others. As for the written reflection, I asked the students to summarize their transition/journey and to explain their understanding of the multiple modes of communication.

Analytical Framework

The analytical framework of social semiotics (Jewitt 2011; Kress 2011) provides a lens through which to understand students' digital multimodal works. Social semiotics is the study of signs and how meaning is made, through the sign makers' design, for purposes of expression, representation and communication. The *social* aspect of social semiotics refers to not only the interpersonal but also the intercultural aspects of meaning-making as well as the inevitable power relations involved.

Kress (2003), drawing from a social semiotics perspective, discussed the affordances of new media, such as digital technologies, as contributing to interactivity and hypertextuality. Interactivity occurs when texts are produced to critique others' texts for their misrepresentation or marginalization, a process made easier as a result of new media, and has 'an effect on social power directly' (5). Hypertextuality refers to when youth producers incorporate others' media texts for their own purposes, and has an influence on 'social power less immediately' (5). Similarly, Stein (2008) highlighted how modal choices can be influenced by the politics of representation:

> The choice of mode may not always be an issue of affordances, a case of whether one mode, technically or formally, is 'better' for meaning-making than another. ... In areas of dread, ambivalence, terror and pain, people can be silent, often seeking beyond language to express what they know and how they feel. (97)

For Stein, power relations, more than affordances, can affect modal choices. The politics of representation can be more easily negotiated and manipulated through multiple semiotic resources for the sign maker. Drawing from both Kress (2003) and Stein (2008) allows the examination of youth-produced multimodal multimedia ensembles for the ways in which they resist dominant relations of power in their lives and re-present themselves through a critical perspective.

Data Analysis

This chapter focuses on the multimodal reports as the main source of data but includes the students' written reflection as additional comparable data for discussion. In analysing the multimodal reports, I followed Hull and Nelson (2005) and Curwood and Gibbons (2010), concentrating mainly on the meaning produced in the interplay between image and text in the students' digital works while also considering the modes which play a minor role in the overall message of the ensemble. Accordingly, a multimodal transcript was made as the first step. To begin with, screen captures were taken of the students' ensembles (i.e. the screen was captured as soon as any additional element is added) and indicated in the following discussion as a slide.

In addition to this slide track in the multimodal transcript, I included an image track and a text track, followed by a music track as there was recurring music (songs or instrumental) in each of the ensembles. In the image track, I summarized the content of the images. The text track included any text on the slide. The music track would show which piece of music was continuously played until the particular point it ended. For the ensembles that included video clips, a video track was added to the transcript which summarized the content of the clips. The students' ensembles did not include voice-over. This multimodal transcript enabled me to focus on the patterns in which the modes were used, and it was found that the images and texts carried the main meaning. In particular, the dynamics between the images and the text and also the order in which they were shown aided in the meaning-making capacity of the ensembles, which is often the case in youth-produced media (e.g. Pandya, Hansuvadha & Pagdilao 2018).

Below, I focus my discussion on the works of two students, Yuan-dao and Hui-rong (pseudonyms). Their ensembles were chosen as examples of the variety of subject positions students took up in relation to gender and sexuality, as well as how they represented themselves through the skilful and intentional orchestration of multiple semiotic resources. In the following, the written text from the students' ensembles are quoted verbatim.

Between the Shown and the Told

Stein (2008) argued that 'although both written narrative and image offer possibilities for the exploration of self, it is within the realm of the image that [one can] find a certain freedom from convention and taboo' (94) because images, as a feature of their distinct epistemological commitment, allow a writer the possibility of remaining ambiguous (Kress 2003). Her discussion of children's depiction of cannibalism demonstrates that it is through the gap between the shown and the told that much can be revealed. This is also the case with Yuan-dao's ensemble.

Yuan-dao began his ensemble by textually narrating his journey in the third person, writing that 'once upon a time, there was a happy boy'. This happy boy gradually lost his happiness because 'boys laughed at his feminine temperament and gestures'. In narrating his childhood, Yuan-dao used the instrumental of Don McLean's *Vincent* as the background music. Then, in the next section of the ensemble, in which he narrated the happiness he found with a group of friends while in high school, Joss Stone's song, *Free Me*, was used. Yuan-dao shared that they did 'many crazy things together' and explained with two photos, superimposed on the slide, placed one after the other on the left and then on the right side. On top of each was a short, written description, including 'super huge marshmallow' and 'laughing wildly'. The placement of the two photos on this slide suggests that they are examples of the 'crazy things' he and his friends did together. He then wrote: 'when he stayed with them, he could retrieve enthusiasm, energy, and the most important of all, freedom'.

On the next slide, rather than on this one, he placed two photos, both of which included himself and another boy. In each photo, one of them is dressed in female apparel. In the photo on the left, Yuan-dao is wearing what could be described as regular male attire while his friend wore a bright patterned top and a short, tight black skirt. The two of them are sitting together on a large sofa, slightly looking up. The background suggests it may be a dressing room of some sort. In the other photo, his friend is wearing regular male attire while Yuan-dao is in an orange strapless dress, holding up one corner of the hem of his dress. The two of them are standing side by side, facing the camera and laughing. Judging from the background of this photo, Yuan-dao and his friend seemed to be at a formal function, such as a gala reception, although this is not clear. Neither of them is wearing any make-up in these photos. The importance of these two photos lies in the fact that they show him (and his friend) in both female attire and 'regular' men's clothing. Through this, Yuan-dao rejects the binary view of gender as only being either one or the other of the only two distinct and opposite ways of being human, and demonstrates Butler's (1990) explanation of gender as performance. Unlike the two photos in a previous slide about the crazy things he did with his friends, not only were these two photos placed on a blank slide without any verbal text, they were also not in any way referred to (such as any explanation of the circumstances under which they wore the female apparel). It is only mentioned, in the preceding slide, that he felt 'freedom' with his group of friends and, in the subsequent slide, that 'there was no need to limit himself for his feminine disposition'. Yuan-dao showed a video clip of him and his friends role-playing the characters in *Sex and the City* as an example of how they 'creat[ed] beautiful memories together'. In the short clip, which was filmed at the senior high school he attended, they show exaggerated feminine mannerisms but are dressed in regular school clothes. After the video clip, the text read, 'I hope that boy could get free because I am that boy. This is my own story and transitions.'

In the subsequent section, Yuan-dao discussed the contextual influences of his experiences: 'Relate my experiences: There are so many stereotypes about what women and men should be.' This is followed by an image,[1] which he referred to as 'man also woman' in the accompanying note. Through this picture, Yuan-dao again refuted heteronormative conceptualizations of gender as binary. As with the photos of him in female attire, this is the only other case in the ensemble in which an image is not explained, although judging from the previous slide, this image could be his way of speaking back to his experiences of 'stereotypes about what women and men should be'. Juxtaposed with other text and image, that is, 'his feminine disposition' and the photo of him in a dress, Yuan-dao further argued for an understanding of gender as fluid rather than binary.

The next slide then stated, 'And, I believe, gender stereotype is a global issue. No matter Asian, White people, or Black people.' Following this, a total of ten photos and images of people of different genders and races are then superimposed on this slide, one by one, around the text, so that after all the images have been placed, the text can still be read. Next, he revealed that he is still trying his best to free himself, explaining in the next few slides, 'Once, I was also suffering with it. But now, I try my best to free myself – make my life more colorful.' He then explained the title 'free me' as 'accept who I am and find my way. Just like the song tells us,' followed by an image[2] of Joss Stone's album, *Color Me Free*, in which a caged girl with one foot and hand poking out of the cage bars is portrayed. This proclamation of his goal to further accept himself and find his way seems like a satisfying ending to the ensemble and the description of his journey. However, Yuan-dao then continued with another revelation:

> Finally, I want to share an interesting question with you. People always ask me, 'Are you gay?' My response is always 'I really don't think about it because I have friends, work, family, and myself in my life.' Did you see that? There is no space for love. Love can flourish our life, but it is not necessary to me. I think sexuality becomes meaningful only when we think about love. So ... I am gay or not gay is not important at all, right? There is no answer! I dream for my own freedom and peace. That's enough for me.

Here, Yuan-dao shared an understanding of sexuality that is consistent with queer theory, that is, as related to attraction, in addition to other variables (van Leent & Mills 2017). Thus, by not engaging with romance, he does not have to be forced to engage with the question about his sexual identity. The ensuing slide then concludes the ensemble by stating his name and department, along with four photos of himself.

Through this ensemble, Yuan-dao revealed his observation of the frequent conflation between gender and sexuality. Because people's question of whether he is gay or not is mostly likely based on his mannerism, that is, 'his feminine temperament and gestures', they are equating his gender expression with sexuality (i.e. feminine disposition implies being gay). Yuan-dao refuted this conflation of gender and sexuality by showing himself in a dress and in a *Sex and the City* skit (further highlighting and complicating the notion of gender performance) and, at the same time, refusing the designation of gay (the notion of sexuality as connoted by particular gender performances). By refusing the concept implied in the question of whether he is gay, and by showing himself in both male and female attire, he is creating room for other conceptualizations of sexuality and gender expression, as well as for himself to further explore his identities outside of the dominant and hegemonic societal understanding of gender (as binary) and sexuality (as gay or straight). To borrow Stein's (2008) term, what might have been *unsayable* through written text became *representable* through the visual storytelling. Yuan-dao's dynamic and ambiguous use of the visual and linguistic modes speaks to the affordances and the epistemological commitment that each mode simultaneously allows and imposes on the sign maker.

An 'Abnormal' Boy

Yuan-dao's written reflection does not reveal any additional information. He merely shared a short paragraph:

> I have suppressed myself to meet others' expectations (do not behave like an 'abnormal' boy) for so long, becoming more and more frustrated. Fortunately, I met my bosom friends in high school and enjoyed the colorful life. We shot many short films, ate special food like a super huge marshmallow and so on. Most important of all, we laughed every day. Laughter returns me to that happy boy, bringing me freedom to live what I want.

In this written reflection, Yuan-dao mentioned the various aspects shown in the ensemble. He also used the phrase 'abnormal boy', which was not used in the ensemble, but does not explain what it is about him that others might designate as 'abnormal'. However, this seems to have been implied in the ensemble, through the photos of him in a dress and the 'man also woman' image. This is further evidence that 'image offers the possibility to make visible a private self which the written text conceals' (Stein 2008: 94) and the importance of providing students not just the opportunity to represent themselves but formalizing multimodality in formal education as a necessary means for identity re-construction.

Hypertextuality and Interactivity

As discussed in the section on the analytical framework, Kress (2003) explained *hypertextuality* as entering into a new relationship with others' texts, and *interactivity* as speaking back to others' texts. Hui-rong's multimodal ensemble exemplifies these ideas that are arguably less frequently explored in empirical research of digital literacy practices.

Hypertextuality

Hui-rong entered into new relations with popular culture texts by positioning her own story as parallel to the story of the protagonist, Andy, in the movie *The Devil Wears Prada*. Hui-rong began her ensemble, entitled 'Girls' Survival Game', by posing the question of whether 'become prettier = better life' and explained that her exploration is 'based on my true story'. However, immediately following these title pages, she described not her own story but Andy's transformation based on which she posed the question about whether 'getting fit and prettier, dressed more fashion like the magazine tells us' equals to 'good relationship with lots of friends, ability to be recognized, wonderful life'. This led to a big red question mark, suggesting her scepticism.

Only after this did she share her own journey in high school, from being a social outcast to becoming one of the popular girls in her class. This transformation was the result of her drastic weight loss, which led to an illness, and then the realization of the importance of a balanced lifestyle. While satisfied that she no longer was marginalized but became one of the popular girls, she also felt 'so perplexed when I conscious that being "prettier" really make me become more popular'. This prompted her to analyse media portrayals (which will be discussed in the next section), after which she concluded her discussion by circling back to Andy's transformation at the end of the movie. Hui-rong then explained that Andy's 'story let me recall my high school's memories when I became popular with the classmates'. The final slide then summarized the lessons to be gleaned from 'these two stories'. For the first part of the ensemble, KT Tunstall's song *Suddenly I See* was played in the background. From the final slide where she summarized the lessons from 'these two stories', the background song was switched to Sweetbox's *Life Is So Cool*.

Both at the beginning and the end of her ensemble, Hui-rong presented Andy's story before sharing her own, comparing herself to and finding many parallels with the journey of an American woman in an American movie. Thus, she entered into new relations with this popular culture text by using it to structure her own story, presenting similar transformations of two women in different racial and geographical contexts. Hui-rong showed, through the juxtaposition of her own 'true story' in the context of Andy's trajectory as well as her own understanding of being beautiful in the context of western beauty standards, that her personal journey is also a transnational narrative, indicative of the survival game that women in many parts of the world go through.

Interactivity

As part of her effort to explain why 'being prettier' helped her to 'become more popular', Hui-rong analysed popular culture texts such as the covers of beauty magazines. An important point in Hui-rong's reflection was that she 'learn[ed] from many magazines, dramas, and advertisements' what it means to be beautiful. Her analysis included a cover page of Elle magazine, as well as a photo of 'the models of Victoria Secret's advertisement', and found that 'the media install the conception of beauty to people, slim body, big eyes, sexy lips, pointed nose become the dream features that girls spare no efforts to pursue'. Her findings are consistent with those of research (e.g. Andsager 2014; Bell & Dittmar 2011), which unvaryingly points to the mass media as responsible for promoting unrealistic ideals of female body and beauty. These repeated media images are powerful, because the naturalization of norms is rarely achieved 'through overt or forceful means, but rather through subtle, yet powerful, messages that repeatedly permeate daily life' (Meyer 2007: 17).

Hui-rong's analysis concluded with a screen capture of a magazine page which ranked the world's most beautiful women. In this image, the photo of a Taiwanese celebrity is featured, which Hui-rong also dissected as having the same facial and body features as those western models. Thus, being able to exemplify through the visual/image the commonalities in the facial and physical features of the so-called sexy beautiful women allowed Hui-rong to present both the process and the results of her analysis. And by critically examining what popular media promotes as beautiful, Hui-rong spoke back to the global media hegemony in establishing the criteria for beauty, that is, the dominance of western standards spreading around the world through the dominance of western media.

Interestingly, even though Hui-rong was born and raised in Taiwan, in the three images that she examined, the first two (Elle cover and Victoria Secret models) were western/Anglo publications, while the third features a Taiwanese celebrity. Hui-rong's discussion of the standards of beauty began with the international, based on which she teased out that 'beauty' as promoted by these media means to have 'slim body, big eyes, sexy lips, [and] pointed nose'. In a subsequent slide, she then showed a page from the Taiwan Asian edition of *For Him Magazine* (FHM) to support this conclusion. This page features the photo of a Taiwanese celebrity alongside FHM's ranking of 'one hundred sexy beautiful women in the world', the title at the top of the page written in Chinese. Hui-rong showed the names of the top ten women in her ensemble, with Anne Hathaway being the fifth on the list, among nine other Taiwanese/Chinese female entertainers. Again, the local is situated in the context of the global 'beautiful women in the world'. Moreover, in this ranking, the local and global are blurred, as Anne Hathaway is placed alongside other Asian 'beautiful women'. Conceivably, Hui-rong's choice to use this particular page, among a variety of other Asian or Taiwanese beauty magazines, shows her intentional design, as the sign maker, to connect the two components of her ensemble, that is, the similarities between her own journey and that of Andy's (portrayed by Hathaway) and Hathaway's being ranked as one of the most 'beautiful women' in the Asian edition of FHM in Hui-rong's analysis of popular magazines and how they represent female desirability.

In both how she framed her personal story (as parallel to that of Andy's) and the materials she used to analyse her understanding of body image, Hui-rong showed a cosmopolitan frame of mind, which 'is primarily about viewing oneself as a part of a world, a circle of belonging that transcends the limited ties of kinship and country to embrace the whole of humanity' (Cheah 2008: 26). Hui-rong was able to express how her meaning-making practices are affected by both global and local forces, that is, her cosmopolitan mindset (Harper, Bean, T. & Dunkerly 2010; Stornaiuolo 2015), as a result of the hypertextuality and especially interactivity afforded by multimodal digital practices.

Analysis versus Personal Story

In her ensemble, through hypertextuality and interactivity, Hui-rong positioned her own journey as springing from global antecedents and analysed the portrayal of attractive women in western fashion magazines. Her written reflection, however, was composed from a purely personal perspective. She did not mention either the movie or the beauty magazines. Instead, she detailed her emotional journey, such as,

> I never known that I was 'not pretty' when I was little, because I had taught I am the prettiest girl in the world from my childhood by my parents, until the moment that I conscious the subtle connection between 'pretty' and one's popularity. … I started thinking whether my unpopular relationship result from my 'not-pretty' face and shape.

Arguably, Hui-rong could have discussed Andy's transformation and analysed the magazine models in her written reflection. After all, this information was textually explained in the ensemble. However, as an English-as-a-foreign-language (EFL) speaker, I can attest to how difficult it is to conduct a simultaneous description and comparison of two stories in a clear and concise manner in

English. In the multimodal ensemble, however, not only can the resources of the visual be called upon to assist in meaning-making, the slideshow format, by its very nature, limits the length of text and, consequently, takes the pressure off the multimodal composer to provide a drawn-out account. This is what the medium of the multimodal ensemble afforded for the storyteller (through restricting extended prose) that the written reflection constrained. In contrast, the format of the written reflection might have allowed Hui-rong a better medium to share her reflections of her life, as such extended narration of her thought process is better supported by the medium of a word processor. Indeed, as Ranker (2008, 2015) and Huang (2019) have shown, the medium influences the message.

Discussion

The discussion above has shown that in Yuan-dao's case, the multimodal ensemble revealed much more about him than his written reflection, exemplifying Stein's (2008) contention that writing 'is more impersonal, distant and associated with official public selves' while the visual 'offers more potential for exploration' (94). However, this is not the case with Hui-rong's ensemble and writing. In fact, Hui-rong's written reflection shared her emotions while the ensemble afforded her an analytical perspective through visual means which may have been more difficult to have achieved linguistically. In addition, it was also through the multimodal nature of the ensemble that Hui-rong was able to frame her story as parallel to Andy's, which she also did not do in her written report. Thus, multimodality, in terms of including both linguistic-based and multiple modes, enables students a more representative means for representing themselves (Govender 2020).

To sum up, Hui-rong's example demonstrated 'the affordances of media production as a space to process, resist, and critique dominant discourse' while Yuan-dao's example demonstrated 'how multimodality in particular allows new practices of social position' (Doerr-Stevens 2015: 336), both of which exemplify the relationship between multiple modes and media and critical literacy.

Conclusion and Pedagogical Implications

The purpose of this chapter was to examine how two students reflected upon their own identity with regard to gender and sexuality politics. The findings suggest that while both the written and the multimodal texts allowed the students opportunities to examine their journeys and transitions, the multimodal format better supported them in expressing their critical perspectives towards the power relations that shaped and reshaped their identities in relation to gender and sexuality. Multimodality, through the medium of digital storytelling, allowed these two students to question the master narratives in their lives in the way that their written reflections did not. Digital storytelling, which permits the incorporation of multiple modes and media, enabled the students to represent themselves differently, that is, more powerfully in terms of speaking back to hegemonic ideologies, and to show sensitive aspects of themselves in a tactful and strategic manner. This study demonstrates that multimodality can contribute to a critical perspective through the gap between the shown and the told and through skilful orchestration which accomplishes hypertextuality and interactivity.

Much can be gleaned from the two students' critical reflections of their subject positions in their multimodal ensembles regarding how gender and sexuality can be explored in the English language classroom. Although highlighting different aspects of gender and sexuality, they both point to what Muren and Don (2012) observed, almost a decade ago but which is still very much true today, that our understanding of gender remains largely binary, and our expectations of behaviours for women and men are still confined by stereotypes of femininity and masculinity. This is not just true for Hui-rong, whose peer interactions were negatively impacted by stereotyped body image ideals. This was also the case for Yuan-dao, who very much suffered from gender stereotypes, being laughed at for his feminine disposition. The students' journeys show that

> *everyone* is constrained by heteronormativity and strict gender conventions, not just those who live outside the norms. These norms restrict everyone by prescribing set limits on the ways we can live and love. (Sandretto 2018: 198, italics in the original)

To fight against heteronormativity, critical scholars suggest an approach to language and literacy education based on the perspective of 'critical literacy with queer intent', the underlying principles of which centre on questioning what counts as normal and who decides (Sandretto 2018). One way to achieve the critique of norms is through pedagogies of inquiry, which Nelson (1999) argued to be preferable to pedagogies of inclusion. She explained that an inquiry perspective does not place responsibility on teachers to have all the answers regarding gender and sexuality diversity. Instead, the teacher's role is 'to frame questions, facilitate investigations, and explore what is not known' (Nelson 1999: 377). An inquiry perspective also foregrounds the discussion of 'how linguistic and cultural practices manage to naturalize certain sexual identities but not others' (Nelson 1999: 378). An inquiry approach may be the key to the wider incorporation of gender and sexuality in the ELT classroom by nature of taking responsibility off teachers to provide all the answers to complex issues which they themselves may be unfamiliar with. Providing space in the classroom for exploring gender and sexuality on a continuum as influenced by social, cultural and political factors, while far from simple, can be a more feasible starting point for many teachers.

An effective way for this to take place is to begin from the work of students, who may already hold a better understanding of these issues as a result of their own experiences. In the case of this study, had the ensembles not been the final assignment of the academic year, they would have been optimal material based on which to embark on further classroom inquiry. For example, even though Hui-rong's discussion of body image highlights 'girls' survival game', body image issues impact negatively upon all gender and sexed identities (Andsager 2014; Brennan, Lalonde & Bain 2010), and is pertinent to everyone regardless of their gender and sexual identification. The issue raised by Yuan-dao regarding the experiences of 'queer-identified people' (O'Mochain 2006: 57) shows that even though there has gradually been more recognition of LGBTQ+ identities, gender and sexual fluidity are still rarely acknowledged. The dominant discourse still considers queer identities in terms of being gay, while heteronormative ideology continues to be imposed on homosexual relationships (van der Toorn, Pliskin & Morgenroth 2020). These issues raised by the students not only question heteronormativity but can be an effective starting point for classroom inquiry because they are founded on the students' lived experiences and concerns.

An inquiry approach that investigates how particular gender and sexual identities are naturalized through dominant linguistic and cultural practices (Nelson 1999) provides direct relevance for the discussion of gender and sexuality in the language classroom. An examination of how gender and sexual identities are assumed and ascribed in language is a possible starting point. Using Hui-rong and Yuan-dao's works as a jumping board, the class could have benefited from a discussion of the assumptions underlying the common practice of ranking women's attractiveness or sex appeal. Students could also explore the ideologies at work when people speculate about whether someone is gay. Extending from this, EFL students can be asked to research the language they come across in their everyday lives, and compare that with discourses in the target language. Nilseon's (1977) observations remain a pertinent point of reference, as well as the work of Livia and Hall's (1997) volume, which 'analyses lexical items, speech acts, grammatical conundrums, discourse strategies, coming-out stories, homophobic slang' (Nelson 2006: 3). O'Mochain's (2006) example is also a useful one, by having learners read out loud the interview transcripts of queer-identifying individuals whose life-history narratives they discussed, focusing on 'approximating the original speaker's expression, pausing, and intonation' (63), all of which are elements of delivery which impact upon the effectiveness of one's communication. These practices reflect the view of language as social and cultural practices at the same time allowing it to remain a linguistic practice, the latter especially important to learners in EFL contexts.

Finally, in terms of interrogating cultural practices, popular media texts as a form of authentic materials can serve as a valuable resource. Apart from using full-length movies, as was the case in this study, situation comedies might permit more focused discussion by nature of their shorter length. For example, *Modern Family* can be used to explore how the portrayal of gay/straight stereotypes (e.g. Season 1, Episode 13) and what it means to be a woman/man (e.g. Season 2 Episode 10) have consequences for different groups of people. Furthermore, teachers can inquire with students the differential responses to these media representations when viewed from a queer lens compared to a heterosexual lens, such as what Sandretto (2018) demonstrated using print materials. These media representations, because they portray homosexuality in heteronormative terms (Merrifield 2016) and gender roles as binary, serve as effective examples of heteronormative ideology and, thus, allow for discussions of alternative conceptualizations of sexuality and gender. However, they do not provide empowering examples of LGBTQ+ representations. In this respect, social media such as Alok Vaid-Menon's digital texts on Instagram can serve as an illustration of gender non-conformity and illuminate how gender needs to be understood as intersecting with other identity categories.

As such, pedagogies of inquiry towards gender and sexuality can begin from students' experiences as reflected upon in their multimodal works. An inquiry approach can also incorporate students' observations of heteronormative ideologies embedded in the languages they are using and learning. Class discussion should also analyse the cultural practices portrayed in the authentic target language materials utilized in the classroom. An inquiry approach that takes into account critical and multimodal perspectives is a necessary way forward for gender and sexuality to become an integral component of (English) language education.

Questions for Change

1. What do multimodal and critical literacy practices mean to you? In what ways do you think they are relevant and applicable to your teaching context?
2. How are your students' literacy practices, both in and out of school, already multimodal and critical? How can you highlight these practices and further build upon them in your teaching?
3. What are some popular culture texts that your students are fond of? How might you discuss them with your students from a critical perspective, particularly in terms of gender and sexuality as well as how they intersect with race, class and other identity categories?

Acknowledgements

This chapter benefited from the funding support of the visiting scholar grant (MOST 106-2918-I-002-002) of the Ministry of Science and Technology (MOST) of Taiwan. Through the grant, while visiting the Department of Second Language Studies at the University of Hawaii at Manoa, the discussions with Dr Graham Crookes and the members of his critical pedagogy group were indispensable in my eventual conceptualization of this chapter. I also want to acknowledge my students, whose poignant works inspire me to continue exploring the power of critical multimodality in the classroom.

Notes

1 Please access the 'man also woman' image from this URL: https://4.bp.blogspot.com/-VGFhXw0uVFs/VjrmdAO--EI/AAAAAAAAH6k/8deq6V9b71Q/s1600/Sex%2Bchange%2Bsurgery.jpg.
2 Please access the cover of Joss Stone's album, 'Color Me Free', from this URL: https://en.wikipedia.org/wiki/Colour_Me_Free!#/media/File:Joss_Stone_-_Colour_Me_Free.png.

8

Gendered Discourses in Global and Glocal ELT Textbooks

Suha Alansari

Introduction

This chapter emanates from a social discursive understanding of gender (after Foucault 1980), whereby gender, as a defining element of identity, is understood to be largely shaped by the circulating discourses within a community. This view foregrounds the role of language in gender construction, allowing gender to be seen as a set of ideas rather than something embodied (Wodak 2015), and, consequently, more as a construct than a fixed category. The discursive conception of gender entails, in theory, a multiplicity of constructions for what is conventionally labelled as *masculine* and *feminine*, some of which complement one another while others do not. *Discourses of gender* in the Foucauldian sense are like other systems of power/knowledge, in that they 'organise texts, create the conditions of possibilities for different language acts and are embedded in social institutions'; therefore, they 'define, delimit and produce' what can be said about gender norms in their contexts (Pennycook 1994: 128). In this light, educational textbooks are but another text that is produced by the gendered discourses of the social institutions they circulate in.

In English language teaching (ELT) textbook research, critics have recognized the role textbooks play in perpetuating gender stereotypes and in promoting one (dominant) gendered construction over others (Holmes 1991; Mustapha 2013; Sunderland 2000). Ever since these criticisms gathered momentum, gendered representations in ELT textbooks are judged to become 'less dire' (Sunderland, Cowley, Rahim, Leontzakou & Shattuck 2002: 224) or to have improved (Gray 2002). This improvement translates into ensuring more gender balance in representations, eliminating 'offensive' representations of women (Blumberg

2007), changing lexical choices and eliminating explicate stereotypical gender representations around gender roles (Sano et al. 2001 in Mustapha 2013).

There is a crucial aspect of ELT textbook production that problematizes such reports of improvement. ELT textbooks are products of a lucrative cultural and educational industry, one that is largely dominated by Anglo-Saxon countries but marketed and consumed internationally (Gray 2012). Like any successful product, ELT textbooks have had to adapt to the forces of market globalization. In ELT research today, the globalization of ELT textbooks is discussed in relation to two topics: first, the expansive reach of the textbooks to ever new markets, which necessitates providing customization services to international customer countries and institutions (Gray 2002; Hicks 2000); and second, the internationalization of the cultural content of the textbooks, especially around the representation of the individuals who populate textbooks (Block 2010; Gray 2010a).

In this chapter, I investigate the phenomenon of localizing global ELT textbooks by their original publishers, analysing how this process impacts gender representations and the discourses that mediate them in these textbooks. The focus of the analysis will be on the linguistic and multimodal constructions of gendered identities represented in a global ELT textbook series and two of its localized editions. Looking at three editions of the same textbooks, a prototype for the global market, a second adapted for a regional market (Middle East) and a third for one country (Saudi Arabia), I ask: what effect does the production of localized editions of global ELT textbooks have on gender representations?

The Globalization and the Glocalization of ELT Textbooks

How globalization is changing the English language and ELT has been the interest of burgeoning critical scholarship within Applied Linguistics. Chief among the effects of globalization nominated by this scholarship is the commodification of the English language (Block, Gray & Holborow 2013; Coupland 2010; Fairclough 2006; Holborow 2015), a condition that marks a shift in the value of English from a symbol of national and cultural identities to what it is worth in a globalized neoliberal world (Block 2010). Consequently, the English language has become a commodity that needs to be 'produced, controlled, distributed, valued and constrained' (Heller 2010: 108), particularly in the growing industry of ELT. In other businesses, the English language is commodified either as a linguistic or communicative job skill, or as an added value to the work products (Heller 2010: 102). Secondly, globalization is seen as a driver for the boom in the

ELT industry, affecting 'people's motivation to learn a language and choice of language to learn' (Block & Cameron 2002: 5).

The commodification of the English language has its consequences on the type of language that is taught to the ever-increasing number of people demanding it. English taught as a skill or English as a job requirement is 'vaguely the same thing in different educational contexts around the world' (Block 2010: 295). The new genre, *global English*, is a lifeless skeletal language built around the minimum communication needs in business and leisure settings (Block 2010). This *global English* is tailored in English-speaking countries, wrapped up in ELT global textbooks, then marketed and consumed in language centres around the world. If *global English* is a commodity, global ELT textbooks are the marketing tools that brand it (Block 2010; Gray 2010b).

One effect of the conditions of globalization on the content of ELT textbooks is the tendency to sanitize the discussion around already limited number of topics. To maximize profits and ensure access to new markets, authors of global ELT textbooks are advised against lists of controversial topics that vary in length from one target market to another (Gray 2010a; Meccawy 2010). Moreover, the type of culture endorsed in modern ELT textbooks is another area affected by the conditions of globalization. Block (2010) notes a shift in the cultural content of ELT textbooks from national cultural content to an 'emergent global culture', which is lived by envisaged global citizens, who need the English language to communicate with one another. Three aspects characterize the global middle-class citizens in ELT textbooks – they are successful (or on the way to success) and they easily talk about their private matters in public. Most importantly, they possess a *cosmopolitan capital*, which motivates them to participate in sports, reading, shopping and travelling, conveying capitalist and consumerist value systems and exhibiting cultural knowledge and appreciation of technological skills, cinema, music and literature (Block 2010: 297–9). When it comes to work, the construction of the global worker in ELT textbooks is congruent with the characteristics valued in the literature describing successful workers in neoliberal economies; these include individuality, commitment, passion for work, mobility, ability to think and act strategically, and the ability to exercise choice (Gray 2010b).

The birth of *the glocal textbook* (Gray 2002), a variant of the global ELT textbook, best encapsulates the influence of globalization on ELT textbook industry. In this trend, textbooks become a package product where the international version represents a core text, the release of which is usually followed by additional add-ons issued at carefully staged times to increase augmentation of the core textbook. The subsequent launch of a localized textbook is part of the add-on option, which is usually accompanied by extra materials such as word lists, workbooks and so on, some of which are offered free to encourage adopting the core textbooks (Hicks 2000). The resulting textbook (i.e. glocal textbook) is an interesting phenomenon where traces of the global, the local and the interaction between the two can be detected.

Unlike the centre-produced ELT textbooks (Canagarajah 1993, 1999), locally produced textbooks (Mahboob & Elyas 2014; Tajeddin & Teimournezhad 2015) or global ELT textbooks (Block 2010; Gray 2002, 2010a, 2010b), the glocal textbook is still an under-researched phenomenon. This study sets out to investigate the glocal textbooks in a sample that represents two levels of localization. It will reveal what localization means for the construction of the global citizen described in the literature, and how the gender of the global citizen is affected in the process.

Data and Methods

I will compare the representations of human individuals in three levels of globality constructed by a single ELT textbook. These levels are realized in a corpus taken from three editions of the same textbook: a Global Edition (GE) *New Headway/Elementary* (Soars & Soars 2003), a regional edition for the Middle East *New Headway Plus/Elementary* (Soars & Soars 2006) and a local edition for Saudi Arabia *New Headway Plus Special Edition/Elementary* (Soars & Soars 2011), all localized by the same publisher. The launching of localized editions is part of an 'add-on' strategy to prolong the shelf life of ELT textbooks and to facilitate their expansion in new markets (Hicks 2000). Since the release of the local edition, the series has been successful, adopted by at least four large Saudi universities for an average period of four years, and is still used in some of its programmes. The example of localization this series represents is significant for another reason; it stands for the first-generation of glocalized textbooks in the country, to which future generations could be compared.

In the sampled series, the differences around human representations between the global coursebook and its two localized editions are numerous, involving changes to the language as well as the visuals. Changes to the visuals are subtle and intricate, including focus, size, colour, the represented characters and elements, and their arrangement on the page; only a multimodal framework of analysis can capture this level of change. To this end, I assembled an analytical framework that is sensitive to the use of colour (Van Leeuwen 2011), layout (Kress & Van Leeuwen

1998), image (Kress & Van Leeuwen 1996) and written language (Halliday & Matthiessen 2014) in the semiotic representation of individuals in ELT textbooks. I integrated multimodal analysis into an adapted version of Fairclough's (1995) framework of critical discourse analysis (CDA), whereby the analysis goes through three stages. In the first stage, I produced a technical description of the data against their analytical systems in multimodality and transitivity; in the second stage, I interpreted the modal values, those uncovered in the first stage, within their respective systems, and clustered the values thematically. The third stage draws connections between the findings and critical theory, with an eye on the wider social context of use for the editions in question.

Individuals who are the primary focus of representation I call Represented Participants (henceforth RP), and non-human elements in the text I refer to as Circumstance (Kress & Van Leeuwen 1996). I counted thirty cases of representation of adult individuals – fourteen for female participants and sixteen for male participants in the GE, and traced their counterparts in the Middle Eastern edition (MEE) and the special edition (SE). All the cases are longer works of visual and verbal representations that were selected for their information richness; representations of fleeting characters were not considered. Representations in ELT textbooks are known to be normative (Gray 2013); therefore, both the analysis and findings here will necessarily follow this. I will adopt the categories *men* and *women* to denote two already discursively differentiated social groups in the data. This step will not only help uncover the different constructions for each category in each edition, but it will also shed light on how *gender difference* is constructed and how it changes in every localization process. I first created a multimodal profile for each adult individual from all editions. Next, I organized the multimodal and linguistic analyses of the individuals from each edition in groups for men and women and employed constant inter- and intra-group comparison, looking for similarities and differences in their multimodal and linguistic constructions. Analytical tables for men and women in each edition were created to facilitate the comparison within and across edition(s). This comparison sometimes led to further codifying of the data based on new recurrent features in one group.

Globalized Women

Women of GE are successful and middle class, who mostly come from Anglo-Saxon countries. Most of them are single; the three married women either have no young children or no children at all. They are pioneers who break moulds (e.g. Joss Stone is a teenage white girl excelling in soul music, Pamela Green is a Canadian doctor in Africa, Josie Dow travelled the world on a bike, Ceri Bevan is a professional rugby player, Shirley Temple is a retired politician) or break records (e.g. Amelia Mary Earhart, first woman to fly alone across the Pacific, Tanya Streeter broke records in freediving). The textual narratives on these women's lives follow a similar plot structure: the female RP picks up an activity that is thought to be new, dangerous, formidable or not suited for girls. The surrounding family or friends are construed with less supportive actions/reactions. Against these odds, she succeeds. The verbal text emphasizes her agency through verbs such as 'love', 'want', 'decided' and 'knew that she wanted to' (Table 8.1). Her talent or passion motivates her to succeed in her chosen field. Someone gets surprised by her success – herself, her parents, her classmates or the teacher. After enjoying some success, some RPs consider teaching the activity (e.g. Tanya Streeter, Shirly Black). Women's *surprising* success is posited to subvert social gendered expectations, which can be taken as a marker of *women's empowerment discourse* that mediates women's representations in this edition.

Indeed, representing all women as successful invokes the notion of the *successful girl* (Baker 2010; Mitchell & Reid-Walsh 2007). The values that the multimodal and linguistic resources take in Table 8.1 all point to an effort to centre the women at the heart of the representational design and can be taken as markers of *the successful girl discourse*. This discourse, which is acquiring currency in contemporary Anglo-American culture, positions women as 'model neoliberal citizen[s] who climb the techno-rationalist ladder to success' (Benjamin 2003: 105), and their educational performance as evidence that 'individual success is attainable … in contexts of Globalization' (Ringrose 2007: 472). Indeed, the narratives on globalized women coincide with the 'new millennium … seductive narrative about girls' educational and workplace success, where girls have become a "metaphor" for social mobility and social change' (Ringrose 2007: 472). The contemporary focus on the *successful girl* often assumes a 'white, heterosexual, middle class, academically capable and childless demographic' (Baker 2010: 2). Female RPs in GE certainly match this description. It is tempting to judge women's representations that realize the *successful girl discourse* as an articulation of the textbooks producers' feminist agenda (Gray 2002), but critics such as Baker (2010) warn that buying into the idea that women are the winners in late modernity pushes back the role of class and gender in attaining success, and Fraser (2013), too, believes that this discourse is an appropriation of the first-wave feminist values such as interdependence, care and social solidarity.

Regionalized Women

Ten new women are introduced in MEE, nine of whom replace nine global women. Not all the British women are white; one is Black and one of South Asian heritage. This is in addition to new women from Portugal and Japan, but none is Middle Eastern (except one young girl). Although not all the new women are heralded as successful in this edition – Ussery is eccentric in living in an old airplane, Miss Bishop and Manuela Da Silva lead ordinary lives –, success remains significant in the representation of most. Yet how success is constructed is different here.

The changes brought about by localization targeted female singleness in the representations of the newly introduced women. Alison Hauser, Keiko Wilson, Bobbi Brown, Joanne Ussery, Mattie Smith and Miss Bishop are all married. This change was accompanied by a modification in the discourse of individuality, realized in the values of both the visual modes (less and smaller-size individualizing photos) and the linguistic modes (an inflation in the domestic roles). Indeed, the new women are constructed with new and additional subject positions that are predominantly domestic. For instance, Bobbi Brown is construed with thirty processes (verbs), more than half of them position her in domestic roles as a wife, a homemaker, a mother and a sister. Ceri Bevan, her counterpart in GE, has only one verb that positions her as a sister and another as a girlfriend out of twenty-eight verbs that construe her identity as a lawyer and a rugby player.

Moreover, the modal changes brought about by localization underlie a reassessment of the public and private spaces in women's representations, bringing into sight the private sphere, thus activating it in the identity construction of the newly introduced women. For instance, most of the activities with which globalized Shirley are constructed are carried out in the public domain, such as 'works', 'goes', 'meets with', and 'discuss'. On the other hand, the verbal text on her counterpart in the glocal editions, Mattie, centres her daily routine on domestic chores such as 'starts her day', 'has a bath', 'cleans', 'sits', 'thinks about' and 'writes'. Such treatment of the dichotomy of private and public spheres in the identity construction of the regionalized women reproduces, rather than challenges, the 'space dichotomy' of gender (Sadiqi 2003), an arrangement that Rosaldo (1974) finds cross-culturally valid. In Arabic communities, this gender-space dichotomy is even more pronounced and bolstered by social and cultural patriarchy (Al-Wer 2014).

The boosting of the domestic roles for regional women is also accompanied by a relegation of work and sports in their visual representations. In the visual design of working RPs in GE, visual attention is always carefully directed to them (Table 8.1). Different design selections are made for the women in MEE (Table 8.2). These selections result in a diffusion of the visual attention across the photo instead of concentrating it on the RP. Conceptually, this has its parallel in introducing *work* rather than *the worker* as the subject matter of the photo. Likewise, the celebratory discourse on successful sporting women in GE is also toned down in MEE. Global professional sportswomen (Tanya and Ceri) are removed. A new sporting woman, car racer Sue Glass, is introduced in the glocalized editions. However, her representation dims when compared to the sporting women in GE. The discourse on Sue Glass makes a shy association between women and car racing. The affair starts with fear, eases into amazement at her ability to do it, but ends with nervousness and more fear. Glass's modest achievement is reached with the help of a man and does not extend to winning: 'I did not win.'

The overall changes to the representations of women in this edition point to an effort to build a hyper-feminine ideal incompatible with the globalized version of preferred femininity – single, athletic and/or with a career. The glocalized woman is a full-time mother who may or may not take a full-time job. The details of her multimodal construction in Table 8.2 can be taken as markers of *the supermom discourse* – a version of femininity that copes with many demands, primarily taking care of children, in addition to taking up domestic tasks and caring of others (Ussher, Hunter & Brown 2000). Overall, localization at this level meant reinscribing the social definition of the category *woman* for the intended users. This attempt is yet another example of the larger social writing of the differences between gender categories through social practices around sex roles (Connell 1987).

Localized Women

Localization for SE meant, in a few instances, replacing the representation of one woman with another (e.g. Mona Halahesh replacing regional Keiko and global Iman). Crucially, and more often, it meant replacing the representation of women with a man's (e.g. Gary Seaman replaces global Ceri Bevan and regional Bobbi Brown; Louise Barnet replaces global Joss Stone and regional Alexandra; Louis Bleriot replaces global Amelia Earhart; and glocal Al Wheeler replaces global Daniella). This brought the number of women represented to seven, down from fourteen in GE and MEE. The changes incurred by the process of localization affected the representation of the social actor, the social practice or both. Keeping on the comparative method, I use Van Leeuwen's concept of 'exclusion' (2008) to better illustrate the phenomenon. Van Leeuwen identifies three possible levels of exclusion of social actors when recontextualizing a social practice. First, *backgrounding* involves distancing the social actor from the social practice while keeping both in the text. Second, *suppression* is removing the social actor but keeping on the social practice. Finally, *radical exclusion* is removing both the social actor and the social practice from the text.

Apart from sports, there are two main sites of exclusion for female RPs in SE – art and profession. The representation of art, in all instances in the three editions, is based on a neoliberal conception (Deresiewicz 2015), where art's value is measured by its market worth and the riches it brings back to the (young) artists and their families. Art in the form of acting for the child star Shirley Black in GE is radically excluded and replaced by poetry writing for adult Mattie Smith in MEE and SE. Art in the form of music making in the representation of global teenager Joss Stone is radically excluded twice. The first is in MEE and replaced there by painting in the representation of Alexandra Nechita; then again in SE and replaced by culinary arts. More importantly, the discourse on neoliberal arts is masculinized in the second level of localization by associating it with a male RP – Louise Barnett.

Three types of profession have become sites of gendered exclusion in SE – legal, political and fashion modelling. The representation of British supermodel and entrepreneur Iman in GE is radically excluded and never replaced in any of the glocal editions. On the other hand, the representation of law practice by a female lawyer in GE has been radically excluded in the two glocal editions. Localization for MEE replaced law practice with television anchoring for a female RP. Yet localization for SE has retained the representation of law practice but masculinized the discourse on it in the representation of Gary Seaman. Thirdly, political posts, as represented in the life of global Shirley Black, are approached differently in the two glocal editions. Localization for MEE retains the social practice but replaced the social actor, downscaled the representation and relocated it on a different page. While localization for MEE employs *suppression*, localization for SE opts for *radical exclusion* where both the social practice and the social actor are removed.

We have seen how the globalized women were constructed with high-profile jobs, symbolic of authority and power, such as the ones in law and politics. The consumers of the multimodal texts on those women were positioned as aspirational and sometimes as less powerful in their relationship with them. Localization for SE kept the reader in the same aspirational, sometimes less powerful position but shifted the object of aspiration to a male persona. Removing women from progressive public sites reinstates restrictions on women representations in these spaces and relegates their positions in the occupational structure (Crompton 1987). These changes correlate with the situation in some Middle Eastern societies where women's access to similar 'sites of power' is limited (Sadiqi 2003).

Lastly, the values assigned to the modes of the interactional structure in localized women's photos (Table 8.3) constitute an important finding. These adjusted values for RPs affect their (imaginary) relationship with the viewers, reducing both RP's contact and engagement with them to the minimum. The adjustments convey an attempt to regulate the viewers' perception of female RPs. Far from being objective representations of reality, photographs are outcomes of multiple selections from among a theoretically infinite set of values and attributes, both aesthetic and ethical (Bourdieu 1990). Producing the RP's image and engineering the viewer's perception of the image are two motivated actions that lie within the agency of the producer of the photo, the page and the textbook. Against this backdrop, we can see that localization, in changing the interactional values for the RPs, embeds an act of staking control over how these women are seen. In this controlled context of photo production, the symbolic attributes introduced in the new photos (e.g. head covering and eyeglasses) assume a vital role in how the female RPs are set to be identified in SE.

Globalized Men

Men in GE are mostly British or European with the exception of one Japanese. They are workers, dressed in all collar-colours – blue, white, gold and pink – in addition to some inventors, entrepreneurs, students and an athlete. Aspiration is a recurrent identity aspect that surfaced in the multimodal analysis of identity formation of men in GE, yet only in the representation of gold collar workers (e.g. music professor, Istvan Kis), inventors (e.g. Kirkpatrick Macmillan and Louis Daguerre), entrepreneurs (e.g. Gorgio Locatelli) and the athlete (David Belle). Gray (2012) analyses aspiration in ELT textbooks in relation to the phenomenon of celebrity profiling, whereby celebrities known for their wealth and success are selected and presented as textbook content. By doing so, ELT textbooks build textual associations between individual wealth and the English language. While agreeing with much of Gray's critique, I argue that the deployment of the neoliberal ethos of aspiration in ELT textbooks is far more intricate than merely profiling celebrities. It is deeply embedded in the structure of the visual and verbal modes of language used in building the identity of the RPs in the textbooks, celebrities or not. These participants are discursively constructed as goal-oriented aspiring individuals who relentlessly work towards achieving their goals, which are normally constructed around study, travel, work or leisure. Aspiration is also key in engineering the relationship between the RPs in the textbooks and the textbooks' users. The multimodal analysis carried out in this study, especially that of layout (utilizing salience and size resources) and the interactional structure of images (visually positioning the viewer in admiring or identifying positions), points to how the users of these textbooks are structurally positioned in an aspirational relationship with the textbooks' characters.

Crucially, the discourse of aspiration does not extend to the representation of white-, pink- and blue-collar workers. For example, the primary teacher, Danny Carrick, is the only male character in this edition who is constructed with a very high angle. This sharply contrasts with the interactional values that chef and entrepreneur Gorgio Locatelli, in the same edition, is imbued with. In their engineered relationship with Danny, the viewers are positioned as having greater power, therefore, in a less admiring or aspiring stance. In a similar vein, the values of the multimodal construction of the only blue-collar worker in GE, Seumas McSporran, set him apart from all other RPs in the book. His visual construction consists of eight small-size photographs; the values of the interactional structure of his photos are all set in medium or long shots, at an eye-level angle. The representational structure of the photos is predominantly narrative with unusually different types of circumstance present all at once. The multimodal values selected for his identity construction are markedly different from the ones typically selected for aspirational characters in the same edition. Indeed, the representation of Seumas is far from aspirational: he is constructed saying, 'My life is not exciting.' While it is unusual to juggle thirteen jobs a day, Seumas says he 'likes' it, a stance consolidated by his smile in some of the photos. Portraying working-class workers as dignified heroes is one neoliberal discursive position in the media, one that is criticized for white washing the workers' working conditions (Walker & Roberts 2017). On the other hand, ELT textbooks are criticized for excluding working-class men and women from their population, thus providing a skewed view of the world (Gray & Block 2014). When they are included, as in the examples above, a discursive tension is created between the generally grim realities of working-class men's working conditions and the discourse of aspiration prevalent in the textbooks. This tension is resolved, as we have seen, in the decisions to exclude working-class men's representation from the aspirational discourse and to conceal if not romanticize their working conditions.

Regionalized Men

Localization for MEE replaced eleven globalized men with new ones and kept on only four. In terms of ethnicity, localization has widened up the pool of the home countries of RPs (Mexico, China, Arabian Gulf), though the Bahraini Hamad Saleh, the closest to the target market, is given a relatively small space. Overall, the changes do not affect the discourse of aspiration that entrenches the representation of highly skilled professionals (e.g. Rafael Ramos, the doctor; Bob Nelson, the flying doctor; Mark Konig; and the BBC journalist), that of young entrepreneurs in their talents (Wesley Chu) or skilled athletes (Clen Quinn). While retaining the representation of blue labourer McSupporn, localization introduced an additional low-skilled labourer, waiter Phillipe Ballon. Like McSupporn, he is constructed with values that construe the least engagement with the viewer – extreme oblique angle, absence of eye contact with the viewer in addition to a narrative representational structure.

More importantly, localization adjusts the gendered boundaries in the representation of some professions and sports. For instance, the pink-collar worker, primary school teacher Danny Carrick, is replaced in MEE with a female RP, Miss Bishop, not surprisingly represented wearing a pink jumper. The values of the Interactional Structure of her visual representation are also adjusted, resulting in changing the power status constructed for the RP from powerlessness in the case of Danny Carrick to equal footing with the viewer in the case of Miss Bishop. Moreover, Bob Nelson is introduced to masculinize the discourse of a happy single professional serving long hours at work, in place of Pamela Green in GE, all the while changing the marital status of the glocalized women to married, their mode of work to part-time, and the discourse on their working identity as one that tries to balance out work and family. In this way, localization rewrites the social differences between the represented men and women in a manner that not only widens the gap between the two categories but also represents masculinity as dependent on the hyper-feminization of women. Consequently, localization subtly brings to the fore the issue of gender power relations through representation in MEE.

Localized Men

Six male RPs are introduced in SE, with five of them, crucially, replacing women in the other editions. Two of the new men have local names and all have successful stories to tell. Some of their stories tell of a curse turning into blessing (e.g. Louis Bleriot). However, unlike the success narratives of globalized women, the success stories of the men in SE are characterized by an absence of any reference to family members opposing or holding different views on their dreams. Therefore, success for these men is constructed to unfold naturally and commonsensically.

Some of the multimodal markers of the discourse of success in the representation of the male RPs in SE (Table 8.4) recall those used in the construction of female RPs in GE. The verbal selections in their constructions serve to boast men's achievements while stressing their agency in telling their success stories. Their visual representations always specify and individualize them. The visual values selected in their photos direct all attention to them.

In addition to reinforcing the discourse of success in the representation of male RPs, localization for SE resulted in masculinizing the discourse on sports and young entrepreneurs. As for the latter, the changes involve an adjustment to the type of entrepreneurship preferred, changing it from masculine musical (Wesley Chu) and feminine artistic (Alexandra Nechita) entrepreneurships in MEE to all masculine small business entrepreneurship (Louis Bleriot) and scalable start-up entrepreneurship (Yahya Stapic) in SE. Regarding sports, localization for SE introduced Gary Seaman in place of global Ceri Bevan. The celebratory discourse on Gary, seen in the optimal positioning of his visual construction in the layout, the size of the photographs and the use of modulated colour pallet, is comparable to global sportswoman Ceri. Although localization for SE maintains the representation of glocalized Sue Glass from MEE, it removes her personalized photograph while keeping a generic photo of car racing, thus assigning a higher level of genericism to the overall representation of Sue, which starkly contrasts with the design selection made for the male athlete Gary Seaman in the same edition. This is on top of the differences between the verbal narratives of the two – Sue is fearful and quits after a while, while Gary is confident and looks forward to more races.

The gendered approach to sportspeople embedded in the act of localization for SE can be seen doing two things. Firstly, it modifies the globalized discourse of feminizing sports which redefines sport away from its hegemonic masculine conception, tilting it more towards its original masculine and masculinizing sense (Markula & Pringle 2006). Secondly, while localization for MEE is concerned with building hyper-feminine ideals, localization for SE is by and large about constructing hyper-masculine ideals. If sport sets ideal masculinity (Connell 1987: 84), then modifying the construction of sports in the local edition articulates the ideal masculinity desired in this context: individualized, robust, competitive and excited by danger. Peddling a glamorous hyper-masculinity in SE is also reliant on the exclusion of women from some sites. Although in some examples the exclusion was overworked (i.e. excluding the female media personality), excluding women from advanced public sites was common in pre-2017 rentier Saudi Arabia. However, recently an increased employment of women in advanced public posts has been noted after the country had adopted *women's empowerment* in its official discourse, part of its recent initiative to diversify its economy (KFCRIS 2021).

Conclusion

This chapter was set out to answer the following question: what effect does the production of localized editions of global ELT textbooks have on their representations of gender? The findings suggest that localization does not alter the neoliberal conception of the global citizen prevalent in the global ELT textbook (Block 2010); it merely redefines the subject positions allocated to men and women within this discourse. Since a significant part of globalization in global ELT textbooks, especially around human representations, is about representing neoliberal values (Block 2010), I suggest framing the changes embedded in the localization processes as contextual and temporal responses to the represented neoliberal values and discourses.

Bound by time and context, the responses are subject to change every time the target market adjusts its position on neoliberal discourses. Indeed, there are signs that the responses have already changed in the case of Saudi Arabia. In 2016, Saudi Arabia introduced its reform plan known as 2030 vision, which aims to diversify the economy and support privatization. The economic side of the plan is accompanied with a host of social initiatives (KFCRIS 2021), some of which resonate with the discourses mobilized in the construction of the globalized women in GE, especially the one on women's empowerment. ELT textbooks have yet to catch up with the new official discourses in Saudi Arabia and it would be interesting to see how the next generation of localized ELT textbooks would accommodate the new pro-neoliberal discourses currently embraced by the kingdom or whether there will be a need to localize global ELT textbooks for the Saudi market in the future.

In any scenario, as in many contexts, teachers and students who use these textbooks come to be at the receiving end of the cycle of production of ELT textbooks and their (gendered) discourses. This is because decisions about selecting and using textbooks do not reside within their agency. Yet there is room for grassroots resistance to ELT textbooks' dominant discourses in the classroom, one that starts with evaluating these discourses, then rejecting or accepting them (Canagarajah 2005). For this to take place, critical knowledge needs to be built in the classroom. In this regard, I propose the design of pre- and in-service training programmes that empower the teachers with visual literacy and discourse analytic skills, tools that will facilitate critical reading and interpreting of complex multimodal texts of modern-day ELT textbooks. Teachers can then convey these skills to their students which will hopefully lead to open classroom discussions about what the discourses are and how they position the readers.

Bearing in mind the constructing and constructed role of textbook discourses and appreciating the role of neoliberal globalization in producing gendered meanings (Salzinger 2016), future studies on gender representation in ELT textbooks are encouraged to further explore the link between the textbooks' selected representations and the economic style of the consuming context, its associated discourses and the positioning of gendered identities within them.

Questions for Change

1. For curriculum developers: what values do we want to associate with the global citizen represented in ELT textbooks? Do these values need to be gendered?
2. For ELT teachers: if you are teaching a glocalized edition, how do gender representations in your book differ from that in other editions? How can you raise students' critical awareness of the fact?

9

Gender, Sexuality and ELT Course Books: Where Are We Now?

Chris Richards

Introduction

The English language teaching (ELT[1]) course book is a tool which is often, despite the range of technological possibilities available, the main resource used by English language teachers. It provides goals, content and methods for individual lessons and whole courses (Richards 2014). In fact, course books are 'part of the assumed furniture in most second-language classrooms', and although they might seem ideologically neutral (Moore 2020: 117), no publication can be; content and editorial decisions are made based on rationales and style guides. Likewise, the activities of teaching and learning languages, and the materials that support this, are not 'ideologically neutral practices' (Curdt-Christiansen & Weninger 2015: 1) but practices that are embedded within social, linguistic, cultural, political and historical moments. Forman (2014) positions the course book not only as 'the curriculum' for many 'majority-world foreign-language teachers' but also as a 'Western import': books published by 'Western companies which embrace Western values, [which] are monolingual in English' and that are promoted in Anglophone and non-Anglophone contexts alike (72).

While teachers may think they are teaching *only* English (see Pakuła, Pawelczyk & Sunderland 2015), the materials they use in their classrooms are populated by gendered representations. The characters are gendered male or female and are heteronormative. The course book, and accompanying materials, allows for the subtle gendering of roles and jobs to go unnoticed; at other times, materials are overtly gendered in a stereotypical and predictable way (see, e.g. Pakuła, Pawelczyk & Sunderland 2015). The lives of LGBTQ+ individuals are generally missing from mainstream course books (see Gray 2013; Pakuła, Pawelczyk &

Sunderland 2015). This latter silence, like that of quietly stereotyping 'mum' in a home-making role and 'dad' in a suit, reinforces a dominant world view in which teachers may be unwittingly complicit. Such a world view relegates the lives and identities of LGBTQ+ individuals to a position reminiscent of *don't ask, don't tell*[2] – their voices unheard, their faces unseen.

Paiz (2019) explains that we cannot regard course books as 'a minor concern' (4). For example, early career educators may not be ready to stray beyond using them (see Richards 2014; Paiz 2017, 2019), and thus, course books may provide the foundation for curriculum design and pedagogy for early career teachers. For some, published material may be considered a form of Continuous Professional Development (CPD) with the teacher's book acting as a guide to pedagogy and methodology. It should also be noted that, in the global context, there are ELT classrooms staffed by teachers whose only teaching qualification is their passport (typically used to indicate an assumed 'native English speaker' status) and who, as a result, might rely on course books even more. Thus, course materials might provide such teachers with both content and pedagogy, teachers who, as a result of their lack of teacher education, might be unaware that they can ask questions about the materials or not know what questions might or should be asked.

For some students, course materials might be the only, or the primary, source of language input they receive other than that from their teacher (see Richards 2014). They are possibly the only input language learners receive about the target culture, and so might 'reinforce certain norms' of that culture (Paiz 2019: 4). Paiz suggests that the identity options presented in a course book give students an idea of what options are available for them to embody their identity in the target culture and language. In my study, participants responded to sample materials taken from my corpus of course book material. For example, one page included four photographs of what the book described as 'different' weddings (each photograph showed a couple presenting as heteronormative). Responding to the material, one participant said that it 'makes you think that 100% of people who get married in the UK are one man and one woman'[3] (Participant 1). An ELT student, therefore, might receive the impression that weddings in the English-speaking world are only for opposite-sex couples. As course materials can be left uncriticized and unquestioned by teachers and students, and as they provide a window onto Anglophone culture, the material that finds its way into classrooms needs to be both inclusive and realistic.

This chapter discusses the findings of a small-scale study conducted as part of the requirements for my masters of education in applied linguistics and addressed these research questions:

1. RQ1: How is gender represented in a sample of ELT course books?
2. RQ2: How is sexuality represented in a sample of ELT course books?
3. RQ3: How do teachers respond to the representations of gender and sexuality in ELT course books?

The chapter aims to position my study within the global context of research on how gender and sexuality are (not) represented in ELT course materials and some of the contemporary grassroots projects that are attempting to address the lack of diverse and inclusive representation. It will also draw attention to what practitioners (can) do in their classrooms.

Literature Review

This section gives an overview of the existing work in this area and includes a discussion of two practitioner projects that are going on. In his introduction to a special issue of *TESOL Quarterly*, Pennycook (1999) painted a utopian picture of inclusivity where we see:

> fewer wholesome White families who look as if they have walked off the back of Kellogg's Cornflakes packets (after another regular dental checkup) and more single-parent families, gay and lesbian parents, people of diverse ethnic backgrounds, and different physical possibilities. (339)

He also argues that this version of inclusivity, merely providing representation, barely goes beyond 'a static sense of possibility' (339). He presents the idea of using classroom debate and discussion to open up the space for issues, but counters that simply engaging rationally with homophobic or racist views (to which we could add sexist and transphobic views, among others) is inadequate. Instead, he suggests that 'an engagement with people's investment in particular discourses' is what is necessary (340).

After all, inclusive practice does not mean having a debate on same-sex marriage rights. Insensitive handling of topics concerning minority groups is likely to be worse than not representing them in the classroom at all. For example, De Vincenti, Giovangneli and Ward (2007) report on a French-language textbook that does include 'homosexual references' but which does so in a way that stereotypes 'homosexuals as diseased' (64). Thus, there is a difference between being represented, well-represented, mis-represented and silenced. In *Quizzes, Questionnaires and Puzzles* (2005, reprinted for the eighth time in 2012) we find an activity called 'The Moral Maze' (60). The activity is found in the chapter called 'Beliefs' and categorized by the book as 'personal ethics'. It presents twelve moral scenarios and asks students to discuss them with their partners. Number 10, for example, asks about lying; number 12 is about theft. Number 11 asks whether same-sex marriage should be permitted.

Gender

While often used interchangeably in daily discourse, 'sex' and 'gender' are now generally accepted to mean, respectively, the biological distinction between men and women (usually classified by a doctor at birth) and the constructed, and often contested, social and cultural differences between men and women (see Pakuła, Pawelczyk & Sunderland 2015). Since Butler (1990), the notion of gender performativity has also problematized the cultural distinction between, and classification of, masculine and feminine gender identities. Pakuła, Pawelczyk and Sunderland (2015) warn about the oversimplification of the terms 'masculinity' and 'femininity' and simply associating the former, for example, with strength and the latter with beauty. Rather, they stress the cultural and contextual variability in these notions. In addition, Miller (2015) notes that today's 'adolescent culture … teaches us that some youth eschew gender and sexual labels' (37) altogether.

The area of gender representation in course books has already generated a body of research. There has been development from traditional representations of men and women in stereotypically gendered roles, with Richards (2014), for example, referring to one publisher who has clear guidelines about giving gender balance and neutrality. Yet, work remains to be done to produce more teaching materials that do not reinforce conservative ideas about which roles and jobs are performed by men and those performed by women. Course books use multimodal depictions (images, audio, and video, for example, alongside text; see also Jewitt 2015) to represent men and women in certain ways and, by doing so, can contribute to the association of certain roles or attributes with men, women or both. Unless challenged by the teacher, these representations limit the discourse of the classroom, and might control what language the learners produce (see Moffat & Norton 2008), for example, where one gendered pronoun is used with one type of role and another pronoun for another type of role (see Jones, Kitetu & Sunderland 1997). As discussed later, this is often found explicitly with materials for younger students (e.g. where women are often nurses and men are often doctors) but may remain the case more implicitly with materials aimed at older learners.

Sexuality

Among the better-known voices and interventions on this topic in ELT are Thornbury (1999) and Gray (2013). Thornbury asked us where we might find the 'coursebook gays and lesbians' before telling us that 'they are nowhere to be found. They are still firmly in the coursebook closet. Coursebook people are never gay' (15). His short but apt contribution was published in 1999. In the modern history of gay rights, this seems like a lifetime ago. Indeed, at that time, I was being educated in a Welsh state school under the infamous Section 28. This legislation was enacted in 1988 and not repealed until 2003 and prohibited local authorities in England, Wales and Scotland from promoting homosexuality or publishing 'material with the intention of promoting homosexuality' (Local Government Act 1988). It further prohibited material that would 'promote the teaching in any maintained school of the acceptability of homosexuality as a pretended family relationship' (Local Government Act 1988). Thus, in Great Britain at least, there was very little incentive to produce pedagogical materials that portrayed homosexual, and other non-conforming, identities or relationships.

Although definitions of heteronormativity differ, they agree that it is the result of social structures that produce heterosexuality as normal, natural and necessary (see Cameron & Kulick 2003; Motschenbacher 2010). In addition, heteronormativity does not simply promote heterosexuality as the default sexuality of all humans but also 'as an institution and the mechanisms by which it is privileged, naturalised, and reproduced' (Gray 2013: 43). Heteronormativity connects with the politics of gender and heterosexuality which themselves depend on normative gender binaries. Such binaries are, as Butler (1990, 2004) argues, performative and rule based. Heteronormativity can also be seen as a question of degrees: the constant representation of nuclear families 'can be seen as *highly* heteronormative', whereas single-sex pairs of teenagers or adults can be described as less heteronormative because they are open to multiple interpretations (Pakuła, Pawelczyk & Sunderland 2015: 11; see also Paiz 2020). Such images can be used to open conversations and provide space for different identities to be discussed or imagined, for students to see people who might be like themselves. Moore (2020) explores heteronormativity and proposes a taxonomy that can be used by material writers and teachers to 'guide their practice away from heteronormativity, towards more critically inclusive materials' (116).

In his chapter 'LGBT Invisibility and Heteronormativity in ELT Materials', Gray (2013) draws the conclusion that the increasing numbers of books, papers and specialist journals dealing with LGBT issues in language teaching mean 'commercial ELT can no longer continue to ignore' (60) them. Yet, he also argues that 'LGBT invisibility and pervasive heteronormativity remain entrenched in mainstream ELT materials' (60–1). This tension is present in much of the literature that deals with this issue: there is demand for such materials, but mainstream publishing does not provide them. Although Gray's work is from 2013, this chapter will show his remarks are still very much relevant today. Indeed, during the last few years, Paiz (2017, 2019, 2020) has been working on 'queering the English language classroom' (2020: 2) and issues specifically related to pedagogical materials (2017).

Rhodes and Coda (2017) examined 'how adult educators in English language classrooms feel regarding the inclusion of Lesbian, Gay, Bisexual, Queer (LGBQ[4]) topics and materials into their curriculum and instruction' (99). They carried out their study in the United States among teachers who taught adult students and found that although participants were 'interested in incorporating these topics into their English language classes, the majority found insurmountable obstacles that prevented them from doing so' (104). Unsurprisingly, they report the lack of appropriate materials to be the chief problem. They also discussed the use of 'teachable moments' in the class, where topics arise organically from the students. Their participants saw value in doing this, 'yet were generally unsure of how to handle the unplanned situations' and this links with their third finding: there is a 'perceived lack of expertise related to the topic of LGBQ-related topics in the English language classroom' (104). As will be discussed later, their findings are very similar to my own.

In addition, a recent MSc project by Tim Hampson investigates a similar area to that considered in my study. He asks to what extent romantic relationships are presented as 'homogamous and heterogamous' (Hampson 2020, n.p.). The study focuses on a sample of four global English language course books (GELCs) and uses a quantitative context analysis of keywords. Hampson's paper 'attempted to evaluate the presence of LGBT people and the LGBT inclusive use of non-gendered language for relationships in GELCs' and concludes that 'no evidence of either was found in the GELCs examined' (10) and so, his findings match those presented here. It is also noteworthy that although Rhodes and Coda (2017) and my study were conducted in different contexts and both claim the limitations from which small-scale studies suffer, their findings and the findings that address my third research question correspond. In short, small-scale qualitative studies (across contexts) reveal issues of power related to gender and sexual diversity in education settings, and how these systems of power develop in different contexts.

Practitioner Projects

While mainstream ELT course book publishing has not changed much despite repeated calls from many within the industry and from academic voices, grassroots projects have begun to fill the void. For example, James Taylor and Ilá Coimbra have launched 'Raise Up for ELT'. Their initiative publishes materials featuring un(der)-represented identities, including women and people who identify as LGBTQIA+. At the time of writing, they have published a pilot book (2019) with inclusive lesson plans aimed at a variety of levels, and further books aimed to supplement courses at B1 and B2. In addition, Tyson Seburn (2019) has produced a 'sample mock-up coursebook unit' based on the principles of inclusion and usualization, demonstrating that what is emphasized in the material is not the included group but rather the language tasks.

At the British Council in Hong Kong, Eduardo Farias and his colleagues have formed a special interest group (SIG) dedicated to 'Mainstreaming EDI [Equality, Diversity and Inclusion] in the Classroom'. The work of what became the SIG began with a classroom incident involving a child aged around four and related to 'him being afraid of [the teacher] because of the colour of [the teacher's] skin' (personal communication). Farias produced a list of storybooks suitable for use with early years students that might help to raise awareness of the six protected characteristics[5] at the British Council. Next, with one other colleague he began producing lesson plans that could exploit those materials and make their early years curriculum more inclusive. Now they have a SIG which sources materials and produces lesson plans for all age groups.

Summary

Miller (2015: 39) writes that 'teachers have great agentive capacity to rupture dangerous dichotomies and myths about gender and sexuality'. Not challenging the status quo with regard to understanding norms of gender and sexuality has been described as 'myopic' because the 'evolving lived realities of people' are unseen (Miller 2015: 41). Indeed, to not recognize these changes would make us complicit in a perpetual delegitimization and stigmatization of those who do not subscribe to gender and/or sexual norms. As will be seen, the participants in my study certainly want to exploit their agentive capacity and challenge narrow, stereotyped views about gender and sexuality. This review suggests that mainstream course materials are unlikely to support them in that goal, and the materials specifically surveyed for my study also fail to provide them with necessary support. It will also become clear that (perceived) power structures can force practitioners to adopt such a myopic stance unwillingly.

Research Methods

This study drew on quantitative data in the analysis of course books and qualitative data obtained from interviews with teachers. This design was inspired by Gray (2013) who used interview data to contextualize data from course book analysis in order to provide a richer picture. This approach is also recommended by Sunderland and McGlashan (2015) who draw attention to the importance of how texts actually get used by teachers in classrooms. Their paper also reminds us of the need to consider multimodality where, for example, a written text might be gender neutral but the accompanying illustration presents a gender stereotype. Today's students are accustomed to making and understanding meaning with multimodal texts in which 'writing provides a partial account only of the overall meaning' (Kress 2017: x). Ignoring modes other than text does not take account of everything the student sees.

To address the first two research questions, I undertook a content analysis of a sample of course materials that quantified the multimodal representations of gender and sexuality. This involved a page-by-page examination, noting gendered representations and representations that implied a romantic relationship. Each occurrence was recorded with page number, brief description and coding. I also noted when one mode contradicted or undermined a meaning presented in another mode and this will be exemplified in the discussion. For the gender representations, codes were assigned that signified gender, whether the representation could be considered positive, negative or neutral and whether it was progressive, traditional or neutral. For example, a smiling man wearing a suit would be considered: male, positive, traditional, whereas an angry female doctor would be coded: female, negative, progressive. With a project of this type, there is inevitable potential for researcher bias, so it is acknowledged that this is a limitation of the project. Moreover, it is recommended that further work in this area considers using a group of researchers who could triangulate their coding decisions.

To obtain data for RQ3, I used semi-structured interviews with teachers about their views on the issues being explored; on specific examples of material; and how the participants might make use (or not) of the exemplars in their classroom. The face-to-face interviews were recorded and lasted about twenty-five minutes. Questions were treated as prompts to permit the participants to explore their ideas in conversation. Extensive notes were taken during the interviews which were then transcribed; participants' comments are quoted throughout this chapter.

Selection of Materials and Participants

As the study was conducted for a masters-level dissertation, it was small scale. Thus, the limitations of the data are acknowledged at the outset. I selected five course books (see Table 9.1) in order to provide a sample of the materials used by different ages including primary aged students, teenagers and adults and at a range of levels from A1.2 to C1 on the Common European Framework of Reference for Languages (CEFR). They were also selected in order to sample material from three major publishers: Oxford University Press, Cambridge University Press and Pearson.

For participants, convenience sampling was used and after approaching seven potential interviewees, five agreed to participate in the study. Table 9.2 provides a summary of how the participants responded when asked how they describe their gender identity, their sexuality, and their teaching experience and current employer. Informed consent was obtained from the participants and the project was ethically approved by my university.

Findings and Discussion

Data Analysis: Course Materials

The first part of my study involved analysing the selected course materials. By choosing to do a multimodal analysis, I was able to add a layer of understanding that a simple text analysis would have missed. For example, in *Objective PET* (Hashemi and Thomas 2010), we find an image showing a female taxi driver (44). The first listening exercise asks students to note the differences between the image and the audio track. One difference is the driver's gender and, consequently, the idea of a female taxi driver suggested by the image is corrected when we listen to the audio.

To discuss the findings that address my first research question, I have divided the data I collected from the sampled books into two groups: those aimed at primary aged students, and those aimed at teens and adults. In the two books designed for the younger students, representations of men and women came to the ratio of 52:48. However, simply having (near) even representation is not the whole story. For example, in one book we find parts of the body being taught using an image of a male superhero and a female princess (*Islands 3*: 24). The two biggest coding groups in the books designed for primary aged students were representations of male-traditional-neutral and female-traditional-neutral representations like an illustration of a woman doing the food shopping (*Islands 3*: 24) or a male chauffeur (*Project 3*: 36). Together, these accounted for 41 per cent of all gendered representations in the books. Interestingly, 12.5 per cent of all gendered representations in both books were positive, progressive representations of women like a female scientist (*Islands 3*: 26) or a female astronaut (81). Based on what we have seen from other recent analyses, perhaps this is not so surprising. It does, however, stand in contrast to the number of times there were positive, progressive representations of men which, in my data, was zero. In other words, while females were seen breaking gender stereotypes, occupying positions of power and smiling about it, men did what men traditionally do.

In the books used by the older students (teens and adults), we see something rather different. The ratio of men to women was 44:56, so unlike the other group of books, we see women more often than men. Only one-third of representations in this part of the data were traditional, neutral men and women. The single biggest coding group was female-positive-progressive with 18 per cent of representations noted: for example, a woman described as 'an international lawyer' (*Objective Advanced*: 11) or the image of a female doctor (34). So, while there have clearly been attempts to present women in what might be regarded as less stereotypical roles and in positions of authority, the opposite cannot be said for men. Just as with the books aimed at younger students, men and boys were generally in positions of power or authority like being a doctor (*Objective Advanced*: 112) or engaging in pursuits typically gendered masculine such as playing football (see *Citizen Z A2*: 27 or *Objective PET*: 12 for two examples, among others). Furthermore, men were rarely found in caregiving roles. It seems that while publishers are ready to show women in non-traditional ways, there remains a reluctance to represent men in progressive ways. This demonstrates the differences between marked and unmarked forms of power, inasmuch as the requirement to produce material that is less gender stereotyped gets interpreted as showing women with more social or economic power; the pre-existing dominant, powerful position of men, however, is not challenged in the same way.

The answer to my second research question about how sexuality gets represented is comparatively simple. In none of the books sampled for this study was there a single instance of a clearly non-heteronormative individual or relationship. Across the sample, course books represented the nuclear family such as in *Citizen Z A2* for example, which features a double spread about television (nuclear) families illustrated by what appears to be husband, wife (with prominent wedding band), son and daughter (44–5). Indeed, students are asked to work in pairs and list examples of 'a TV husband and wife' (44).

Data Analysis: Participant Interviews

In order to answer my third research question, I analysed the transcripts of the five interviews and three themes stood out: awareness, time and training. As the themes cross over, they are addressed here together and discussed with other voices from the literature.

While there was agreement among the respondents that they would subvert or avoid materials they consider to be sexist, there was also general agreement that with a busy timetable they might not notice more subtle sexism. This issue of insufficient time to 'review and update materials' has already been raised because 'many language educators are typically overburdened with teaching and service to their institution' (Paiz 2017: 352). For example, while looking at the aforementioned page from *Objective: PET* which shows four 'different weddings', all showing couples presenting as male–female, participant 1 stated: 'it depends on the day whether – especially me as a straight woman – whether I would necessarily pick up on that'. Participants remarked that they had not been trained to tackle these issues. Training serves a myriad of purposes, but among them should be to draw trainees' attention to things that might have otherwise eluded them. As this is a systemic issue, LGBTQ+ erasure can happen subtly and without malicious intent, yet it can be so easily prevented. 'Latent heteronormative bias may manifest in seemingly benign ways', Paiz argues (2017: 357), such as when teachers assume the gender of a student's partner and use gendered language to ask about them.

Just as was found by Rhodes and Coda (2017), a participant in my study suggested that there should be 'teacher training about how to approach these themes' (participant 1). Not knowing how to talk about gender or sexuality in the classroom means that the topics get avoided, and so erasure and silence are inadvertently maintained. The topic could also be addressed in the spaces provided by initial teacher education or later CPD. However, queer research is also 'conspicuously absent from the syllabi of many TESOL core courses' (Paiz 2017: 355), meaning that it is often left to teachers to choose elective courses that cover the topics (see also Govender 2018).

One of the main issues identified was teachers' schedules and the lack of paid non-teaching time. Many teachers do not have time to vet everything they use. Forman (2014) also notes that, for the teachers in his study, the combination of heavy workload and low pay obliged many teachers to take on private work, which further reduced their available time to develop materials. Even if teachers have sufficient time to check everything, they may not have time to make changes should they so wish. Participant 2 remarked that she would like to create more of her own materials, but does not 'have the time', and so 75 per cent of what she uses in class is that which has been assigned. She added: 'unfortunately when we're busy and we think right this is what we've got and we're doing this – this is what's for the class – you don't take the time to think of these things'.

Participant 4 highlighted the related issue of classroom time. This participant, who identifies as queer, stated, 'I know it's relevant but lesson time is usually limited and unfortunately classes often get derailed by polemical topics such as LGBTQ+ issues and gender.' This comment points to something that I suspect remained unsaid during these interviews. A sense that while, as participant 1 stated, 'I would love to see better representation of real life in my book', the teachers I talked to are aware of the explicit language tuition that students are seeking and do not want to be seen to be wasting time. Who might be critical of such wasted time? While talking generally about the issues of diverse representation at the end of the interview, participant 1 remarked that she is 'employed by somebody ... there's a certain amount of ... well I don't want to say the wrong thing'. While unable to speculate on what there was a certain amount of, nor what would be the wrong or right thing to say, I can contextualize this remark. At this point in the interview, she was talking about moments when her ideas as a teacher diverge from those of her employer; the tension between doing what she feels to be right as opposed to what she has been directed to do. If we see this discussion in Freire's (1970) terms, pedagogy is seen according to a banking model in which teachers deliver the content prescribed by the course book. For each of the participants in my study, that course book was chosen for them and was purchased by students/parents. Thus, there are further tensions present for these teachers. Firstly, an employer took the decision about what materials to use. Either covertly not using them or overtly criticizing them could be construed as criticism of, or challenge to, the manager's authority. Furthermore, if students have spent money purchasing a resource that was required for a course, they are unlikely to appreciate a teacher who chooses not to use it. So, traditional ideas about teaching as praxis continue to enable the persistence of normative discourses around gender and sexuality by not allowing space for a critical discussion.

These understandable tensions sit in juxtaposition with participant 2's remarks about a fourteen-year-old male student who had recently come out as gay and who, as much as his peers, makes reference to his personal life in discussion. It seems problematic that the topic of LGBTQ+ identities and lives only enters the classroom by chance, should there be an individual who identifies as LGBTQ+ and is sufficiently confident to be out in the classroom. Surely, that space should be made for them by their teachers and the courses that they follow. Returning to the theme of training, inadequately prepared educators are unable to signal to LGBTQ+ students that they can safely be themselves in classes. Individuals who are not able to be their authentic selves might feel themselves 'shut out of the educational space' (Paiz 2017: 2).

Concluding Thoughts

As we have seen, although mainstream published material might leave practitioners short, teachers are trying to redress the deafening silence they find. However, there are still too many classrooms where teachers are unable to go beyond the printed materials. Forman (2014: 85) argues that foreign publications have prestige and that 'local teachers may not feel they have the legitimacy to question' them. Thus, the question remains: if teachers see this lack of inclusive representation, why do mainstream course books not represent these diverse identities? The accepted response identifies a 'robust economic imperative' for publishers to conduct business in a global marketplace (Paiz 2020: 73). Moore (2020: 117) agrees, arguing that as course books are generally produced by publishers 'with the ultimate intention of generating profit, they tend to be aligned with … dominant ideologies'. Gray (2013: 62) called for publishers to 'begin to segment markets along lines which are no longer determined by the entrenched prejudices of their most conservative customers'. However, as Richards (2020) remarks, some publishers already produce material specifically for certain markets. Cambridge University Press produces versions of its material specifically for Spanish speakers, for example. In 2020, the *New York Times* published a feature discussing how some publishers, Pearson included, produce different editions of the same textbooks to meet the requirements of the review boards in different states.

Looking at where we are now, we can no longer describe course books as a source of authority 'beyond criticism' (Luke, de Castell & Luke 1983: 198) as both practitioners and academics are criticizing them. Textbook studies, however, obscure the reality. It is likely that there are many ELT classrooms around the world that do make use of more representative and inclusive materials, perhaps because an individual teacher or director of studies recognizes that this is important. For example, in an earlier article about this study, I focused on what teachers said about the published materials they use and how they supplement them in order to be more representative (Richards 2020). Participant 1 said she regularly and subtly queered materials or inverted gender stereotypes. For example, unhappy with the flashcards provided for teaching vocabulary for the family, she created her own using images showing a range of kinship relationships between famous people. As 'twins' was in the target vocabulary list, she included a picture of Neil Patrick Harris, his husband and their twins. No mention was made that the twins had two dads because this was not the focus of the lesson, but the image chosen usualized the idea of two dads. The same teacher was frustrated that the flashcards provided for teaching jobs did so in a stereotypically gendered way:

> I had a picture of a doctor and a nurse and I found it really annoying that the doctor was male and the nurse was female. So, as [the students] were three years old, I decided to tell them the nurse was a doctor. There wasn't really much difference. Both of them were wearing white coats and, you know, were obviously related to the medical profession. (participant 1)

Nonetheless, it remains the case that for many teachers in many different settings, for many different reasons, course books *are* the course.

This chapter set out to discuss where we are now, but it has also looked at where we have been and has begun to look at where we might go next. Govender (2018: 8) has suggested that our classrooms 'can become creative spaces for social transformation, awareness and justice'. In order to take this vision seriously, we have to ask ourselves serious, critical questions. Do our classrooms present opportunity or restriction? Is our pedagogy that of the oppressor or the oppressed? Can our students be themselves in our classrooms and feel empowered to express their authentic voices?

Further Research

Paiz (2020: 20) argues that 'perhaps the most disturbing gap in current disciplinary knowledge about LGBTQ+ issues is related to transgender concerns. The almost complete omission of trans lives in the ELT literature is disturbing'. Regrettably, given the scope of a master's thesis, my study did not address this topic explicitly, but my data can make a limited contribution. The open-ended questions used in the interviews would have allowed participants to bring up any materials that included trans representation, but they did not. In addition, there is a further gap when it comes to non-binary identities and experiences. Thus, it is clear that much work remains to be done to introduce more diverse identities into the classroom, and in particular, non-heteronormative identities and gender non-conforming identities. Future scholarly work in this area might usefully investigate how these identities are represented, if at all, in ELT materials and how this particular silence can be addressed in an inclusive way. It might also explore the experiences of trans and non-binary practitioners and students in the world of ELT.

Furthermore, my data found that while women are represented in positions of responsibility, men are rarely depicted in caregiving roles. Thus, a future project might specifically investigate how traditional identities and positions of power are represented, making visible the unquestioned assumptions that men are naturally found only in more powerful positions.

Questions for Change

1. What identities are currently represented in the materials you use in your classroom, and which are absent?
2. What training do you, or your team, need in order to feel confident about using more inclusive materials and pedagogies in your classroom(s)? Do you know where you can find that training?
3. What changes to working practices in your institution might be necessary if you are going to allow teachers time to ensure materials are inclusive?

Notes

1 The context of the study, and this chapter, is English being taught as a foreign or additional language. Thus, throughout, ELT refers to the practice of teaching English to those who do not speak the language at home.
2 DADT was the official US policy on gay men, lesbians and bisexuals serving in the military between 1994 and 2011.
3 When quoting participants in my study, I have added punctuation to aid the reader. I have also used '…' to indicate a lengthy pause and also where I have removed words.
4 Later in the paper, while describing the methodology, the authors note that one survey item asked participants about 'their experience with openly lesbian, gay, bisexual, trans, queer (LGBTQ) students and their responses to three classroom scenarios involving unplanned inclusion of LGBTQ topics' (101).
5 (1) Age; (2) Gender; (3) Sexual orientation; (4) Race, Ethnicity and Culture; (5) Religion and Belief; (6) Disability.

10

Addressing Critical Perspectives in Language Teacher Education: Challenging Norms and Structures

David Gerlach

Introduction

Every teacher remembers at least one teacher educator who has had an impact on them during certain courses in universities or professional development seminars: be it in a negative way, so that they become inclined to do things differently, or be it in a positive way, when the teacher educator served as a role model, challenged assumptions about learning and teaching, and respected the views of others. Although this conception of 'the good teacher educator' already has normative assumptions and implications within discussions about critical language teacher education that in itself carries questions of morality (e.g. see principles for language teacher educators in Hawkins & Norton 2009), my argument in this chapter will be as follows: We need to look more closely at the role(s) of teacher educators and how they work within given structures and institutions. Gender in general can only be addressed in language classrooms if teachers and, therefore, teacher educators become critically aware of the relevance of gender and sexual identities through their own education and professional development. Let me say this in advance: With the help of the data I collected in open interview settings with teacher educators, it became apparent that the reflection of gender or sexuality within both teacher education and language teaching did not play a role whatsoever.

The crucial and not always unproblematic role(s) of teacher educators became apparent when I was a trainee language teacher myself, years ago. I was heavily influenced by two very different teacher educators: One was very confident and convinced of his views and changed my view of language teaching in a positive way to a degree that, today, I love to educate future language teachers myself; therefore, I like to question aspects such as heteronormativity in language teaching materials. The other teacher educator made me question whether I even understood the subject principles and was meeting the demands of my second subject. As it turned out, most of my colleagues had the same impression of the latter.

Within teacher education systems, a critical mind might want to ask questions such as: What roles should teacher educators perform? Should they be just good teachers and serve as role models? Should they be colleagues in the broadest sense of the term? Or do they need to be (professional or close) friends? Is there a need for hierarchy between the educator and a trainee to effectively ensure teacher *education* or teacher *training*? Such questions were also raised by scholars on teacher education and teacher professionalism who focus on teacher identity research and the interconnectedness between emotional and pedagogical content knowledge (e.g. Mockler 2010; Widodo, Fang & Elyas 2020; Zembylas 2007) or/and intend to incorporate a critical and justice-oriented approach into educational programmes (e.g. Medina 2020; Widodo, Fang & Elyas 2020).

The differentiation between the terms teacher *education* and *training* is therefore important. While one might tend to view the act of becoming a teacher as a part of (higher) *education*, there are instances of teacher *training* which – other than education – rather resembles a traditional, transmission-oriented way of developing teachers that, in many cases, neglects socio-constructivist views, interactive practices and pedagogical values that should be adopted in future classrooms of the same teacher candidates who undergo that training (e.g. Gerlach 2020; Gray 2019). Training, therefore, undermines the autonomy (and professional identity) of future language teachers and language teacher educators, disrupts a democracy-oriented discourse in teacher education, leading to an uncritical reception and ideologic implementation of practices (Freire 1970). If such training is maintained, one might run the risk of not implementing innovative practices, that is, keeping gender stereotypes and heteronormative traditions, discrimination of sexual identities of the teachers themselves (as well as students) and thus ignoring socio-political developments. Innovations, for example, from a social rights or gender perspective that the contributions in this volume discuss, could be undermined by the beliefs and convictions of teacher educators within the system, thus indirectly shaping the practices of teachers, irrespective of whether these beliefs are communicated explicitly or implicitly.

In Germany, the difference between education and training becomes apparent through two fairly different institutions for teacher education, universities (first phase) and *Studienseminare* (second phase; see below). These two institutions have different expectations and approaches based on different ideologies (transmission-oriented versus critical and democratic orientation): On the one hand, there is the freedom of research and teaching in university settings; on the other hand, there is a need to implement state curricula and train teachers to become vital parts of the state-run education system. Unfortunately, cooperation between the two phases is rather weak or depends heavily on individuals who try to bridge teacher education in regions or cities where cooperation is possible due to local proximity. Critical language teachers who are aware of gender (in)equalities may only develop through a teacher education system that is based on the principles of democracy, autonomy, participation and gender sensitivity. If not, *Studienseminare* might continue to reproduce gender inequality and heteronormativity.

In order to explore whether gender sensitivity and a critical perspective can be found within language teacher education, I re-analysed the data of a long-term study from the perspective of critical language teacher education. I want to strengthen the idea that it is necessary to enhance the development (or *education*) of teacher educators and equip both them and student teachers with critical perspectives to challenge norms and structures within educational systems, curricula, schools and classrooms that promote injustice and problematic power relations. In order to make teachers and, therefore, teacher educators aware of the role of gender in language education, this chapter will look at the (un)critical system of teacher education in Germany and its premises before confronting those pillars with results from my research. The ensuing discussion will show which role teacher educators (would have to) fulfil to implement this critical perspective regarding the system – or at least to maintain it. This chapter should, thus, also contribute to teacher educators reflecting on their own practice.

Critical Language Teacher Education

In order to educate (language) teachers for a critical perspective that also focuses on gender, one must consider implementing innovation and questioning structures, norms and power relations within educational systems or even the system of teacher education itself (de Costa & Norton 2017; Kubanyiova & Crookes 2016). A special focus has been the growing awareness among teachers or student teachers about discriminatory practices or social inequality (e.g. gender inequalities through portrayals in textbooks, the lack of inclusion of learners' sexual identities) and conceptualizing ways to transform these disadvantageous structures by making language (teacher) education more critical and gender sensitive (Akbari 2008; Hawkins & Norton 2009; Norton 2005; Pennycook 2004). While many of these often language-specific approaches, such as critical literacy (e.g. Abednia & Crookes 2018), which can also be seen as a crucial part of the pedagogy of multiliteracies (e.g. Breidbach, Medina & Mihan 2014; The New London Group 1996), are based on the work of Freire (1970) and critical pedagogy (e.g. Abednia 2012; Gerlach & Fasching-Varner 2020), others open up the discussions to specific intersectional perspectives (e.g. feminist or anti-racist) that are often targets of discrimination such as gender, sexuality, class, religion and so on (e.g. Crookes 2013).

As a prerequisite for addressing gender in language classes, teacher candidates need to be able to reflect on their own views and develop their own teaching, identity and agency, which can in part be achieved through critical teacher educators. Aligned with this, many authors (e.g. Ahmadian & Maftoon 2016; Fairley 2020; Zeichner 2009, 2011) stress the need to introduce dialogic practices in language teacher education. They maintain that besides the integration and development of critical materials, it is specifically a practice of critical discourse and engaging with each other in critical concepts that seem to be vitally important for a critical language teacher education (Sharma & Phyak 2017).

In a similar fashion that gender, for example, is connected to everyone's identity and based on the assumption that there is a general need to create an atmosphere that allows the addressing of learners' identities (and their development) in language classrooms (Norton 2013), teacher identities need attention as well. According to Norton (2013: 45), identity is defined as 'how a person understands his or her relationship to the world, how that relationship is structured across time and space, and how the person understands possibilities for the future'. If we consider critical awareness (about, e.g. gender) a vital part of teacher identity construction since one's relationship to the world should constantly be reflected (e.g. Fairley 2020; Widodo, Fang & Elyas 2020), teacher educators working with language teachers, who are to consider gender in language classes in the future, would need to address and foster this awareness to a degree that allows for positive, social change and innovation in education.

The question that arises is what happens if this critical perspective is neglected, impaired or disturbed by structures or elements within institutions of teacher education. What happens if members of the staff in teacher education appointed by the state create their own individual practices in such a way that a critical examination becomes impossible? This will be the focus of the following sections that investigate language teacher educator practices in a practical training phase in German language teacher education. The data collection took place from February to May 2015 in different Hessian teacher education institutes and included data from eleven language teacher educators in total. To understand the structures, I describe teacher education in Germany at a general level first, before analysing the role of teacher educators within this system.

(Language) Teacher Education in Germany

Teacher education in Germany works similarly across all sixteen federal states: Normally, students obtain a teaching degree through four or five years of university education, studying at least two subjects for a specific type of school (primary or secondary schools, middle or high schools, schools for vocational training). After spending eighteen to twenty-four months of in-practice training at state-run institutions, they get their second (final) teaching degree and can apply for teaching positions in the schools of their chosen fields. While student teachers in universities do have some choice regarding the seminars they pick, despite – depending on the institution – some modularized obligatory courses, this changes in the second phase, where state-run institutions, *Studienseminare*, are introduced to train teachers to function in schools across the state and according to state curricula. Although international experts on teacher education once concluded that this second phase in Germany was both unique and had the potential to integrate theory-based university training and a career entry phase (OECD 2004), the immense differences between teacher *education* in German universities and teacher *training* in state-run institutions in the second phase do not arise from nowhere (for differences between the two institutions see above).

Criticism of practices in these *Studienseminare* is widespread: Apart from the second phase being characterized as highly stressful due to constant examinations and lesson monitoring by teacher educators, teacher trainees, on the one hand, have to work half-time in school and prepare lessons just like a regular teacher, and, on the other hand, they fall back into their roles of learners in seminars held in the training institutions. Thus, teachers-in-training in Germany have to switch and reflect on being teachers and learners and, at the same time, being persons who judge and who are being judged. *Studienseminare* have been characterized as places of 'self-idealization' (Lenhard 2004) that provide a banking concept of teaching and education, which is supposed to be staged by the teachers-in-training and evaluated by teacher educators. The perspective within courses in the *Studienseminare* is often viewed as 'playing school' (Kunze 2014) and this is diametrically opposite of the actual teaching practices in schools. Dzengel, Kunze, K. and Wernet (2012) even found a 'disappearance of the matter', that is, a high level of formalization in the training institutions, leading to a neglect of the actually relevant questions for teaching and prospective teachers.

In this second phase, teacher educators play a major role both in the training and assessment of the teachers-to-be since they work with rather small groups and accompany their trainees mostly throughout the eighteen to twenty-four months. The interaction takes place during seminars in the training institutions and lesson monitoring for which the teacher educators visit the candidate at their school and base their assessment on the planning, execution and reflection of that lesson. Before becoming teacher educators in the *Studienseminare*, teacher educators have been teachers themselves and, in most cases, then apply for more lucrative and responsible positions at the teacher education institutions. Most teacher educators within this system are not formally trained or prepared for their work, although there exist non-mandatory professional development opportunities. In addition, the *Studienseminare* are not connected to teacher education in university and communication between the two institutions is rather poor (see below).

De-pedagogizing Practices in Language Teacher Education: The Role of Teacher Educators in the German 'Second Phase'

The goal of this section is to briefly describe the larger research project that I conducted between 2014 and 2019 (Gerlach 2020), which is to a degree necessary to understand the ensuing reinterpretation of the data, given a critical perspective that is a precondition for addressing gender in language education and that uncovers de-pedagogizing practices embedded in this second phase, executed (willingly or unwillingly) by the teacher educators and, finally, implemented in public schools through the trained teachers.

Owing to the obvious high impact of teacher educators and yet a lack of research on their roles and practices within the second phase of teacher education in Germany, my goal was to 'reconstruct' (Bohnsack 2010) their beliefs and practices in order to learn more about this particular group of professionals.

The Study

The study followed a professional development theory based on a structural and professional biographical approach (Helsper 2014; Terhart 2011). It implies that the goal was not only to find out about the current practices of eleven teacher educators through their own descriptions of their work but also to learn about how they became the individuals they were, based on their motivations and the challenges they had faced in school, university, teacher training and professional development. The teacher educators were asked the same questions in narrative-episodic interviews (Schütze 1983). This laid the basis for the reconstruction of the interviewees' practices in an explorative approach (cf. Nohl 2010) to gain insights into 'the biographical subject's explanatory models and interpretations' (Schütze 1983: 284) and 'their reconstructed biography' (ibid.; translations according to Nohl 2010: 196). The resulting interview transcripts were analysed using the documentary method (Bohnsack 2010) to work out the implicit and habitual orientations of the staff in terms of their training practice. In methodological terms, the documentary method is less concerned with the explicit level of *what* is being said but rather with implicit structures and orientations that can be recognized by means of interpretation and contrastive case comparisons (cf. Bohnsack 2010; Mannheim 1982): 'It is the change from the question *what* social reality is in the perspective of the actors, to the question *how* this reality is produced or accomplished in these actors' everyday practice' (Bohnsack 2010: 102). Consequently, the importance of implicit knowledge as guiding the action is emphasized here, which can be shown along the individual processing of, for example, institutional norms in the field of the second phase of language teacher education.

The goal of the documentary method is to develop, through a contrastive-reconstructive analysis of cases, distinct types that show characteristics of how professionals act in certain situations: their habitus. Following Bourdieu (1977) and Bourdieu & Wacquant (1992), habitus in the documentary method is understood as an orientation framework in the narrower sense, which, primarily reconstructed on the basis of the documentary (implicit) meaning of the utterances, is in a tense relationship with the orientation schemes on an explicit level of the evoked utterances. This tension and the individual's handling of the orientation frameworks in the narrower sense (the habitus) and, for example, relevant training/teacher education content, knowledge or norms of the interviewees at the explicit level allow for the reconstruction of the practices and orientations of the teacher educators interviewed.

For the study, the fact that reconstructive methods aim at eliciting narratives of interviewees to reach a level of implicitness in their utterances was made difficult through one phenomenon: Most of the teacher educators described their own teacher education practice in a highly reflective and argumentative way that included justifications for their own actions. This was, in the end, considered to be a characteristic of the field in general, which is under a lot of pressure to justify any measures taken, any curricula being implemented and any teacher trainee assessed against the background of certain standards. This characteristic might be due to neoliberal trends in education leading to over-standardization (e.g. Bonnet & Hericks 2020; or in the UK see Block & Gray 2016). Only through rigorous comparisons of the teacher educators' talking about certain situations, the way they dealt with teacher trainees, could I establish a typification of teacher educators valid for that context of second-phase language teacher education in Germany. The typification is presented below.

Types of Language Teacher Educators

In the methodology of the documentary method, types can be reconstructed based on sense construction of individuals or communities, and on the basis of relations and differences. In my original study, the teacher educators could be divided into two groups having two different subgroups each: First, they differed in the way they designed their teacher education in a transmission-oriented or a constructive/moderating way, that is, either they set certain aspects as individual standards and taught them very explicitly to teacher trainees or let the trainees partake in their education to a much fuller extent, decide on topics to cover, construct lesson plans together and so on. The subgroups consisted of a type of teacher educator who identifies very clearly with the goals of this second phase of teacher education and also their teacher candidates, while the other type is rather critical of the system and also distances themselves from the teacher trainees. The contrastive analysis is shown in Table 10.1.

Most teacher educators in this case study shared the implicit self-concept that they viewed themselves as teachers and their teacher trainees as learners. Though this might seem normal in any educational setting, the question is how large this gap between perceived expertise and novicehood 'in practice' was and the extent of its implications for teacher educator practice(s). Conversely, the question arises to what extent a critical examination of gender issues or sexual identities is made (im)possible when teachers-in-training are hierarchically conceptualized as learners.

Based on the division into these four types, showing clear differences in terms of training practice and their ability to identify with the system, there were potential difficulties for interactional practices with prospective teachers: A trainee who has not received a good education in the university phase might lack a sufficient knowledge base about language teaching. If this lack of knowledge is not assessed and addressed through a transmission of concepts, professional development might be hampered. In a sharp contrast, a trainee who has had a good and fruitful university education might not develop further if confronted with a highly transmission-oriented teacher educator, who just wants to get across his/her own beliefs about good language teaching. If they share widely different views, this might even lead to conflicting situations. Teacher educators with constructivist orientations, on the other hand, might design very open seminar settings that allow for diverse discussions on teaching issues, problems and working on their solutions, so that students can construct meaning themselves. Yet, as soon as the system demands an evaluation of the teaching practice (in classroom observations), the teacher educator must have certain criteria aligned to the intended learning aims to evaluate these practices that he/she might not have made transparent in seminar settings before (Biggs & Tang 2011).

It seems, therefore, that some trainees might need special – or, rather, specific – teacher trainers to develop within these interactive training practice settings. In addition to that, one needs to consider that this training, the seminars and lesson debriefings, especially, are held under the pressure of being assessed and graded. And these grades might even decide on the job chances of teacher candidates and, maybe, even on the tenured positions in their 'dream school'.

A Lack of Criticality?

Re-analysing the data and results of the study, I have to admit that there is no evidence of criticality, nor of gender sensitivity based on the assumptions discussed in the beginning of this contribution in the way language teacher education is being designed by the teacher educators. The topics in the seminars and counselling sessions oscillated between purely didactic issues of foreign language learning and general, formal-institutional challenges such as the assessment of student performance. Even those teacher educators who are very critical of the second phase and the structure itself do not try to foster a critical awareness among their trainees and thus never question heteronormativity or stereotypical language teaching materials. I will present a few examples to illustrate this.

One teacher educator, Jörg Reger (pseudonym), who belongs to both the transmission-oriented and distinctive type, said,

> But, where it becomes problematic for me is, um, if there are six people sitting in front of me. That's also good, so the more the better. But they come from completely different contexts and, of course, bring in their own problems and think quite often: 'Gee, I should really be preparing classes right now and then we sit here and talk about uh literary didactics, but actually there's a fire somewhere else.' (Gerlach 2020: 298; my translation)

The design of the module sessions was presented here as problematic, as Jörg Reger personally found it difficult to respond individually to the various concerns of the trainees. He assumed that they often had other problems (such as lesson preparation for the next day) and were, therefore, less able to concentrate on the normatively prescribed content of a seminar. It remained unclear whether the group size (six people) or the structure of the session was the cause of the problem. The educator evaluated the group size in the sense that more trainees were better (alluding to a transmission orientation). Yet, different contexts, problems and backgrounds made this transmission of knowledge challenging. One colleague of his made it very clear that the institutional norms and curricula were the basis for his practice:

> I accompany (.) them (.) in training, with regard to a goal set by the HLBG [the state law for teacher education; D.G.], or a standard, and, uh, in the seminars, in training, or even after lesson observations, it is always communicated to them how far, uh, there is a discrepancy between the actual state and the target state and what can I do for them, what can we do together, and what you can do for yourself personally to, uh, minimize the discrepancy between the actual state and the target state, uh, to, uh. (Gerlach 2020: 307–308; my translation)

With the formality of this description the teacher educator tried to be transparent about his criteria in a competence- and goal-oriented fashion. Yet, within these strict confines, there seemed to be little room for criticality with regard to gender issues about the state law and the standards that he upheld. Like him, most teacher educators referred to language competence as being the most important quality in their candidates, a competence that they had already acquired before entering the second phase. Teacher educator Stefanie Ferrer said,

> So if we have as our goal good English lessons at schools, (.) we want pupils with uh, English skills, which is what makes them not only competitive economically, as is often erroneously justified today, but also to this claim to education um

(.) or meets this social um requirement. Then we really need umm really umm (.) very good English teachers. And not very good in the sense that they have a 'very good' on but that they bring a human quality to the table (...) (...) And that's where it comes apart again, right? (Gerlach 2020: 291; my translation)

Human qualities were mentioned by some teacher educators as necessary prerequisites, but it became apparent that these are innate – or, at least, already developed – qualities that one cannot change within the course of the second phase. There were either (future) teachers who had good human qualities and will help create good English language classes or those who will not. Therefore, there seemed to be no need to integrate a (critical) pedagogic practice perspective into one's own counselling. One teacher educator in the sample, Regina Meier, even stated,

But the other, uh, let's say, pedagogical problems, such as classroom management or other things, are also, uh, brought into the knowledge of trainees through other seminars. So I do not do this so often anymore. (Gerlach 2020: 346; my translation)

The *language* teacher educator relied on colleagues who taught general pedagogical principles (subject-independent) and how to deal with these seemingly less important 'pedagogical problems'. Therefore, she could ignore them in her own educator practice. Pedagogy, caring for individual learners or groups of learners in a pedagogic, caring way, which is a prerequisite for focusing on gender issues in language teaching, seemed not to be part of the language teacher curriculum. Instead, the formalization of teacher training led to a focus on teachable (and assessable) skills and content that was deemed important within language curricula. Learner orientation and authenticity as principles of language teaching remained mostly unmentioned in the interviews with the teacher educators.

The Role of Norms and Structures

My main argument in the following will be that the aforementioned and identified 'lack of criticality' is not a result of the teacher educators' lack of caring about high-quality (critical and reflective) language teaching or a good teacher education programme. The reason for this lack is rather systemic in nature, which is why this section rather goes beyond the specific aspect of critical language teacher education and gender. Bourdieu's habitus theory proceeds on the assumption that practices are acquired through mimesis, that is, socialization with and integration into a certain social field based on implicit orientations of that field (Bourdieu 1977; Bourdieu & Wacquant 1992). The group of individuals, or in this case, professionals in education, share characteristics that have been developed over time through a constant iteration of norms and expectations that this group has experienced in the field of language teacher education in the German second phase. Although the habitus theory has sometimes been considered too static and too deterministic, there is a profound influence of existing structures within a system that have deep-rooted impacts on individuals – and most of the time without the knowledge of its social beings.

The teacher educators in my sample share an orientational dilemma: They are, on the one hand, rather autonomous in the way they design their courses and counselling. Yet, on the other hand, they also share the implicit need to implement both institutional norms dictated by the state and identity norms that they deem necessary for future language teachers. The latter might be the result of professional development, that is, distancing oneself from the 'normal' teachers, or a biographical process in which they reflect on their own second-phase experience, earlier trainees, development opportunities, current educational and professional development and so on. Therefore, based on implicit, or atheoretical, knowledge, teacher educators as social groups create their practice: 'Atheoretical knowledge thus connects people' (Nohl 2010: 202). In this process of socialization, becoming a teacher educator seems to require and enforce strict rules in the second phase of language teacher education in the German system (cf. also Dzengel Kunze & Wernet 2012): The standardized expectations, certain rules of conduct, rules of behaviour, the power relation between the educator and trainee as well as the heteronormative approach in language teaching (cf. Banegas, Jacovkis & Romiti 2020) lead to an implicitly valid code of conduct that most educators will adapt to. This is in sharp contrast to some of the research on teacher educators that is available internationally (e.g. Lunenberg, Dengerink & Korthagen 2014; Swennen, Jones & Volman 2010). Yet, the contrastive image of teacher educators can be explained fairly easily: No teacher education system around the world has integrated a state-bound 'middle' phase that conditions a certain kind of teaching, teacher and teacher educator habitus. The pressure on both groups of staff, teachers-in-training and teacher educators, is extremely high due to the structures they find themselves in – and they cannot escape from them easily.

If we take seriously the different types of language teacher educators that were identified based on the reconstruction of the implicit orientations in this sample, these different educators necessitate different types of teacher trainees. One could imagine that trainees with certain orientations which in turn represent a fit with the trainers could ensure successful training. Thus, a transmissive/distinctive teacher educator might work very well with a teacher trainee who is himself/herself insecure about interacting with the educator but still needs certain basics and feedback on language teaching. On the other hand, a very engaged and competent trainee might be best served by a moderating/identification type of teacher educator, who provides him/her with enough room to experiment in his/her language classrooms but will still give valuable feedback in consultation settings. This fit could help dissolve the hegemonic inequality between the parties.

But this would only create an optimized training situation – it is not language teacher *education*, and it is definitely not (yet) *critical* language teacher education in the way described above, which would be necessary for addressing the role of gender and sexuality in language education and, thus, language teacher education. Apart from the fact that the second phase as a system is structured in such a way that it maintains itself with its norms, expectations, contents and goals, a fit of the people involved alone does not, therefore, contribute to the fact that it becomes (critical) teacher education. Yet, more critical teacher educators might change the rigid system of indoctrination, which is going to be discussed below. In sharp contrast, teacher trainees who already show a high critical awareness (about gender) heightened during the first phase have to face uncritical teacher educators and will still have a very hard time going through the second phase. Thus, this might necessitate a shift requiring at least one generation of critically equipped teacher educators who question the norms and structures of the second phase as well as the power structures related to gender and allow for more critical perspectives both in terms of the topics to be taught and talked about as well as the potential and necessary innovations within the system of language teacher education.

Developing Critical and Gender-Oriented Language Teacher Educator Education

International research on critical (language) teacher educators (and their education and professional development in general) is becoming more widespread and diverse but, in most cases, investigates teacher educators in higher education, that is, university settings (for an overview, see Gerlach & Fasching-Varner 2020 or Hawkins & Norton 2009). As this piece has shown so far, critical teacher educator education addressing gender is crucial not only in university settings but also in the second phase of teacher education in Germany. The reason for focusing on gender in teacher educator education can be explained by research showing that addressing gender in teacher education is helping visibility of LGBTQ on the one hand and is enhancing teacher reflections on their beliefs and personal experiences as well as their awareness of their own identity on the other hand, which makes it necessary for teacher educators to critically address gender (Banegas, Jacovkis & Romiti 2020; Collier, Bos & Sandfort 2015; Ollis, Harrison & Maharaj 2013; Robinson & Ferfolja 2008; Vavrus 2009; for the concept 'language teacher identity' see Barkhuizen 2017; Gao 2017; Golombek 2017; Varghese 2017).

One of the challenges often described in the literature is teacher educators' transformation from first-order practitioners as teachers themselves (Murray 2002) to second-order teachers, for which teacher educators need to reflect on their own identity and practice (Swennen, Jones & Volman 2010). However, this transformation is infrequently hampered by inadequate structures of professional development opportunities, that is, teacher educators are often left alone and seek opportunities to develop, for example, through mentoring, action research, self-study and by joining existing communities of practice (Izadinia 2014; Lave & Wenger 1991). Nonetheless, gender-oriented and critical teacher educator education must be enhanced within these structures. To foster criticality (Banegas & Villacañas de Castro 2016), for example, about gender, teacher educators could be introduced to principles of critical pedagogy and critical literacy (e.g. Abednia & Crookes 2018; Crookes 2013) through workshops, which may be organized by universities. In accordance with such principles, teacher educators could begin with integrating reflective phases in which student teachers and teacher educators reflect on the role of gender and sexuality in language teaching together and, along the way, in language teacher education. With such activities, teacher educators as well as student teachers could become more aware of their own identity and, therefore, of their sexual identity, one's role within structures and systems and gain a sense of progression towards a professional goal, that is, the education and development of future language teachers (and their own agency) (Beauchamp & Thomas 2019; Miller & Gkonou 2018; Ruohotie-Lyhty & Moate 2016).

Besides, teacher educators could engage in collaboratively designing language teaching materials in seminars preparing for classroom observations (Govender 2019), which is already a familiar approach in language classrooms that are based on critical pedagogy principles (e.g. Crookes 2013; Miller & Endo 2016).

Designing teaching materials collaboratively could promote discussions about gender in language teaching, reduce hierarchical relationships between educators and student teachers, explore one's own teaching practices and, eventually, enhance student teachers' agency and empowerment (Govender 2019; Banegas, Jacovkis & Romiti 2020). With the integration of (critical) reflective phases as well as collaboratively designing critical and gender-oriented materials, the transfer of knowledge and, maybe, the cooperation between teacher education in university and *Studienseminare* could also be advanced. All in all, and apart from specific activities,

> it becomes necessary to have teacher education that does not merely pass on a body of knowledge, but rather one that is dialogically constructed by participants who think and act critically. (Kumaravadivelu 2006: 182)

Conclusion

A tale that has been circulated in Germany regarding the second phase of teacher education is that many trainers would tell their trainees in their very first seminar session: 'You can now forget everything you learned in the university. Now, you'll face reality and practice – this is what really counts.' And although this dictum has been around for a long time (but is probably, hopefully, no longer being uttered), it does give us an idea of the normative self-enactment of the second phase, which could be endangered by a more critical and gender-sensitive perspective. A gender-sensitive perspective cannot be adopted since the basic critical attitude towards teaching practice is missing. If the first, university-based phase wants to produce a critical habitus that critically reflects both forms of knowledge, theory and practice, the second phase increases the importance of given convictions of supposedly 'correct practice' and self-idealizes itself without being able to meet the demands of what might be necessary given societal developments.

One might sum up the arguments about critical language teacher education in one question: What do we want to be – teacher *trainers* or teacher *educators*? It is a question of a professional stance that implies and requires reflective practice, openness, and both identity and agency development. If language teacher educators become enabled to think critically about their own work and their relationship with (future) teachers, they might serve as role models for their own students, despite certain state-regulated structures, curricula and normative demands. And I would like to follow up on Morgan (2017: 205), who emphasizes, 'Critical awareness (i.e. reflexivity) of the situated limits that power/

knowledge imposes enables new possibilities, the transformative dimension in which identity itself can become a strategic resource.'

And, maybe, it is not so much about *what* we teach, although aspects such as gender and sexuality are, obviously, vitally important. Maybe, it should be more about *how* we teach and educate future language teachers, for example, through dialogic practices, methods that help build teacher identity and agency (e.g. Fairley 2020), action research, and open discussions on formerly tabooed and critical issues in university courses and language classes.

Questions for Change

1. How critical am I about my own practices when I educate future teachers?
2. Can my work considered to be language teacher *education* or language teacher *training*?
3. How do I achieve a 'professional fit' with my student teachers or teacher trainees?
4. Where do I allow my teachers to become critical of their own and my own practices, topics and materials? What criteria do we use when we talk about them?
5. How can I integrate aspects of critical language teacher education into my professional practice?

11

Gender Diversity and Online English Language Teaching during the Covid-19 Pandemic in Bangladesh

Sayeedur Rahman and Mohammad Hamidul Haque

Introduction

Historically and culturally, women in Bangladesh are relegated to a marginal socio-economic status because of existing gender inequalities based on traditional gender roles and patriarchal socio-cultural norms imposed on their mobility and participation in public and other social spheres. The United Nations Development Programme (UNDP 2007) in its human development and gender-related development report ranked Bangladesh as the lowest in human development index and one of the lowest (next to Pakistan) in gender-related development in the South Asian region. As noted by Jennings (2009), there are many barriers that inhibit women and girls' access to basic services as well as their full participation in developmental activities in patriarchal societies in South Asian countries. The report clearly indicated that gender disparity still poses a major challenge for development in most of these countries in the region. This gender disparity is even more evident in existing digital divide in Bangladeshi society. For example, Tandon (2006) and Melhem, Morrell and Tandon (2009), in their studies on information and communication technologies (ICTs) in Bangladesh and their implications for women workers, enumerated enormous challenges such as low levels of literacy, restricted access to and control over resources, less flexibility in balancing income-generating and household activities, less access to training and education, economic imbalances, inequality in working conditions and remuneration that underpins the quantification of the impact of ICTs on women's work, livelihoods and overall opportunities. According to them, unless gender considerations are incorporated into employment policies, ICT diffusion strategies or national policies, all measures may inadvertently result in negative unintended consequences that compound gender and income disparities. Covid-19 pandemic increases reliance on digital technologies, and hence, in education male teachers are more likely to benefit disproportionately to female teachers. The greater access to digital technology and information may further reinforce existing digital gender divide.

The widespread pandemic has brought significant and distinct challenges to education, increasing reliance on technology and digital transformation in traditional classrooms. The pandemic has exposed the existing inequalities in areas such as education, especially those related to connectivity, access and use of technology. The readiness to face these challenges on the part of government and other stakeholders has been rather limited. The decision to switch to online education overnight failed to consider the wide-ranging digital gender divide that persists in society. Limited resources, lack of infrastructure and asymmetrical access to technology are some of the key factors that limit the attempt to bridge the existing gender digital divide. Against this backdrop, this chapter is an attempt to find out how the social divide based on technological access and existing gender gap in accessing knowledge still prevails in crises or emergencies like pandemics. With this aim, this chapter explores whether teaching practices used by male and female English teachers differ in any respect when it comes to teaching English online during Covid-19 as a unique situation.

As for female English teachers who are one of our major concerns, the digital classroom through both synchronous and asynchronous platforms like Zoom, MS Teams, Google Meet and other learning management systems (LMSs) has been transformative. The domestic private space has been converted into an education station to conduct and attend classes amidst a chaotic situation for both teachers and learners. Teachers of English, over a period of more than a year, went through mental trauma of adapting to new technological tools and while facing various insecurities including being marginalized in their teaching domain. Compared to other countries, Bangladesh government has given inadequate attention to help the teachers to teach online effectively. To avoid being left out and to become professionally proficient, teachers had to learn to make technology an essential part of their teaching-learning and educational lives mostly without adequate training, proper infrastructure or much support.

Digital Inclusion and Gender in Education

There is a growing conviction in today's world that without 'knowledge' and 'technology' no country or individual can achieve economic independence and sustainable economic growth. For Bangladesh, it is even more challenging as the country is aiming to achieve sustainable economic growth while being a developing nation. The world today has witnessed a massive change because of ICTs that have revolutionized the dynamics of social systems and human relations. Addressing this aspect, Tandon (2006) ascribes *the knowledge economy, the digital revolution* and *the information society* as terms that effectively illustrate the swiftness and vitality with which the decoding and transference of information take place in the current world, while expounding on its impact on global commerce and manufacturing practices.

ICTs have created new economic and social opportunities all over the world. Their use, however, continues to be governed by existing power relations whereby women frequently experience relative disadvantage. Because of deep-rooted gender inequalities, female teachers with lack of technological orientations, as researchers reported (Tandon 2006; Tyers 2012), are assumed to face several disadvantages.

The Covid-19 pandemic and the subsequent containment measures by the authorities are affecting our societies, triggering substantial changes for different facets of well-being across dimensions, including education. Educational institutions at all levels are challenged by the extraordinary consequences of this pandemic in various ways. In the face of the prospective deficit in individual and collective capabilities, the education sector resorts to technology that offers a worthwhile alternative to freedom of movement. ICTs are also essential and an integral part to bring about revolutionary changes to the education system. In this regard, OECD (2020) has emphasized the need to address the needs of vulnerable students during this pandemic.

According to the World Bank (2020) note, many countries have adopted different technological means and digital resources to satisfy the various needs of vulnerable students simultaneously, considering their socio-emotional needs and utmost support and cooperation on behalf of the teachers. Some countries are adopting initiatives like partnerships with free online learning resources and other digital educational platforms. For example, China has made exemplary achievements through digital education by reaching out to 200 million primary- and secondary-level students. The Ministry of Education of China has launched an initiative titled, 'Ensuring undisrupted learning when classes are disrupted'.

This initiative comprises of mobilizing online education through boosting internet connectivity all throughout the country, especially in underprivileged regions. China has introduced more than 24,000 online courses for university students along with providing flexibility and appropriate methodologies. Teachers have access to high-quality training programmes to better equip them with the latest technology, digital and pedagogical skills, required to deliver online lectures. India has also made exceptional progress in online learning by offering various courses in e-learning across various digital platforms. India has also synced video lessons, worksheets, textbooks and other assessments with students, parents and teachers. All of this content has been prepared by more than 250 teachers who speak multiple languages. Indonesia has created provisions for online tests and assessments for students, which were marked in accordance with their class performances and previous records. Indonesia has also made use of Education TV to demonstrate online learning systems sponsored by LMS. Europe too has maintained consistent progress with online teaching while Asian countries like Singapore and Korea have perhaps surpassed many western countries.

Our theoretical framework draws on Amartya Sen's (1985, 1999) capability approach and West and Zimmerman's (1987) *Doing Gender* to shed light on the way technology–gender relationships work for English teachers. That is, how teachers manipulate circumstances in order to exploit digital technology, experiences and so on, in ways that either create educational advantage or, on the contrary, restrict their ability to adopt technology and participate in educational processes. According to Sen (1985, 335), an individual's capabilities are, in part, determined by the resources they have access to as well as 'the freedom to achieve'. This is hindered by what they term the 'conversion problem', whereby the personal and environmental situations of individuals complicate how well resources might be used to develop capabilities. According to Sen (1985), this holds particularly true for marginalized communities and social positions, including those related to gender in contexts of patriarchy. The use of LMS, Zoom, Google Meet/Classroom and other online educational platforms enables teachers and students to carry out their classes and other academic activities from distant locations. Therefore, the virtual video/audio conferencing characteristic of these platforms expands teachers' and students' capabilities to teach and learn remotely. Functionings (Sen 1985) are achieved outcomes – what people actually succeed in doing – in this case, teaching English online in a difficult circumstance. The conversion from resources (in this case technology) into a capability set (in this case ability to teach and learn remotely, etc.) or from capabilities to functionings is subject to certain 'conversion factors' that play positive or negative roles. Thus, the need to evaluate freedom to formulate capabilities requires investigating the personal (e.g. personality traits, physical disability, computer literacy), social (e.g. social norms, power relations in workplace, political climate) or environmental (e.g. climate, pollution, geographical locations) conversion factors that obstruct or facilitate the expansion of capabilities by means of these technologies. In this chapter, we will mainly focus on social conversion factors related to gender diversity and social class (urban/rural) that influence the appropriate use of online technology in teaching English during the extended university closures and remote academic instruction during the Covid-19 pandemic.

In addition, Sen (1985) defines agency as 'what a person is free to do and achieve in pursuit of whatever goals or values he or she regards as important'. An agent, on his account, is 'someone who acts and brings about change, and whose achievements can be judged in terms of her own values and objectives, whether or not we assess them in terms of some external criteria as well' (Sen 1999). Klugman et al. (2014) define agency and, by extension, empowerment as 'the ability to make decisions about one's own life and act on them to achieve a desired outcome, free of violence, retribution, or fear'. Following Ross, Shah and Wang (2011), Ahmed and Hyndman-Rizk (2018) expanded the analysis of the impact of education on the agency development by distinguishing between instrumental and intrinsic empowerment. Intrinsic empowerment is the power within – the impact of critical understanding of one's own aspirations, capabilities and rights – and instrumental empowerment is the power to influence in decision-making.

For our understanding of the gender roles, we also applied poststructuralist approaches to gender ideologies and identities put forward by West & Zimmerman (1987). They argue that gender is not a set of traits, not a variable, not a role but the product of continuous creation of the meaning of gender through human actions. The study intends to contribute to our understanding of any reversion to gender roles in light of new experiences in the context of online teaching in higher education sector of Bangladesh.

Regarding gender and use of ICT in the context of Bangladesh, Tyers (2012) reported that the main barrier to participation for women was the lack of access to ICTs. There are three main underpinnings of this issue of access: control, social norms and language. Patriarchal norms and constraints over mobility mean that in Bangladesh many women are restricted to the domestic sphere and are not able to visit a cyber cafe to use the internet unchaperoned. In addition, due to domestic responsibilities, women often have time constraints and cannot visit public facilities during daytime, while public mobility at night is restricted for many women, often due to male relatives' fears of sexual harassment. As well as control over mobility, control over finances and decision-making in Bangladesh is also exerted by male relatives who often pay phone and internet bills and are often the primary users of shared mobile phones and computers. Therefore, women frequently have less autonomy with regard to ICTs and related expenses. In addition, men are often gatekeepers of technology and control women's use of mobile phones and computers, or television. Her findings also show that learning English through these ICTs helped break down some of these barriers.

Our Study

This chapter has two objectives: firstly, to identify and highlight the issues related to gender in teaching English during the unprecedented Covid-19 pandemic, specifically investigating the gender-related issues of online English teaching where male and female teachers have access to the same technology, that is, the way they use digital space for the purpose of teaching English. The second objective is to illustrate how online English teaching practices are connected to gender issues. In this research we addressed the following research questions:

1) What teaching practices do male and female English teachers pursue during online teaching of English language?
2) Is there a gender digital divide for the use of technology in online English language teaching at the tertiary level?

Our study is linked to some of the private universities (selected based on the ranking by University Grants Commission, Bangladesh) located in Dhaka that continued their educational programmes online even after the shutdown due to the spread of Covid-19. The study included four male and four female English language teachers who were teaching in these private universities and data were collected from them through in-depth interviews. Our contact with the English teachers interviewed was through our professional acquaintance.

Participants of the Study

The sampling technique was purposive as only private universities were conducting online English classes during the pandemic. When the data were collected, most of the private universities had started online classes from March 2020; however, government universities migrated to online teaching more slowly. Participant teachers from different private universities in Dhaka who taught 'English Skills' courses were approached. The departments of English in private universities offer many modules emphasizing English skills (e.g. academic spoken English, academic English writing, etc.) for undergraduate students of various disciplines. Table 11.1 shows the participants' profiles including their school orientation and teaching experience ranging from three to fifteen years. The participants were selected from various private universities only in Bangladesh for the reasons mentioned above. Given the situation, this was the only group that could provide enough information as their wealth of experience makes them imminently suitable to comment on the issues under discussion. The selected participants belong to diverse socio-economic backgrounds and have varied degrees of technological competence, which is an important distinction to consider when investigating mindsets and ease-of-access across multi-communal realities.

The eight interviews, one with each participant, were conducted in Bangla (participants' L1) and lasted approximately forty-five minutes to one hour. Before the interview, the teachers were briefed about the main objectives of the study. Firstly, they were asked relevant demographic questions and then open-ended questions to elicit their experience of teaching English online during the pandemic. The interviews were conducted through Zoom and Google Meet in observance of social distancing protocols limiting face-to-face contact. The interviews were recorded, and written permission was obtained from each interviewee. They were assured about the confidentiality of the information and anonymity of their identity. Codes were used to anonymize the participants.

The participants were interviewed based on a semi-structured questionnaire; interviewees were offered clarifications and explanations whenever they were not clear about the intended outcome of the questions by the interviewers. Along with the responses, field notes were taken by the researchers when necessary. The interview data were then transcribed and coded for identifying the emerging themes guided by the objectives of the study. This process involved repeated reading, underlining and annotating of the transcript to comprehend the data profoundly.

Digital Gender Divide in Teaching Practices in Online English Classes

While we studied the teaching practices in light of this singular situation, we aspire to focus on and gain insight into the complexities both male and female teachers are likely to experience. Data were analysed and interpreted thematically to help process and understand the lived experience of English teachers working in tertiary education. As both researchers went through similar experiences as participants, individual lived experiences and stories were interpreted through the lens of the researcher's own experiences (Creswell 2014). In the following subsections, we present excerpts that illustrate the major themes that emerged.

Use of ICT Tools and Learning Platforms

The applications and platforms used by the participants interviewed in the study fall into three categories: (1) LMS for sharing content (both synchronous and asynchronous learning), (2) social media groups and Messenger for communication and (3) video conferencing platforms for live sessions. Some participants also used platforms and applications in addition to the ones prescribed by their universities to supplement their teaching. For online teaching, the participants are reported to use different learning platforms like Moodle or Google Classroom. All participants interviewed, irrespective of their gender, mentioned using some additional electronic platforms, including social media, to complement the limitations of live classroom sessions. Both male and female teachers were found to use social media such as Facebook, WhatsApp, Messenger and YouTube for staying connected with the students.

Apart from the availability of well-quipped technological support, some teachers were found to have better teaching platforms and technological orientations since their respective universities were better equipped. One male participant extolled the innovation instituted by their university, which developed its own platform modelled after the ones used by MIT and Harvard. The platform is an integrated one that is equipped to share content, administer tests, publish grades and the like. In addition, the use of Slack was also instituted, making it convenient to communicate with students as well as colleagues.

At the outset, the availability and access to ICT instructional tools used for teaching and learning seem to be equitable. Viewed from a capability perspective, the availability of ICT tools as resource or input alone cannot be emphasized as much; rather, what the teachers and students are able to do or be, such as to be educated, by exploiting these technologies or capabilities is the main focus. The capability approach changes the focus from means to ends because ICT tools by themselves do not ensure that all are able to transform them into actual doings and beings. Male and female participants, for example, with similar technology input may nevertheless be able to achieve very different ends depending on their circumstances.

Classroom Activities and Materials Used

Most of the participants in the study reported using pre-recorded videos or lectures and other audiovisual materials in addition to live sessions on Zoom, Google Meet, Microsoft Team and so on. The majority also reported using different social media platforms to maintain regular communication with their students outside the e-classrooms. Almost all of them felt that the live sessions have limitations and emphasized using social media platforms additionally. All of them reported to have faced challenges due to poor internet connectivity, lack of privacy at home and poor infrastructure. They had to take these into account with due consideration and adopted various means, used multiple platforms or applications and innovations to overcome these challenges. Privacy at home during online class was reported to be a serious concern by both male and female participants.

The majority, irrespective of their gender, received no formal training or had no previous experience of online teaching. In the initial phase of online classes, most of them faced problems and struggled to overcome these difficulties. Compared to face-to-face classrooms, the online English classes could not provide them similar opportunities for interaction among the students and teachers that they felt was crucial for learning English. So, teachers tried to ensure student engagement in various ways by nominating individual students randomly for opinions, turn taking, asking questions, using the chat box for opinion, eliciting different types of responses and so on. However, female teachers are reported to have a tendency to use audiovisual materials more often compared to their male counterparts. One female teacher mentioned, 'I personally use more audio-visual materials now to engage the students in classroom activities online' (Participant 7, female).

In response to the inquiry on how the participants balanced the deficiencies of online live sessions compared to physical face-to-face classes, everyone felt that they had to put in extra efforts and relied on various teaching practices. The majority also found social media to be a useful alternative in addition to live classrooms and more convenient platform over traditional forms of communication, such as telephone that allowed 'real-time' communication. Within the capability approach, this can be interpreted as the participants making a choice and exerting agency to achieve functionings under the circumstances. Here again, the findings place emphasis on the 'ends', or outcomes, that participants were able to achieve. The participants by their efforts or extending their skill set, or in Capability terms 'personal conversion factors', transform ICT resources into capabilities and together with agency and choice help attain functionings.

Online Teaching Practices

Concerning the type of teaching practices or adjustment in online classes, neither female nor male participants noticed any significant differences regarding gender and believed that the type of teaching techniques and practices is hardly dependent on gender identity. Adapting to the changing demands of online teaching has proved quite difficult for them, not only due to the need for adapting to the use of technology for online classes but also the additional responsibilities (like monitoring students, submitting reports for online class progress, even taking care of student enrolment, etc.) given to them by their respective institutions. Hence, the responsibilities of the participants in online teaching have multiplied. A female participant mentioned how she had to spend at least ten hours a day on the computer to fulfil responsibilities assigned to her by the institute during this pandemic time. This is true about all participants. It was evident that teachers' attempt to adapt to the new technologies also took a physical toll on the teachers. The same teachers mentioned, 'I have to wear glasses now as a consequence of spending long hours on the computer' (Participant 1, female).

Teachers also brought innovation in their teaching style based on student feedback. A male teacher (Participant 2, male) shared how he tried to provide lots of resources to the students as he felt that providing additional resources would benefit the students. He also added that the use of L1 has increased significantly in online teaching-learning.

All participants strongly agreed that online classes cannot be replacements for physical classes. However, classes had to be shifted online, as a kind of emergency response. Participant 3, a male teacher, shared his experience: 'The biggest challenge I faced was facing the camera and making videos for my class without the presence of my students. But I could adapt to the technology successfully.' Adapting to online class was a continuous process for all the participants. One of our female participants mentioned:

> I used to map out how to give assignment to the students, where they would submit, how I will effectively conduct classes at the initial stages when we started the online classes. The first month was a struggle. (Participant 8, female)

Some participants had access to the LMS provided by the university to upload short lecture videos of the following week's classes and a handout explaining the contents in the lecture video so that students with difficulty in comprehending the lectures may consult the handout. Participant 3, a male teacher for a leading private university, used the LMS and explained the process as to how he uploaded video lectures starting from brainstorming to outlining, followed by all other steps. Because of better understanding he in fact transfers all these to a scribe who prepares detailed handouts for students. As a result, if some students fail to understand the lectures fully, they could read the handouts and understand the concepts. Then the students used to come prepared in the live sessions on Zoom or Google Meet where we used to have live sessions like regular classes. In discussions in the live sessions, student could ask questions and teachers could clarify any confusion. He also mentioned how students used to receive instructions in different stages through LMS, then handouts followed by live sessions: 'Even then if some of them have problems, they could ask for help in Slack where the teachers used to reply throughout the day.'

Teachers also shared some interesting explanation videos on relevant topics in the form of cartoons and animations prior to class through Messenger:

> For example, in the last semester I taught English Skills course at Textile Engineering Department ... I shared a video on e-fiber and asked students to speak on the topic for one minute in the following class. (Participant 1, female)

Female teachers were also found using anecdotes, share personal experiences and humour to make lessons interesting and engaging. One female teacher elaborates:

> I use lots of humor, anecdotes and ask students to share their experience … to keep their attention going. These are really effective. Apart from all these, I always try to be connected with them through Messenger and share interesting short video clips in from time to time. (Participant 1, female)

The use of social media in few cases also created inconveniences for both male and female teachers. One female participant shared her experience and she also empathized with her male colleague:

> Although I use social media extensively for academic purposes it creates a lot of inconvenience for me. Usually, I'm connected to social media 24 hours through Wi-Fi. Students often disregard the time … especially students of this generation … they often called me at 3:00 AM in the morning for some silly reasons. Honestly speaking, a male married colleague faces even more inconveniences because of this. If some female student calls him at night, it causes huge embarrassment for him in front of his spouse. I as a female colleague sympathize with his plight. (Participant 1, female)

Gender Aspects in Teaching English Online at the Tertiary Level

In answering RQ2 (Is there a gender digital divide for the use of technology in online English language teaching at the tertiary level?), it was found that there is no significant difference between female and male teachers in their instructions in their online English classes at the tertiary level.

There is a general perception as reported in the existing literature on ICT and gender that there is a sharp dichotomy between the technological skills of men and women where men hold the upper hand (Tandon 2006; Tyers 2012; Rahman 2017). Consequently, males in society receive diverse professional benefits in the workplace. However, our participants presented a very encouraging picture altogether. They felt that in academia there is no marked difference in the technological skills between men and women. Rather, Participant 3 (male) revealed his own experience of learning from his female colleagues about different technological knowledge necessary for smooth conduct of online classes:

> I learn many new things from my female colleagues regarding technology. So, I do not feel there is a big discrepancy between male and female regarding IT knowledge. (Participant 3, male)

Responding to the interview questions, almost all the teachers voiced similar opinions regarding the gender difference in the use of technology in English language classrooms. They did not observe any significant difference between female and male teachers in teaching instructions in online English classes.

One female teacher rather strongly believes that previous exposure to technology and training matters more than anything else:

> I have participated in a number of training sessions on regular basis. These trainings have helped me tremendously. And I believe without these trainings I would not have conducted online classes so confidently. I can specifically mention the numerous trainings I received on online teaching through American Centre time to time. Because of my previous experiences, I was already familiar with online courses thoroughly including assessment and engagement. (Participant 7, female)

Taking a keen personal interest in using technology was found to be more important in determining the level of competence as reported by one participant:

> I was already aware of many online technologies we are using now ... I was always genuinely interested in learning new technology. I helped many of my colleagues to operate new technologies whenever they struggled. (Participant 4, female)

When it comes to teaching practices, the female teachers could ensure interactive pedagogy by actively engaging students inside and outside the online classrooms. One female participant even opined that online classroom increases interaction:

> I feel that I pay even more attention to individual students in case of online teaching. I think my students are more participative in my online classes ... those who were shy and not participative in physical classes are active and talking in online classes. I identify and address them by names individually and this strategy has worked for me tremendously in online classes. I even shared this experience with my colleagues in a presentation. (Participant 7, female)

Social Structure and Capabilities

The capability approach acknowledges that individuals are not equally placed to realize their human capabilities, owing to barriers arising from structural inequalities of class, gender and so on. Inequality in terms of gender and social class, in this study urban–rural divide, can be considered as capability deprivation as it may at times interfere with individuals' capabilities to make valued choices and participate fully in higher education processes online. Participants, regardless of their urban–rural backgrounds, responded in similar fashion – they all faced dilemmas initially but later overcame it with their efforts and perseverance.

> I had to change my teaching style to cope up with the online classes. I struggled a bit with the technological tools initially as I had no orientation and prior training. The online classes are mostly lecture based … there are not much interactive things. I had to adjust my teaching strategies accordingly. I tried to engage the students into different presentations, provided individual topic of presentation. (Participant 4, rural/female)

> My university started online teaching just within one week of the lockdown in March 2020 … without any prior preparation or training on online teaching, I faced some problems in using the technological tools … but I eventually overcame it. I had to change in my teaching style … the level of teacher-student interaction is low in online classes. Most of my classes are now kind of one-way flow of information and students are totally grade oriented. (Participant 5, rural/male)

The agency aspect, especially intrinsic agency, seems to be related to empowerment capabilities. Teachers were able to effectively convert resources into achieved functionings; more precisely, they were able to exploit technologies for effective English teaching practices. This intrinsic empowerment was demonstrated through their equal participation in teaching irrespective of their social backgrounds by extending their capabilities in difficult circumstances.

Discussion

Contrary to general findings in the existing literature on ICT and gender in Bangladesh (e.g. Ahmed & Hyndman-Rizk 2018; Tyers 2012), where women in Bangladesh are assumed to face a number of disadvantages due to 'deep-rooted' gender inequalities present in society, the study revealed that female English teachers in higher education experienced very similar experiences compared to their male counterparts in relation to accessibility, digital literacy and skills, and the adoption of digital technology for online education in the context of the Covid-19 pandemic. Almost all the participants were very positive and confident about female participants' use of digital technology for the purpose of English education online. Moreover, female English teachers were often found to be more active and engaging as they excelled in embracing different digital technologies, especially social media, for teaching-learning of English. This raises an interesting issue of women's agency in line of Kabeer, Mahmud, and Tasneem (2011) that

> it is the kind of paid work women do, rather than the fact of paid work, that influences women's voice, agency and relationships both within the home, and to some extent outside it. (30)

That means, employment in higher education sector helped women strengthen their agency which, according to the study, not only contributes to economic change but also can have spill-over effects on other aspects of their lives.

Ahmed and Hyndman-Rizk (2018) found instrumental agency to be incomplete among the female students in higher education in Bangladesh and suggested a gap. In our study, the results indicated that female English teachers in higher education were able to minimize this instrumental gap. This can be attributed to female teachers' engagement in higher education for an extended period of time and the opportunities it offered.

The qualitative findings of this study clearly indicated that male and female teachers both were able to adapt to online English classes in a similar fashion and, by extension, to the use of technology in their classes. However, female teachers were more innovative in their approach and teaching practices as they constantly tried a wider range of learning activities and were also more engaged with the students inside and outside the online classroom. They were more active in teaching and learning through different applications to mobilize students' learning processes. In the interview, female teachers were more vocal about engaging with the students and reported that they were more aware of learning through the instructive use of digital applications that meant a shift from traditional, face-to-face classroom to virtual environment.

Tyers (2012) rightly pointed out three underpinning factors such as control, social norms and language work as major barriers to participation for women. Our research reconfirms her findings that the women who overcome the barrier of social norms and control do so in terms of their decision-making and, gaining access to ICTs, are successfully able to compete with their male counterparts in higher education. Our study on gender issues in teaching English language online also supports West and Zimmerman's (1987) idea that gender is not a set of traits; rather, it is 'the product of continuous creation of the meaning of gender through human actions'. Since findings show that there is insignificant digital gender divide, the nature of gender roles and English teachers' identities in the higher education should be reconceptualized.

For future research, it may be interesting to see how norms prevent or restrict frequent interaction between the opposite gender, especially teachers' and students' engagement in conversation using social media, as emerged from the discussion of a female participant on social media and gender. The investigation on the restrictions on teachers' interaction with adult students in one-to-one interaction and public sphere in general could be interesting. These restrictions may include teachers' commenting on their students' status updates, joining the groups with their students and hours deemed appropriate for communication. Furthermore, male teachers' social inconvenience to communicate with their adult female students, especially in the presence of their female partner and other family members at home and other similar inconveniences, could be identified and further researched. Hence, gender-discriminating norms and active/passive roles of teachers and students in interaction and participation in discussion on social media and online educational platforms could be the focus of future studies.

Conclusion

The findings of the study make an indelible contribution to critical perspectives on gender issues in English language education during emergencies. This research is particularly important in the context of a developing country like Bangladesh which is frequently hit by natural calamities that seriously affect education in general. We looked into the gender inequality issues in English language education considering Covid-19 as an epitome of teaching in difficult circumstances (like war, disasters, natural calamities) that potentially disrupts education. Finally, this will help researchers everywhere, as well as policymakers, to reconceptualize gender issues in developing contexts and will provide useful insights for the planning of sustainable intervention strategies for English education in similar crises.

In general, technology has created immense opportunities for all, but more so for marginal components of society, whether during a crisis or beyond. While it is true that technology has the potential to ensure equitable growth and opportunity, how this potential can be utilized is largely an unexplored territory in Bangladesh's context, and, by extension, in other similar contexts. There is a wide gamut of factors like livelihood, women's empowerment, women's agency development and gender roles during pandemic in a society where genders roles are fixed – all these factors need to be in cognizance when we consider a policy about online education. Without careful planning and policy implementation, we will not be able to ensure equality for the stakeholders in the knowledge economy that we envisage. If we fail to have a well-balanced policy, ICTs may exacerbate differences between the rich and the poor, and the men and the women. However, further research is required as these findings may not hold true for the primary and secondary education sector and teachers, or for public higher education institutions.

Questions for Change

(1) For all readers: To what extent, and in what ways, do teaching and learning online enable you to negotiate, reconstruct, or transform traditional gender roles?
(2) For English as a second/foreign language (ESL/EFL) teachers: To what extent, and in what ways, can online technologies be used for effective and meaning learning in future English language classes breaking the traditional gender roles? Are you willing to do so? If yes, how?
(3) For ESL/EFL teachers and students: How can online and social media technologies be used as an educational tool to increase teacher–student and student–student interactions overcoming the limitations of gender disparity?

12

New Transnational Voices on Gender Diversity in English Language Education: Moving Forward

Joanna Pawelczyk

Introduction

As evidenced in the robust extant research, various instantiations and forms of sexism, heteronormativity and homophobia still persist in education across the world, including in the field of teaching and learning English as a foreign and second language (EFL/ESL) (e.g. Sauntson 2021a, 2020; Pakuła, Pawelczyk & Sunderland 2015). Perhaps paradoxically, even in those societies that openly and systemically support LGBTQ+ inclusive education, there is still a degree of social resistance and sometimes explicit rejection of any attempts to interrupt normativities in general, and specifically to challenge ubiquitous heteronormativity in school contexts. This points to a disconnect between the implemented or ongoing structural changes and their seeming lack of acceptance by at least part of the general population, which often results in their incomplete adoption by specific institutions, in our case educational. Additionally, there continues to be very little understanding (or even strategic rejection) of the salience of foreign language education when it comes to issues around students' identities (Paiz 2021; see Chapter 4 in this volume). Such an attitude contradicts the fact that 'in the language classroom, students are more likely to be expected to talk about themselves than in any other subject classroom' (Sunderland 2021: 217). There is, however, an increasing number of teachers across the globe who are fully cognizant of the fact that how educational texts will be 'consumed' (Fairclough 1992), and consequently whether students' *various* identities beyond the gender binary and heterosexuality will be acknowledged and heard, is largely contingent on them.

These are just a few of the complex and multifaceted issues around gender and sexual diversity in the context of English language education addressed and explored by the chapters presented in the current volume. All the chapters are driven by a social justice agenda, and in that spirit, they offer relevant suggestions for real change/transformation, often by allowing teachers and educators to become reflective and reflexive about their teaching practices (and rapport) with their students. The studies draw on various types of data relevant to English language education and apply a range of methodological frameworks and critical methods in revealing and further unpacking heteronormativity. That critical lens is necessary to identify the invisible power of heterosexuality in English language education, leading to its implicit normalization in the classroom.

The volume draws on examples from ten countries and five continents to reveal the local challenges facing teachers, educators and also students in their respective struggles to queer the classroom and have their *various* identities acknowledged and respected. The thought-provoking questions offered at the end of each chapter aim not only to inspire teachers and educators to be reflective about their practices but also may instil in them much-needed reflexivity in their future work. As such, the questions, although embedded in the local context of the respective countries, carry strong global and practical implications.

In this closing chapter, I summarize the main findings and conclusions offered by the authors. I will also demonstrate how the volume extends the existing research and our thinking on gender and sexual diversity in English language education by offering further suggestions and ideas for consideration.

Main Takeaways

The chapters evidence *a transnational struggle to recognize a diversity of gender and sexual identities* in English language education systems. Overall, English language teaching (ELT) materials explicitly and implicitly promote dominant gender roles and heterosexuality (Pakuła, Pawelczyk & Sunderland 2015) and concurrently symbolically annihilate people who do not conform to traditionally prescribed gender roles or conservative gender relations and non-heterosexual people by leaving them out (Tuchman 1981). On the other hand, however, there are teachers and language educators contesting and challenging official ELT materials by offering new readings (Sunderland 1994, 2021), thus opening up the ESL/EFL classroom space to queering. As demonstrated in Chapter 9, students are keen and willing to enter a critical reading of heteronormative teaching materials and consider non-heterosexual perspectives. Richards (Chapter 9, this volume) discovered that students (and also teachers) wish to exercise their *agentive capacity* and enter a true dialogue with teaching materials with the support of their teachers.

In fact, such a dialogue, or I would say *interaction*, is the foundation of a successful foreign (including English) language learning for all types of learners (Menard-Warwick, Mori & Williams 2014: 472). What connects all the chapters – although perhaps not initially evident – is their demonstration that change/transformation in the English language classroom can happen when both participating parties, teachers and students, are involved in dialogue. This is the place where meanings are co-produced but also challenged, resisted, contested and constructed anew (Fairclough 2003). Through dialogue, heteronormativity can be revealed and questioned, allowing non-heterosexual voices to be represented. Communication then allows teachers to interrupt the heteronormativity and cisnormativity of the English language classroom by 'queering knowledges, texts and discourses' (Chapter 1, this volume).

The growing salience of and reliance on *multimodality* in education generally, and in English language education specifically, opens up new affordances for queering the ESL/EFL classroom as detailed in Chapters 3, 4 and 7 (see also Paiz 2021). The quotation from Chapter 3, that 'the space between the words (what is said) and the pictures (what we see) offers a particular imaginative and multimodal space' (Magnet and Dunnington 2020: 3), aptly illustrates the potential of multimodal communication in topicalizing and exploring the non-normative. Dominant and normative images found in ELT materials can be read anew and discursively (and critically) deconstructed by students and teachers, thus breaking the 'heteronormative prosody' (Chapter 4, this volume) of the classroom. As the authors of Chapters 3 and 4 argue, such exploration and discovery of gender and sexual diversity needs to be aligned with students' 'affective and linguistic needs' (Chapter 3) as well as 'the social and situational contexts in which teaching and learning are taking place' (Chapter 4; see also Paiz 2020).

I would now like to elaborate on *the key role of the teacher* in making the English language classroom a more gender and sexuality diverse space. I will begin, however, with the assertion that teachers, similarly to other practitioners, might not be adequately aware of the kind of realities they are constructing for their students in classroom interactions with their language use and discursive practices (see Peräkylä and Vehviläinen 2003). They may hold, for example, certain stereotypical dominant views concerning femininity and masculinity, and remain unaware of how they rely on them during their interactional work with students in the classroom. This calls for a development of teachers' reflectivity but also critical reflexivity (Lazar 2014) to examine anew – among others – their constructions of various identities in the classroom (Chapters 1, 4 and 5, this volume) that may involve uncritical production of a highly heteronormative world for their students. Teachers may need to think of themselves as agents with situated power 'to introduce certain topics and manage them with learners' (Chapter 4, this volume). This situated agency is particularly important in societies where homophobia is widespread and implicitly or explicitly condoned by the authorities and those who hold institutional power. In such contexts, teachers' individual bottom-up interventions in challenging heteronormativity are especially crucial. Yet even in countries that openly recognize (the rights of) the LGBTQ+ community and celebrate multiculturalism and diversity, learners still need to manage practices of marginalization on the ground (Paiz 2021: 7), and teaching materials may not reflect their diverse reality (Chapter 1) at all. There as well, the teacher can 'rescue' (Sunderland 1994) these normative texts by engaging students in entering a safe dialogue with them. Following Sunderland's (2021: 218) remark, 'even the most heteronormative text can be critically queered'. Furthermore, we are living in times of unprecedented or even highly unpredictable social changes. One therefore needs to ask: Do the ELT materials used globally give justice to the highly complex and ever-changing social world? I am afraid the answer is no or not yet (Chapter 8, this volume; see also Gray 2013), and thus students are not likely to identify with that EFL content, which in turn may have a detrimental effect on their learning experience and outcomes.

In fact, research on gender and language in the context of English language education has consistently recognized the crucial position of teachers in contesting heteronormativity and making ESL or EFL more inclusive to learners (Sauntson 2021b; Pakuła, Pawelczyk & Sunderland 2015). However, there seems to be an assumption that all ESL/EFL teachers are as if a priori equipped with the necessary critical and reflective skills that can be instantly tapped into and used effortlessly to somehow break the institutionally imposed heteronormativity of the ESL/EFL classroom.

What the current chapters (e.g. Chapters 1 and 10) call for is the need for specifically designed *education programmes for English language educators/teachers* that will allow them to *acquire* the necessary skills to engage their students in queering dialogues. Teachers need support in the first place before they are able to problematize and challenge the notions provided in ELT materials leading to their reflexive transformation of heteronormative content (Chapters 4 and 10). Queer critical literacies (Chapter 1), visual literacy, discourse-analytic skills and critical reading (Chapter 8) are just a few tools recommended to be used by teachers to interrupt heteronormativity and let all marginalized voices speak up and be reflected in the classroom 'reality' co-constructed by teachers and learners. To this set, following Sauntson (2021a: 342, 2021b), I would add the 'queer applied linguistics' (QAL) framework, that is, critical applied linguistics 'informed by queer theory/queer linguistics and which is applied to addressing social concerns with inequalities around gender and sexuality'. The application of such a critical, questioning lens always leads to some kind of transformation, even if it is gradual and extended over time (Sauntson 2021b).

I also wish to underline the importance of *examining language use* more broadly in attempts at identifying and confronting gender and sexuality-based discrimination. As documented by extensive research, discriminatory behaviours have increasingly often taken on more subtle and nuanced forms (Caldas-Coulthard 2020; Holmes 2020; Mills 2008), making them difficult to contest. Sauntson (2020: 145, see also Sauntson 2018) illustrates this pattern with reference to bullying: 'gender and sexuality-based discrimination often does not happen through overt bullying, but operates at a more discursive level which is difficult to challenge'.

Being equipped with critical skills allows teachers to feel confident 'to frame questions, facilitate investigations, and explore what is not known' (Nelson 1999: 377) and then over time, queering practices may progressively become their praxis. Teachers empowered with critical knowledge and powerful tools of inquiry can then in turn empower their students. This is also to say that there should be a serious investment in the development of critical skills in language teacher education before we can observe a tangible transformation in English language education towards becoming a gender and sexuality diverse space. To sum up, teachers need a toolkit of critical methods to fully understand what social realities they are constructing for their learners with their handling of teaching materials and to be able to reflect on their classroom practices. Only then will they be able to engage in critical reflexivity by self-monitoring their use of language (practices) in constructing social realities for students/learners.

The importance of *intercultural experience* in exploring topics around gender and sexual diversity (Chapter 2) needs more emphasized recognition (see also Xue 2014). By being involved in a dialogue, English language learners around the globe can engage in unpacking the meaning and significance of issues around gender and sexuality in their respective countries. In this sense, the experience of learning English will also become real for them (Banegas 2013). As the authors of Chapter 4 compellingly demonstrate, 'intercultural learning … enhances understanding of gender issues'. It can be claimed that in such contexts the role of teachers is to (closely) monitor student interactions, while the exploration of issues around gender and sexuality is somehow facilitated by students' different cultural backgrounds and their curiosity to get to know one another.

Ideally, *the gender and sexual diversity perspective should be included in the process of designing teaching materials* (Chapter 11, this volume). It should become a guiding principle for all ELT stakeholders if they want the English language learning experience to become enriching and satisfactory and above all ensure that learners of all identities are (somehow) represented there. As argued by Banegas and Evripidou (2021: 127), 'research-informed classroom strategies should be offered in order to support educators in their quest for adopting a gender perspective in their ELT practices'. However, in view of what was discussed above, our hope is that teachers and students/learners on the ground will be willing and keen to acquire the second/foreign language in a communicative environment that more closely resembles the highly diverse world they are living in.

Possible Ways Forward

What then are the possible ways forward to make the English language classroom a truly diverse and inclusive space for all students?

To start with, diversity and inclusion do not happen by talking about them, and thus they cannot be merely buzzwords (Melaku 2019) floating around in education contexts. Diversity and inclusion need *doing*. What if we start talking about *doing* normalizing diversity and inclusion in English language education? That normalizing, as the chapters in this volume have convincingly argued, needs teachers and educators who are equipped with critical skills and extensively rely on the affordances of multimodality to include and respect the voices and (intersectional) identities of all students. Teachers and educators need to be prepared to do normalizing diversity, as without training it is almost impossible to remain completely unbiased and reflexive (Chang 2018: 18). We can also observe in these studies students' keen interest in exploring and discussing the unknown and unpacking the normative in a safe and respectful environment. Researchers are also encouraged to look outside the school context to explore how (queer) migrants attempt to learn English and are challenged by various ideologies, for example, linguistic nationalism and heteropatriarchy (Chapter 6, this volume). These ideologies may also be present in the actual school context and the classroom.

Diversity brings a real-ness into English language education, a real-ness that reflects the multi-type of the world we are living in. This type of world far better reflects the lived experiences of students and learners (as well as teachers) and thus can translate into students' satisfaction and felt respect, leading to positive learning outcomes. Above all, what all English language education stakeholders should also remember is that diversity brings creativity into classroom.

References

Abednia, A. (2012). Teachers' professional identity: Contributions of a critical EFL teacher education course in Iran. *Teaching and Teacher Education, 28*, 706–17.

Abednia, A., & Crookes, G. (2018). Critical literacy as a pedagogical goal in English language teaching. *Second Language Studies, 37*(1), 1–33.

Adams, T. E., & Holman Jones, S. (2011). Telling stories: Reflexivity, queer theory, & autoethnography. *Cultural Studies < – > Critical Methodologies, 11*(2), 108–16.

Ahmadian, M., & Maftoon, P. (2016). Enhancing critical language teacher development through creating reflective opportunities. *Journal of Asia TEFL, 13*(2), 90–101.

Ahmed, R., & Hyndman-Rizk, N. (2018). The higher education paradox: Towards improving women's empowerment, agency development and labour force participation in Bangladesh. *Gender and Education, 32*(4): 447–65.

Akbari, R. (2008). Transforming lives: Introducing critical pedagogy into ELT classrooms. *ELT Journal, 62*: 276–83.

Aldridge-Morris, K. (2016). *How to Write ESOL Materials*. ELT Teacher 2 Writer.

Al-Wer, E. (2014). Language and gender in the Middle East and North Africa. In S. Ehrlich, M. Meyerhoff & J. Holmes (Eds), *The Handbook of Language, Gender, and Sexuality* (pp. 396–411). New York: Wiley-Blackwell.

Amelina, A., Boatcă, M., Bongaerts, G. & Weiß, A. (2021). Theorizing societalization across borders: Globality, transnationality, postcoloniality. *Current Sociology, 69*(3), 303–14.

Andrews, G. (2019). The emergence of black queer characters in three post-apartheid novels. *Tydskrif vir Letterkunde, 56*(2), 1–9.

Andrews, G. (2020). Teaching gender & sexuality in the wake of the Must Fall Movements: Mutual disruption through the lens of critical pedagogy. *Education as Change, 24*(1), 1–20.

Andsager, J. L. (2014). Research directions in social media and body image. *Sex Roles, 71*, 407–13.

Antony, S. (2019). Why I made the picture book they said wouldn't sell. Booktrust, Retrieved from: https://www.booktrust.org.uk/news-and-features/features/2019/february/steve-antony-why-ive-made-the-picture-book-they-said-wouldnt-sell/ (accessed 23 May 2021).

Anzaldúa, G. (2012). *Borderlands/La Frontera: The New Mestiza* (4th edn). San Francisco, CA: Aunt Lute.

Apple, M. (2000). *Official Knowledge: Democratic Education in a Conservative Age*. New York: Routledge.

Apple, M., & Oliver, A. (2003). Becoming right: Education and the formation of conservative movements. In M. Apple (Ed.), *The State and the Politics of Knowledge* (pp. 25–50). New York: Routledge Falmer.

Armstrong, H. (2021). *Encyclopaedia of Sex and Sexuality: Understanding Biology, Psychology and Culture*. Santa Barbara, CA: ABC-CLIO.

Ashwin P., & McVitty, D. (2015). The meanings of student engagement: Implications for policies & practices. In A. Curaj, L. Matei, R. Pricopie, J. Salmi & P. Scott (Eds), *The European Higher Education Area* (pp. 343–60). Cham: Springer.

Bader, B. (1976). *American Picturebooks from Noah's Ark to The Beast Within*. New York: Macmillan.

Baker, J. (2010). Great expectations and post-feminist accountability: Young women living up to the 'successful girls' discourse. *Gender and Education, 22*(1), 1–15.

Bandura, A. (1997). *Self-Efficacy: The Exercise of Control*. New York: Freeman.

Banegas, D. L. (2013). The integration of content and language as a driving force in the EFL lesson. In E. Ushioda (Ed.), *International Perspectives on Motivation: Language Learning and Professional Challenges* (pp. 82–97). Basingstoke: Palgrave.

Banegas, D. L. (Ed.) (2017). *Initial English Language Teacher Education: International Perspectives on Research, Curriculum and Practice*. London: Bloomsbury.

Banegas, D. L., & Evripidou, D. (2021). Introduction: Comprehensive sexuality education in ELT. Special issue on Comprehensive sexuality education in ELT. *ELT Journal, 75*(2), 127–32.

Banegas, D. L., & Gerlach, D. (2021). Critical language teacher education: A duoethnography of teacher educators' identities and agency. *System, 98*, 102474.

Banegas, D. L., & Villacañas de Castro, L. S. (2016). Criticality. *ELT Journal, 70*(4): 455–7.

Banegas, D. L., Jacovkis, L. G., & Romiti, A. (2020). A gender perspective in initial English language teacher education: an Argentinian experience. *Sexuality & Culture, 24*(1), 1–22.

Barkhuizen, G. (Ed.). (2017). *Reflections on Language Teacher Identity Research*. New York: Routledge.

Barone, C. (2011). Some things never change: Gender segregation in higher education across eight nations and three decades. *Sociology of Education, 84*(2), 157–76.

Barrios, G. (2011). El tratamiento de la diversidad lingüística en la educación uruguaya (2006–2008). *Letras 21*, 42, 15–44.

Beacon, G. (2019). Contemporary fairy tales: A queer perspective. *Ágora UNLaR, 4*(9), 43–47.

Beauchamp, C., & Thomas, L. (2019). Identity learning in teacher education. In M. A. Peters (Ed.), *Encyclopedia of Teacher Education* (pp. 1–5). Cham: Springer.

Bell, B., & Dittmar, H. (2011). Does media type matter? The role of identification in adolescent girls' media consumption and the impact of different thin-ideal media on body image. *Sex Roles, 65*, 478–490.

Benjamin, S. (2003). What counts as success? Hierarchical discourses in a girls' comprehensive school. *Discourse, 24*(1), 105–18.

Beyer, S. (2014). Why are women underrepresented in Computer Science? Gender differences in stereotypes, self-efficacy, values, and interests and predictors of future CS course-taking and grades. *Computer Science Education, 24*(2–3), 153–92.

Biggs, J., & Tang, C. (2011). *Teaching for Quality Learning at University: What the Student Does*. Glasgow: Society for Research into Higher Education & Open University Press.

Blaise, M. (2009). 'What a girl wants, what a girl needs': Responding to sex, gender, and sexuality in the early childhood classroom. *Journal of Research in Childhood Education, 23*(4), 450–60.

Bland, J. (2018). Introduction: The challenge of literature. In J. Bland (Ed.), *Using Literature in English Language Education: Challenging Reading for 8-18 Year Olds* (pp. 1–22). London: Bloomsbury.

Bland, J. (2020). Using literature for intercultural learning in English language education. In M. Dypedhal & R. E. Lund (Eds), *Teaching and Learning English Interculturally* (pp. 69–86). Oslo: Cappelen Damm Akademisk.

Bland, J. (2022). Picturebooks that challenge the young English language learner. In Å. M. Ommundsen, G. Haaland & B. Kümmerling-Meibauer (Eds), *Exploring Challenging Picturebooks in Education*. London: Routledge.

Bland, J. (Forthcoming). *Compelling Stories for English Language Learners – Creativity, Interculturality & Critical Literacy*. London: Bloomsbury.

Block, D. (2003). *The Social Turn in Second Language Acquisition*. Edinburgh: Edinburgh University Press.

Block, D. (2007). The rise of identity in SLA research, post Firth and Wagner (1997). *Modern Language Journal, 91*(5), 863–76.

Block, D. (2010). Globalization and language teaching. In N. Coupland (Ed.), *The Handbook of Language and Globalization* (pp. 287–304). Malden: Wiley-Blackwell.

Block, D., & Cameron, D. (Eds) (2002). *Globalization and Language Teaching*. London: Routledge.

Block, D., & Gray, J. (2016). 'Just go away and do it and you get marks': The degradation of language teaching in neoliberal times. *Journal of Multilingual & Multicultural Development, 37*(5), 481–94.

Block, D., Gray, J. & Holborow, M. (2013). *Neoliberalism and Applied Linguistics*. Routledge.

Blumberg, R. (2007). *Gender Bias in Textbooks: A Hidden Obstacle on the Road to Gender Equality in Education*. Paris: UNESCO.

Blunt, A. (2007). Cultural geographies of migration: mobility, transnationality and diaspora. *Progress in Human Geography, 31*(5), 684–94.

Bohnsack, R. (2010). Documentary method and group discussions. In R. Bohnsack, N. Pfaff & W. Weller (Eds), *Qualitative Analysis and Documentary*

Method: International Educational Research (pp. 99–124). Opladen: Verlag Barbara Budrich.

Bollas, A. (2021). A critical discussion of inclusive approaches to sexualities in ELT. *ELT Journal, 75*(2), 133–41.

Bonnet, A., & Hericks, U. (2020). *Kooperatives Lernen im Englischunterricht. Empirische Studien zur (Un-) Möglichkeit fremdsprachlicher Bildung in der Prüfungsschule*. Tübingen: Narr.

Bourdieu, P. (1977). *Outline of a Theory of Practice*. Cambridge: Cambridge University Press.

Bourdieu, P. (1986). The forms of capital. In J. G. Richardson (Ed.), *Handbook of Theory and Research for the Sociology of Education* (pp. 241–58). Westport, CT: Greenwood Press.

Bourdieu, P. (1990). *Photography: A Middle-brow Art*. Cambridge: Polity Press.

Bourdieu, P. (1991). *Language and symbolic power* (G. R. M. Adamson, Trans.). Cambridge: Polity Press.

Bourdieu, P., & Wacquant, L. J. D. (1992). *An Invitation to Reflexive Sociology*. Chicago: The University of Chicago Press.

Bourke, A., & Maunsell, C. (2016). Teachers matter: The impact of mandatory reporting on teacher education in Ireland. *Child Abuse Review, 25*(4), 314–24.

Breidbach, S., Medina, J. & Mihan, A. (2014). Critical literacies, multiliteracies and foreign language education. *Fremdsprachen Lehren & Lernen, 43*(2), 91–106.

Brennan, M. A., Lalonde, C. E. & Bain, J. L. (2010). Body image perceptions: Do gender differences exist? *International Honor Society in Psychology, 15*(3), 130–8.

Brown, S., Berry, M., Dawes, E., Hughes, A. & Tu, C. (2019). Character mediation of story generation via protagonist insertion. *Journal of Cognitive Psychology, 31*(3): 326–42.

Bucholtz, M. (2001). The whiteness of nerds: superstandard English and racial markedness. *Journal of Linguistic Anthropology, 11*(1), 84–100.

Bucholtz, M. (2011). *White Kids: Language, Race and Styles of Youth Identity*. Cambridge: Cambridge University Press.

Butler, J. (1990). *Gender Trouble*. Abingdon: Routledge.

Butler, J. (2004). *Undoing Gender*. New York: Routledge.

Butler, J. (2007). *Gender Trouble: Feminism & the Subversion of Identity*. New York: Routledge.

Butler, J. (2011). *Bodies That Matter. On the Discursive Limits of 'Sex'*. New York: Routledge.

Byram, M. (2008). *From Foreign Language Education to Education for Intercultural Citizenship*. Clevedon: Multilingual Matters.

Byram, M., & Wagner, M. (2018). Making a difference: Language teaching for intercultural and international dialogue. *Foreign Language Annals, 51*, 140–51.

Caldas-Coulthard, C. (Ed.) (2020). *Innovations and Challenges. Women, Language and Sexism*. London: Routledge.

Cameron, D. (2001). *Working with Spoken Discourse*. London: SAGE.

Cameron, D. (2005). Language, gender, and sexuality: Current issues and new directions. *Applied Linguistics*, 26(4), 482–502.

Cameron, D., & Kulick, D. (2003). *Language and Sexuality*. Cambridge: Cambridge University Press.

Cameron, J. E. (2004). A three-factor model of social identity. *Self and Identity*, 3(3), 239–62.

Canagarajah, S. (1993). American textbooks and Tamil students: Discerning ideological tensions in the ESL classroom. *Language, Culture and Curriculum*, 6(2), 143–56.

Canagarajah, S. (1999). *Resisting Linguistic Imperialism in English Teaching*. Hong Kong: Oxford University Press.

Canagarajah, S. (Ed.). (2005). *Reclaiming the Local in Language Policy and Practice*. London: Routledge.

Canagarajah, S. (2013). *Translingual Practice: Global Englishes and Cosmopolitan Relations*. New York: Routledge.

Canale, G. (2015). Mapping conceptual change: The ideological struggle for the Meaning of EFL in Uruguayan Education. *The L2 Journal*, 7(3), 15–39.

Canale, G. (2019). *Technology, Multimodality and Learning: Analyzing Meaning across Scales*. Cham: Palgrave Macmillan.

Canale, G., & Furtado, V. (2021). Gender in EFL Education: Negotiating Textbook Discourse in the Classroom. *Changing English*, 28(1), 58–71.

Cao, L. (in press). Intersectional structural constraints and delegitimized language learner in the making: An ethnographic case study of a bisexual migrant's language learning in Western Canada. In J. M. Paiz & J. Coda (Eds), *Intersectional Perspectives on LGBTQ+ Issues in Modern Language Teaching and Learning*. Cham: Palgrave Macmillan.

Carolin, A., & Frenkel, R. (2019). Transnational imaginaries and the negotiation of sexual rights during the South African transition. *African Studies*, 78(4), 510–26.

Carr, J., & Pauwels, A. (2006). *Boys and Foreign Language Learning: Real Boys Don't Do Languages*. Basingstoke & New York: Palgrave Macmillan.

Chaffee, K. E., Lou, N. M. & Noels, K. A. (2020). Does stereotype threat affect men in language domains? *Frontiers in Psychology*, 11, 1302.

Chaffee, K. E., Lou, N. M., Noels, K. A. & Katz, J. W. (2020). Why don't 'real men' learn languages? Masculinity threat and gender ideology suppress men's language learning motivation. *Group Processes & Intergroup Relations*, 23(2), 301–18.

Chang, E. (2018). *Brotopia. Breaking up the Boys' Club of Silicon Valley*. New York: Portfolio/Penguin.

Chaskalson, J., Bhana, D., Brouard, P., Hodes, R., Ngabaza, S., Silbert, P. & Zungu, N. (2019). Knowledge is power: The case for Comprehensive Sexualities Education in South Africa. Daily Maverick. Retrieved from: https://www.dailymaverick.co.za/article/2019-11-26-knowledge-is-power-the-case-for-comprehensive-sexualities-education-in-south-africa/ (accessed 25 November 2020).

Cheah, P. (2008). What is a world? On world literature as world-making activity. *Daedalus, 137*(3), 26–38.

Chun, E. W. (2013). Ironic blackness as masculine cool: Asian American language and authenticity on YouTube. *Applied Linguistics, 34*(5), 592–612.

Chung, B. G., Ehrhart, M. G., Holcombe Ehrhart, K., Hattrup, K. & Solamon, J. (2010). Stereotype threat, state anxiety, and specific self-efficacy as predictors of promotion exam performance. *Group & Organization Management, 35*(1), 77–107.

Coda, J., Cahnmann-Taylor, M., & Jiang, L. (2020). 'It takes time for language to change': Challenging classroom heteronormativity through teaching proficiency through reading and storytelling (TPRS). *Journal of Language, Identity and Education, 20*(2), 90–102.

Cohen, J. (1988). *Statistical Power Analysis for the Behavioural Sciences Hillsdale* (2nd ed.). New York: Routledge.

Collier, K. L., Bos, H. M. W., & Sandfort, T. G. M. (2015). Understanding teachers' responses to enactments of sexual and gender stigma at school. *Teaching & Teacher Education, 48*, 34–43.

Collins, P. (2019). *Intersectionality as Critical Social Theory*. Durham and London: Duke University Press.

Connell, R. (1987). *Gender and Power*. Cambridge: Polity.

Connell, R. W. (2005). *Masculinities*. Polity Press.

Council of Higher Education. (2021). *Number of undergraduate students according to classification of fields of education and training, 2020–2021*. Retrieved from: https://istatistik.yok.gov.tr/ (accessed 3 March 2021).

Coupland, N. (Ed.) (2010). *The Handbook of Language and Globalization*. Malden: Wiley-Blackwell.

Coyle D., Hood P. & Marsh, D. (2010). *CLIL: Content and Language Integrated Learning*. Cambridge: Cambridge University Press.

Craven, M. (2005). *Quizzes, Questionnaires and Puzzles: Ready-made Activities for Intermediate Students*. Cambridge: Cambridge University Press.

Creswell, J. W. (2014). *Research Design: Qualitative, Quantitative, And Mixed Methods Approaches* (4th ed.). Thousand Oaks, CA: Sage Publications.

Crompton, R. (1987). Gender, status and professionalism. *Sociology, 21*(3), 413–28.

Crookes, G. (2013). *Critical ELT in Action: Foundations, Promises, Praxis*. New York: Routledge.

Curdt-Christiansen, X. L. & Weninger, C. (2015). Introduction: Ideology and the politics of language textbooks. In X. L. Curdt-Christiansen & C. Weninger (Eds), *Language, Ideology and Education: The Politics of Textbooks in Language Education* (pp. 1–15). London: Routledge.

Curwood, J. S., & Gibbons, D. (2010). 'Just like I have felt': Multimodal counternarratives in youth-produced digital media. *International Journal of Learning and Media, 1*(4), 59–77.

Darvin, R., & Norton, B. (2014). Social class, identity, and migrant students. *Journal of Language, Identity & Education*, *13*(2), 111–17.

Darvin R., & Norton, B. (2015). Identity and a model of investment in applied linguistics. *Annual Review of Applied Linguistics*, *35*, 36–56.

Dawson, J. (2021). *What's the T?* London: Wren & Rook.

De Costa, P. I., & Norton, B. (2017). Introduction: identity, transdisciplinarity, and the good language teacher. *The Modern Language Journal*, *101*, 3–14.

De Vicenti, G., Giovanangeli, A. & Ward, A. (2007). The queer stopover: How queer travels in the language classroom. *Electronic Journal of Foreign Language Teaching*, *4*(1), 58–72.

Delanoy, W. (2018). Literature in language education: Challenges for theory building. In J. Bland (Ed.), *Using Literature in English Language Education: Challenging Reading for 8-18 Year Olds* (pp. 139–58). London: Bloomsbury.

DePalma, R. (2016). Gay penguins, sissy ducklings ... and beyond? Exploring gender and sexuality diversity through children's literature. *Discourse: Studies in the Cultural Politics of Education*, *37*(6), 828–45.

Deresiewicz, W. (2015, September). The Neoliberal Arts. *Harper's Magazine*. Retrieved from: https://harpers.org/archive/2015/09/the-neoliberal-arts/ (accessed 15 February 2021).

Dervin, F., & Gross, Z. (2016). Introduction: Towards the simultaneity of intercultural competence. In F. Dervin and Z. Gross (Eds), *Intercultural Competence in Education. Alternative Approaches for Different Times* (pp. 1–10). London: Palgrave Macmillan.

Dewale, J. M. (2018). Why the dichotomy 'L1 versus LX user' is better than 'native versus non-native speaker. *Applied Linguistics*, *39*(2), 236–40.

Dodge, B., Herbenick, D., Friedman, M. R., Schick, V., Fu, T. J., Bostwick, W., Bartelt, E., Muñoz-Laboy, M., Pletta, D., Reece, M. & Sandfort, T. G. (2016). Attitudes toward bisexual men and women among a nationally representative probability sample of adults in the United States. *PloS One*, *11*(10), e0164430.

Doerr-Stevens, C. (2015). 'That's not something I was, I am, or am ever going to be': Multimodal self-assertion in digital video production. *E-learning and Digital Media*, *12*(2), 164–82.

Doiz, A., Lasagabaster, D., & Sierra, J. M. (2014). CLIL and motivation: The effect of individual and contextual variables. *The Language Learning Journal*, 42(2), 209–24.

Douglas, K., & Poletti, A. (2016). *Life Narratives and Youth Culture. Representation, Agency and Participation*. London: Palgrave Macmillan.

Dzengel, J., Kunze, K., & Wernet, A. (2012). Vom Verschwinden der Sache im pädagogischen Jargon: Überlegungen zu einem Strukturproblem der Ausbildungskultur im Studienseminar. *Pädagogische Korrespondenz*, *45*, 20–44.

Education Scotland (2019). Relationships, Sexual Health & Parenthood. Education Scotland. Retrieved from: https://rshp.scot/about-the-resource/#rshpandcfe (accessed 6 August 2020).

Ellis, C., Adams, T. E. & Bochner, A. P. (2011). Autoethnography: An overview. *Historical Social Research*, 36(4), 273–90.

Ellis, G. (2018a). The picturebook in elementary ELT: Multiple literacies with Bob Staake's Bluebird. In J. Bland (Ed.), *Using Literature in English Language Education: Challenging Reading for 8-18 Year Olds* (pp. 83–104). London: Bloomsbury.

Ellis, G. (2018b). The communication triangle: voices from the home, the school, and the child. In F. Copland & S. Garton (Eds), *TESOL Voices: Insider Accounts of Classroom Life – Young Learner Education*. New York: TESOL International.

Ellis, G. (2019). Social model thinking about disability through picturebooks in primary English. *Children's Literature in English Language Education*, 7(2), 61–78.

Ellis, G., & Brewster, J. (2014). *Tell it Again! The Storytelling Handbook for Primary Teachers* (3rd ed.), London: British Council. Retrieved from:https://www.teachingenglish.org.uk/article/tell-it-again-storytelling-handbook-primary-english-language-teachers (accessed 23 May 2021).

Ellis, G., & Ibrahim, N. (2021). Teachers' image of the child in an ELT context. In A. Pinter & K. Kuchah (Eds), *Ethical and Methodological Issues in Researching Young Language Learners in School Contexts*. Clevedon: Multilingual Matters.

Ellis, G., & Mourão, S. (2021). Demystifying the read-aloud. *English Teaching Professional*, 136.

Eslen-Ziya, H., & Koc, Y. (2016). Being a gay man in Turkey: Internalised sexual prejudice as a function of prevalent hegemonic masculinity perceptions. *Culture, Health & Sexuality*, 18(7), 799–811.

Evripidou, D. (2018). The interrelationship among sexual identity, learning and sexualisation: Primary EFL teachers' attitudes in Cyprus. *TESOL Quarterly*, 52(4), 1062–72.

Evripidou, D. (2020). Effects of heteronormativity on Cypriot EFL classroom participation: Students' experiences. *Gender and Education*, 32(8), 1019–33.

Ezcurra, A. (2011). *Igualdad en Educación Superior: Un Desafío Mundial*. Buenos Aires. Ediciones UNGS.

Fairclough, N. (1992). *Discourse and Social Change*. Cambridge: Polity Press.

Fairclough, N. (1995). *Critical Discourse Analysis: The critical study of language*. Harlow: Longman

Fairclough, N. (2001). *Language and power*. Harlow: Pearson Education.

Fairclough, N. (2003). *Analysing Discourse. Textual Analysis for Social Research*. London/New York: Routledge.

Fairclough, N. (2006). *Language and globalization*. London: Routledge.

Fairley, M. J. (2020). Conceptualizing language teacher education centered on language teacher identity development: A competencies-based approach and practical applications. *TESOL Quarterly*, 54(4), 1037–64.

Farrar, J., Arzipe, E. & McAdam, J. E. (2022). Challenging picturebooks and literacy studies. In Å. M. Ommundsen, G. Haaland & B. Kümmerling-Meibauer (Eds), *Exploring Challenging Picturebooks in Education*. London: Routledge.

Fernández, M., & V. Frade. (2019). *Ocho pasos hacia la transformación. Un modelo de educación en género.* Montevideo: ANEP/Embajada de los Estados Unidos de América.

Forman, R. (2014). How local teachers respond to the culture and language of a global English as a foreign language textbook. *Language, Culture and Curriculum, 27*(1), 72–88.

Foucault, M. (1980). *The history of Sexuality: An Introduction*, volume I. Trans. R. Hurley. New York: Vintage.

Fox, R., Corretjer, O., Webb, K. & Tian, J. (2019). Benefits of foreign language learning and bilingualism: An analysis of published empirical research 2005–2011. *Foreign Language Annals, 52*(3), 470–90.

Francis, D. A. (2017). Homophobia and sexuality diversity in South African schools: A review. *Journal of LGBT Youth, 14*(4), 359–79.

Francois, E. J. (2016). What is transnational education? In E. J. Francois, M. Avoseh & W. Griswold (Ed.), *Perspectives in Transnational Higher Education* (pp. 3–22). Rotterdam: Sense.

Fraser, N. (2013). Fortunes of Feminism: From State-managed Capitalism to Neoliberal Crisis. London and New York: Verso Books.

Freeman, D. (2020). Arguing for a knowledge-base in language teacher education, then (1998) and now (2018). *Language Teaching Research, 24*(1), 5–16.

Freire, P. & Macedo, D. (1987). *Literacy: Reading the Word and the World.* London: Routledge and Kegan & Paul.

Freire, P. (1970). *Pedagogy of the Oppressed.* London: Penguin.

Freire, P. (1994). *Pedagogy of Hope.* New York: Continuum.

Furtado, V. (2018). De niñas y niños: Las políticas lingüísticas de género en la educación primaria uruguaya. *Lingüística, 34*(2), 9–31.

Gao, X. (2017). Questioning the identity turn in language teacher (educator) research. In G. Barkhuizen (Ed.), *Reflections on Language Teacher Identity Research* (pp. 197–202). New York: Routledge.

Gatehouse, T. (Ed.). (2019). *Voices of Latin America: Social Movements and the New Activism.* U.K: Monthly Review Press.

Gee, J. P. (1989). Literacy, discourse, and linguistics: Introduction. *Journal of Education, 171*(1), 5–17.

Gerlach, D. (2020). *Zur Professionalität der Professionalisierenden: Was machen Lehrerbildner*innen im fremdsprachendidaktischen Vorbereitungsdienst?* Tübingen: Narr.

Gerlach, D., & Fasching-Varner, K. (2020). Grundüberlegungen zu einer kritischen Fremdsprachenlehrer*innenbildung. In D. Gerlach (Ed.), *Kritische Fremdsprachendidaktik: Grundlagen, Ziele, Beispiele* (pp. 217–34). Tübingen: Narr.

Gilmore, A. (2007). Authentic materials and authenticity in foreign language learning. Nottingham University, UK & Kansai Gaidai University, Japan.

Goh, C. C. (2016). Cognition, metacognition, and L2 listening. In E. Hinkel (Ed.), *Handbook of Research in Recond Language teaching and Learning* (pp. 214–28). New York: Routledge.

Golombek, P. (2017). Innovating my thinking and practices as a language teacher educator through my work as a researcher. In T. S. Gregersen & P. MacIntyre (Eds), *Innovative Practices in Language Teacher Education* (pp. 15–31). Cham: Springer.

Goodwin, M. H., & Alim, S. H. (2010). 'Whatever (Neck Roll, Eye Roll, Teeth Suck)': The situated coproduction of social categories and identities through stancetaking and transmodal stylization. *Journal of Linguistic Anthropology, 20*(1), 179-94.

Govender, N. (2017). The pedagogy of 'coming out': Teacher identity in a critical literacy course. *South African Review of Sociology, 48*(1), 19–41.

Govender, N. (2019). Negotiating gender and sexual diversity in English language teaching: 'Critical'-oriented educational materials designed by pre-service English teachers at a South African university. In M. E. Lopez-Gopar (Ed.), *International Perspectives on Critical Pedagogies in ELT* (pp. 125–49). Cham: Palgrave Macmillan.

Govender, N. N. (2015). *Negotiating the Gendered Representations of Sexualities through Critical Literacy*. [Unpublished PhD thesis]. Johannesburg, South Africa: University of the Witwatersrand.

Govender, N. N. (2018). Deconstructing heteronormativity and hegemonic gender orders through critical literacy and material design: A Case in a South African school of education. In E. Walton & R. Osman (Eds), *Teacher Education for Diversity* (pp. 36–52). Milton Park: Routledge.

Govender, N. N. (2019). Critical literacy and critically reflective writing: navigating gender and sexual diversity. *English Teaching: Practice & Critique, 18*(3), 351–64.

Govender, N. N. (2020). Critical transmodal pedagogies: Getting student teachers to play with genre conventions. *Multimodal Communication, 9*(1), 1–23.

Govender, N., & Andrews, G. (2021). Queer critical literacies. In J. Z. Pandya, R. A. Mora, J. Alford, N. A. Golden & R. S. de Roock (Eds), *The Critical Literacies Handbook*. London: Routledge.

Gray, J. (2002). The global course book in English language teaching. In D. Block & D. Cameron (Eds), *Globalisation and Language Teaching* (pp. 151–67). London: Routledge.

Gray, J. (2010a). *The Construction of English. Culture, Consumerism and Promotion in the ELT Global Coursebook*. New York: Palgrave Macmillan.

Gray, J. (2010b). The branding of English and the culture of the new capitalism: Representations of the world of work in English language textbooks. *Applied Linguistics, 31*(5), 714–33.

Gray, J. (2012). English, the industry. In A. Hewings & C. Tagg (Eds), *The Politics of English* (pp. 137–63). Abingdon and Milton Keynes: The Open University/Routledge.

Gray, J. (2013). LGBT invisibility and heteronormativity in ELT materials. In J. Gray (Ed.), *Critical Perspectives on Language Teaching Materials* (pp. 9–43). Basingstoke: Palgrave Macmillan.

Gray, J. (2019). Critical language teacher education. In S. Walsh & S. Mann (Ed.). *The Routledge Handbook of English Language Teacher Education* (pp. 68–81). London: Routledge.

Gray, J. (2021). Addressing LGBTQ erasure through literature in the ELT classroom. *ELT Journal, 75*(2), 142–51.

Gray, J., & Block, D. (2014). All middle class now? Evolving representations of the working class in the neoliberal era: The case of ELT textbooks. In N. Harwood (Ed.), *English Language Teaching Textbooks* (pp. 45–71). Basingstoke: Palgrave Macmillan.

Güthenke, C., & Holmes, B. (2018). Hyperinclusivity, hypercanonicity, and the future of the field. In M. Formisano & C. Shuttleworth Kraus (Eds), *Marginality, Canonicity, Passion*. Oxford: Oxford University Press.

Habegger-Conti, J. (2021). 'Where am I in the text?' Using positioning in refugee comics for intercultural education. *Children's Literature in English Language Education, 9*(2).

Hall, S. (1996/2003). Introduction: Who needs 'identity'? In S. Hall & P. Du Gay (Eds), *Questions of Cultural Identity* (pp. 1–17). London: Sage Publications.

Halliday, M., & Matthiessen, C. (2014). *An Introduction to Functional Grammar*. London: Routledge.

Hampson, T. (2020). *LGBT Representation in Textbooks*. [Unpublished essay].

Han, H. (2009). Institutionalized inclusion: A case study on support for immigrants in English learning. *TESOL Quarterly, 43*(4), 643–68.

Han, H. (2012). Becoming a 'new immigrant' in Canada: How language matters, or not. *Journal of Identity Language and Education, 11*(2), 136–49.

Han, H. (2013). Individual grassroots multilingualism in Africa Town in Guangzhou: The role of states in globalization from below. *International Multilingual Research Journal, 7*(1), 83–97.

Han, H. (2014a). 'Westerners,' 'Chinese,' and/or 'us': Exploring the intersection of language, race, religion and immigrantization. *Anthropology and Education Quarterly, 45*(1), 54–70.

Han, H. (2014b). Access English and networks at an English-Medium multicultural church in East Canada: An ethnography. *Canadian Modern Language Review, 70*(2), 220–45.

Han, H. (2019). Making 'second generation,' inflicting linguistic injuries: An ethnography of a Mainland Chinese church in Canada. *Journal of Language, Identity & Education, 18*(1), 55–69.

Harper, H., Bean, T. & Dunkerly, J. (2010). Cosmopolitanism, globalization and the field of adolescent literacy. *Canadian and International Education, 39*(3), Article 2.

Hashemi, L., & Thomas, B. (2010), *Objective PET: Students Book*. Cambridge: Cambridge University Press.

Hawkins, M. R. (2011). *Social Justice Language Teacher Education*. Bristol: Multilingual Matters.

Hawkins, M., & Norton, B. (2009). Critical language teacher education. In A. Burns & J. C. Richards (Eds), *Cambridge Guide to Second Language Teacher Education* (pp. 30–9). Cambridge: Cambridge University Press.

Hayes, A. F. (2013). *Introduction to Mediation, Moderation, and Conditional Process Analysis: A Regression-based Approach*. New York: The Guliford Press.

HBO Documentary Films (2020). *Transhood*.

Heller, M. (2010). The commodification of language. *Annual Review of Anthropology*, *39*, 101–14.

Heller, M., Pietikäinen, S., & Pujolar, J. (2017). *Critical Sociolinguistic Research Methods: Studying Language Issues that Matter*. London: Routledge.

Helsper, W. (2014). Lehrerprofessionalität – der strukturtheoretische Professionsansatz zum Lehrberuf. In E. Terhart, H. Bennewitz & M. Rothland (Eds). *Handbuch der Forschung zum Lehrerberuf* (pp. 149–70). Münster: Waxmann.

Hermann-Wilmarth, J. M., Lannen, R., & Ryan, C. L. (2017). Critical literacy and transgender topics in an upper elementary classroom: A portrait of possibility. *Journal of Language and Literacy Education*, *13*(1), 15–27.

Hibbard, L. (2020). Out in the classroom: A transgender pedagogical narrative. *Journal of the Coalition of Feminist Scholars in the History of Rhetoric & Composition*, *22*(4). Retrieved from: https://cfshrc.org/article/out-in-the-classroom-a-transgender-pedagogical-narrative/ (accessed 15 January 2021).

Hicks, D. (2000). English Language Teaching Teachers' Guides: A Critical Discourse Analysis of Three Texts. Unpublished doctoral dissertation, University of Bristol, UK.

Hill Collins, P. (2019). *Intersectionality as Critical Social Theory*. Durham/London: Duke University Press.

Hirsu, L., Arizpe, E. & McAdam, J. E. (2020). Cultural interventions through children's literature and arts-based practices in times of disaster: A case study of reading mediators' response to the Mexican earthquakes (September 2017). *International Journal of Disaster Risk Reduction*, *51*, 101797.

Holborow, M. (2015). *Language and Neoliberalism*. London: Routledge.

Holmes, J. (1991). Language and gender: A state-of-the-art survey article. *Language Teaching*, *24*(4), 207–20.

Holmes, J. (2020). 'Until I got a man in, he wouldn't listen'. Evidence for the gender order in New Zealand workplaces. In C. R. Caldas-Coulthard (Ed.), *Innovations and Challenges: Women, Language and Sexism* (pp. 96–112). London: Routledge.

Hope, J. (2017). *Children's Literature About Refugees: A Catalyst in the Classroom*. London: Trentham Books.

Huang, S.-y. (2015). The intersection of multimodality and critical perspective: Multimodality as subversion. *Language Learning & Technology, 19*(3), 21–37.

Huang, S.-y. (2017). Critical multimodal literacy with moving-image texts. *English Teaching: Practice & Critique, 16*(2), 194–206.

Huang, S.-y. (2019). EFL learners' critical multimodal reflections on the politics of English. *TESOL Journal, 10*(3), 1–17.

Hull, G., & Nelson, M. E. (2005). Locating the semiotic power of multimodality. *Written Communication, 22*, 224–61.

Ibrahim, N. (2020). The multilingual picturebook in English language teaching: Linguistic and cultural identity. *Children's Literature in English Language Education, 8*(2), 12–38.

Irvine, J. T., & Gal, S. (2000). Language ideology and linguistic differentiation. In P. V. Kroskrity (Ed.), *Regimes of Language* (pp. 35–83). Santa Fe, NM: School of American Research Press.

Izadinia, M. (2014). Teacher educators' identity: A review of literature. *European Journal of Teacher Education, 37*, 426–41.

Jagose, A. (1996). *Queer Theory*. New York: New York University Press.

Jamieson, J. P., & Harkins, S. G. (2007). Mere effort and stereotype threat performance effects. *Journal of Personality and Social Psychology, 93*(4), 544.

Janks, H. (2010). *Literacy & Power*. London/New York: Routledge.

Javaid, A. (2020). Reconciling the Irreconcilable Past: Sexuality, Autoethnography, & Reflecting on the Stigmatization of the 'Unspoken'. *Sexualities, 23*(7), 1199–1227.

Jennings, J. (2009). *Asia and the Pacific Education for All (EFA) Mid-Decade Assessment: South Asia Sub-Region Synthesis Report*. Bangkok: UNESCO Bangkok.

Jewitt, C. (2011). An introduction to multimodality. In C. Jewitt (Ed.), *The Routledge Handbook of Multimodal Analysis* (pp. 14–27). New York: Routledge.

Jewitt, C. (2015). Multimodal Analysis. In A. Georgakopoulou & T. Spilioti (Eds), *The Routledge Handbook of Language and Digital Communication* (pp. 69–84). London: Routledge.

Johnson, K. E., & Golombek, P. R. (2020). Informing and transforming language teacher education pedagogy. *Language Teaching Research, 24*(1), 116–27.

Johnson, M. (2004). *Philosophy of Second Language Acquisition*. Yale: Yale University Press.

Jones, M. A., Kitetu, C. & Sunderland, J. (1997). Discourse roles, gender and language textbook dialogues: Who learns what from John and Sally? *Gender and education, 9*(4), 469-90.

Kabeer, N., Mahmud, S. & Tasneem, S. (2011). Does Paid Work Provide a Pathway to Women's Empowerment? Empirical Findings from Bangladesh. *IDS Working paper 375*. Brighton: IDS.

Kajee, L. (2011). Multimodal representations of identity in the English-as-an-additional-language classroom in South Africa. *Language, Culture and Curriculum, 24*(3), 241–52.

Keller, J. (2007). Stereotype threat in classroom settings: The interactive effect of domain identification, task difficulty and stereotype threat on female students' maths performance. *British Journal of Educational Psychology, 77*(2), 323–38.

KFCRIS. (2021). Vision 2030 and Reform in Saudi Arabia: Facts and Figures (April 2015 – April 2021). Riyadh: King Faisal Center for Research and Islamic Studies. Retrieved from: https://www.kfcris.com/pdf/6ad1a03b25b4e104d7c3821f7623a9016093ca96d624b.pdf.

Kilodavis, C., & DeSimone, S. (2009). *My Princess Boy.* KD Talent, LCC.

King, B. (2008). 'Being gay guy, that is the advantage': Queer Korean language learning and identity construction. *Journal of Language, Identity, and Education, 7*(3), 230–52.

King, B. (2017). Hip Hop headz in sex ed: Gender, agency, and styling in New Zealand. *Language in Society, 47*(4), 487–512.

Klugman, J., Hanmer, L., Twigg, S., Hasan, T., McCleary-Sills, J., & Santamaria, J. (2014). *Voice and Agency: Empowering Women and Girls for Shared Prosperity.* Washington: World Bank Publications.

Koraan, R., & Geduld, A. (2015). "Corrective rape" of lesbians in the era of transformative constitutionalism in South Africa". *Potchefstroom Electronic Law Journal/Potchefstroomse Elektroniese Regsblad, 18*(5), 1930–52.

Koster, D., & Litosseliti, L. (2021). Multidimensional perspectives on gender in Dutch language education: Textbooks and teacher talk. *Linguistics and Education, 64*(1), 100953.

Kress, G. (2003). *Literacy in the New Media Age.* Abingdon: Routledge.

Kress, G. (2011). What is mode? In C. Jewitt (Ed.), *The Routledge Handbook of Multimodal Analysis* (pp. 54–67). New York: Routledge.

Kress, G. (2017). Preface. In K. Donaghy and D. Xerri (Eds), *The Image in English Language Teaching* (pp. ix–x). Valetta: ELT Council.

Kress, G., & van Leeuwen, T. (1996). *Reading Images: The Grammar of Visual Design.* London: Psychology Press.

Kress, G., & van Leeuwen, T. (1998). Front Pages: (The critical) Analysis of Newspaper Layout. In A. Bell & P. Garrett (Eds), *Approaches to Media Discourse* (pp. 186–219). London: Blackwell.

Kress, G., & van Leeuwen, T. (2001). *Multimodal Discourse: The Modes and Media of Contemporary Communication.* London: Arnold.

Kubanyiova, M., & Crookes, G. (2016). Re-envisioning the roles, tasks, and contributions of language teachers in the multilingual era of language education research and practice. *The Modern Language Journal, 100*, 117–32.

Kubota, R., & Lin, A. (Eds) (2009). *Race, Culture, and Identities in Second Language Education: Exploring Critically Engaged Practice.* London and New York: Routledge.

Kumaravadivelu, B. (2006). *Understanding Language Teaching. From Method to Postmethod.* London: Lawrence Erlbaum.

Kumashiro, K. K. (2002). *Troubling Education: Queer Activism and Antioppressive Pedagogy*. London: Routledge.

Kunze, K. (2014). Professionalisierungspotenziale und -probleme der sozialisatorischen Interaktion im Studienseminar. *Zeitschrift für interpretative Schul- & Unterrichtsforschung, 3*, 44–57.

Kutuk, G., Putwain, D. W., Kaye, L. & Garrett, B. (2020). Development and Validation of a New Multidimensional Language Class Anxiety Scale. *Journal of Psychoeducational Assessment, 38*(5), 649–58.

Lähdesmäki, T., & Koistinen, A. K. (2021). Explorations of linkages between intercultural dialogue, art, and empathy. In F. Maine & M. Vrikki (Eds), *Dialogue for Intercultural Understanding: Placing Cultural Literacy at the Heart of Learning* (pp. 45–58). Cham: Springer.

Lamb, T., Hatoss, A. & O'Neill, S. (2019). Challenging social injustice in superdiverse contexts through activist languages education. In R. Papa (Ed.), *Handbook on Promoting Social Justice in Education* (pp. 1–38). Cham: Palgrave.

Lara Herrera, R. (2015). Mexican secondary school students' perception of learning the history of Mexico in English. *Profile: Issues in Teachers' Professional Development, 17*(1), 105–20.

Lave, J. (1988). *Cognition in Practice*. Cambridge: Cambridge University Press.

Lave, J., & Wenger, E. (1991). *Situated Learning: Legitimate Peripheral Participation*. New York: Cambridge University Press.

Lawrence, M., & Taylor, Y. (2020). The UK government LGBT Action Plan: Discourses of progress, enduring stasis, and LGBTQI+ lives 'getting better'. *Critical Social Policy, 40*(4), 586–607.

Lawson, M., & Lawson, H. (2015). New conceptual frameworks for student engagement research, policy, and practice. *Review of Educational Research, 83*(3), 432–79.

Lazar, M. (2014). Feminist critical discourse analysis: relevance for current gender and language research. In S., Ehrlich, M. Meyerhoff & J. Holmes (Eds), *Handbook of Language, Gender, and Sexuality* (pp. 180–99). Oxford: Wiley-Blackwell.

Le, V. C. (2020). Remapping the teacher knowledge-base of language teacher education: A Vietnamese perspective. *Language Teaching Research, 24*(1), 71–81.

Lehner, A. (2019). Trans self-imaging praxis, decolonizing photography and the work of Alok Vaid-Menon. *Refract: An Open Access Visual Studies Journal, 2*(1), 45–77.

Lenhard, H. (2004). Zweite Phase an Studienseminaren und Schulen. In S. Blömeke, P. Reinhold, G. Tulodziecki & J. Wildt (Eds), *Handbuch Lehrerbildung* (pp. 275–289). Bad Heilbrunn: Klinkhardt.

LGBT Youth Scotland (2018). *Life in Scotland for LGBT Young People*. Retrieved from: https://www.lgbtyouth.org.uk/media/1354/life-in-scotland-for-lgbt-young-people.pdf.

Li, J., McLellan, R. & Forbes, K. (2021). Investigating EFL teachers' gender-stereotypical beliefs about learners: A mixed-methods study. *Cambridge Journal of Education, 51*(1), 19–44.

Lippi-Green, R. (2012). *English with an Accent: Language, Ideology, and Discrimination in the United States* (2nd ed.). London/New York: Routledge.

Little, D., Dam, L. & Legenhausen, L. (2017). *Language Learner Autonomy: Theory, Practice and Research*. London: Multilingual Matters.

Litwin, E. (2016). *El Oficio de Enseñar: Condiciones y Contextos*. Buenos Aires: Paidós.

Livia, A., & Hall, K. (1997). *Queerly Phrased: Language, Gender, and Sexuality*. Oxford: Oxford University Press.

Local Government Act (1988). Section 28. Available at: https://www.legislation.gov.uk/ukpga/1988/9/contents.

Love, J. (2018). *Julián is a Mermaid*. New York: Candlewick Press.

Love, J. (2020). *Julián at the Wedding*. New York: Candlewick Press.

Luke, C., Castell, S. & De, L. A. (1983). Beyond criticism: The authority of the school text. *Curriculum Inquiry*, *13*(2): 111–27.

Lunenberg, M., Dengerink, J. & Korthagen, F. (2014). *The Professional Teacher Educator. Roles, Behaviour, and Professional Development of Teacher Educators*. Rotterdam, Boston & Taipei: Sense.

Madalena, E. & Ramos, A. M. (2022). Gender diversity in picturebooks: challenges of a taboo topic in Portuguese schools. In Å. M. Ommundsen, G. Haaland, B. Kümmerling-Meibauer (Eds), *Exploring Challenging Picturebooks in Education*. London: Routledge.

Magnet, S., & Dunnington, C.-L. (2020). Necessary discomfort: Three preschool classrooms break open the heart and the bottle and sit with hard feelings. *Bookbird: A Journal of International Children's Literature*, *58*(1): 1–14.

Mahboob, A., & Elyas, T. (2014). English in the Kingdom of Saudi Arabia. *World Englishes*, *33*(1), 128–42.

Mannheim, K. (1982). *Structures of Thinking*. London: Routledge.

Markula, P., & Pringle, R. (2006). *Foucault, Sport and Exercise: Power, Knowledge and Transforming the Self*. London: Routledge.

Martino, W., & Cumming-Potvin, W. (2016). Teaching about sexual minorities and 'princess boys': A queer and trans-infused approach to investigating LGBTQ-themed texts in the elementary school classroom. *Discourse: Studies in the Cultural Politics of Education*, *37*(6), 807–27.

Massei, S. (2014). France gives way to opponents of 'gender theory' in schools. *The Conversation*. Retrieved from: https://theconversation.com/france-gives-way-to-opponents-of-gender-theory-in-schools-28641 (accessed 23 May 2021).

Mayer, D. M., & Hanges, P. J. (2003). Understanding the stereotype threat effect with 'culture-free' tests: An examination of its mediators and measurement. *Human Performance*, *16*(3), 207–30.

Mayhew, S. (2015). *Oxford Dictionary of Geography* (5th ed.). Oxford: Oxford University Press.

McClung, N. A. (2018). Learning to queer text: Epiphanies from a family critical literacy practice. *The Reading Teacher*, *71*(4), 401–10.

Meccawy, Z. (2010). Language, culture & identity: A qualitative study of Saudi female students' perceptions of EFL current practices and textbook use. Unpublished Doctoral dissertation, University of Nottingham, UK.

Medina, R. A. (2020). Designing, facilitating, & supporting for the critical engagement of self-reflection, critical dialogue, & justice-oriented teaching. *Teacher Education Quarterly, 47*(1), 117–22.

Mehdinezhad V. (2011). First year students' engagement at the university. *International Online Journal of Educational Sciences, 3*(1), 47–66.

Meighan, R. (2014). *John Holt*. London: Bloomsbury.

Melaku, T. (2019*). You Don't Look Like a Lawyer: Black Women and Systemic Gendered Racism*. Lanham-London: Rowman & Littlefield.

Melhem, S., Morrell, C. & Tandon, N. (2009). Information and Communication Technologies for Women's Socioeconomic Empowerment. *The International Bank for Reconstruction and Development*. The World Bank. Retrieved from: https://openknowledge.worldbank.org/handle/10986/5935 (accessed 21 February 2020).

Menard-Warwick, J., Mori, M. & S. Williams. (2014). Language and gender in educational contexts. In S. Ehrlich, M. Meyerhoff & J. Holmes (Eds), *Handbook of Language, Gender, and Sexuality* (pp. 471–90). Oxford: Wiley-Blackwell.

Merriam-Webster (2021). *Online dictiorary*. New York: Merriam-Webster. Available at https://www.merriam-webster.com/

Merrifield, R. L. (2016). *Developing the harmless homo: Representations of gay men on U.S. television*. University of Colorado Springs Colorado, Department of Sociology Graduate Archives, 12/1/16: 3-61.

Meyer, E. (2007). 'But I'm not gay': What straight teachers need to know about queer theory. In N. Rodriguez & W. Pinar (Eds), *Queering Straight Teachers: Discourse and Identity in Education* (pp. 15–32). New York: Peter Lang.

Meyerhoff, M., & Ehrlich, S. (2019). Language, gender, and sexuality. *Annual Review of Linguistics, 5*, 455–75.

Miller, E., & Gkonou, C. (2018). Language teacher agency, emotion labor and emotional rewards in tertiary-level English language programs. *System, 79*, 49–59.

Miller, J. (2019). For the little queers: Imagining queerness in 'New' queer children's literature. *Journal of Homosexuality, 66*(12), 1645–70.

Miller, P. C., & Endo, H. (2016). Introducing (a)gender into foreign/second language education. In sj Miller (Ed.), *Teaching, Affirming, and Recognizing Trans and Gender Creative Youth: A Queer Literacy Framework* (pp. 163–84). London: Palgrave Macmillan.

Miller, sj. (2015). A queer literacy framework promoting (a)gender and (a)sexuality self determination and justice. *The English Journal, 104*(5), 37–44.

Mills, S. (2008). *Language and Sexism*. Cambridge: Cambridge University Press.

Mitchell, C., & Reid-Walsh, J. (2007). *Girl Culture: An Encyclopaedia*. Connecticut/London: Greenwood Publishing Group.

Mockler, N. (2010). Beyond 'what works': Understanding teacher identity as a practical & political tool. *Teachers & Teaching, 17*(5), 517–28.

Moffatt, L., & Norton, B. (2008). Reading gender relations and sexuality: Preteens speak out. *Canadian Journal of Education, 31*(31), 102–23.

Mojica, C. P., & Castañeda-Peña, H. (2021). Helping English language teachers become gender aware. *ELT Journal, 75*(2), 203–12.

Moore, A. R. (2016). Inclusion and exclusion: A case study of an English class for LGBT learners. *TESOL Quarterly, 50*, 86–108.

Moore, A. R. (2020). Understanding heteronormativity in ELT textbooks: a practical taxonomy. *ELT Journal, 74*, 2, 116–25.

Morgado, M. (2019). Intercultural mediation through picturebooks. *Comunicação e sociedade*. (Special Issue).

Morgan, B. (2017). Language teacher identity as critical social practice. In G. Barkhuizen (Ed.), *Reflections on Language Teacher Identity Research*. (pp. 203–9). New York: Routledge.

Morrish, E. (2002). The case of the indefinite pronoun: Discourse and the concealment of lesbian identity in class. In L. Litosseliti & J. Sunderland (Eds), *Gender Identity and Discourse Analysis* (pp. 177–91). Amsterdam/Philadelphia: John Benjamin.

Motschenbacher, H. (2010). *Language, Gender and Sexual Identity: Poststructuralist Perspectives*. Amsterdam: John Benjamins.

Motschenbacher, K. (2011). Taking queer linguistics further: Sociolinguistics and critical heteronormativity research. *International Journal of the Sociology of Language, 212*, 149–79.

Mourão, S. (2016). Picturebooks in the primary EFL classroom: Authentic literature for an authentic response. *Children's Literature in English Language Education, 4*(1), 25–43.

Mpike, M. (2019). Diversity and positive representation in Nordic children's literature. In N. Josef & K. Pellicer (Eds), *Actualise Utopia* (pp. 53–70). Oslo: Kulturrådet.

Msibi, T. (2011). The lies we have been told: On (homo)sexuality in Africa. *Africa Today, 58*(1), 55–77.

Munro, M. (2003). A primer on accent discrimination in the Canadian context. *TESL Canada Journal, 20*, 38–51.

Murnen, S. K., & Don, B. P. (2012). Body image and gender roles. In T. Cash (Ed.), *Encyclopedia of Body Image and Human Appearance* (pp. 128–34). New York: Academic Press.

Murray, J. (2002). *Between the Chalkface and The Ivory Towers? A Study of the Professionalism of Teacher Educators Working on Primary Initial Teacher Education Courses in The English Education System*. [Unpublished Dissertation]. University of London.

Mustapha, A. (2013). Gender & language education research: A review. *Journal of Language Teaching and Research, 4*(3), 454–63.

National Geographic (2017). *Gender Revolution: A Journey with Kate Couric.*

Nelson, C. (1993). Heterosexism in ESL: Examining our attitudes. *TESOL Quarterly, 27*, 143–50.

Nelson, C. (1999). Sexual identities in ESL: Queer theory and classroom inquiry. *TESOL Quarterly, 33*(3), 371–91.

Nelson, C. (2006). Queer inquiry in language education. *Journal of Language, Identity, and Education, 5*(1), 1–9.

Nelson, C. (2009). *Sexual Identities in English Language Education: Classroom Conversations*. New York: Routledge.

Nelson, C. (2010). A gay immigrant student's perspective: Unspeakable acts in the language class. *TESOL Quarterly, 44*(3), 441–64.

New London Group. (1996). A pedagogy of multiliteracies: Designing social futures. *Harvard Educational Review, 66*, 60–92.

Nguyen, H., & Yang, L. (2015). A queer learner's identity positioning in second language classroom discourse. *Classroom Discourse, 6*, 221–41.

Nikolajeva, M. (2014). *Reading for Learning: Cognitive Approaches to Children's Literature*. Amsterdam: John Benjamins.

Nilseon, A. P. (1977). Sexism as shown through the English vocabulary. In A. P. Nilsen, H. Bosmajian, H. L. Gershuny, & J. P. Stanley (Eds), Sexism and language (pp. 27–42). Urbana: National Council of Teachers of English.

Nohl, A. (2010). Narrative interview and documentary interpretation. In R. Bohnsack, N. Pfaff & W. Weller (Eds), *Qualitative Analysis and Documentary Method in International Educational Research* (pp. 195–218). Opladen & Farmington Hills: Barbara Budrich.

Norton Peirce, B. (1995). Social identity, investment, and language learning. *TESOL Quarterly, 29*(1), 9–31.

Norton, B. (1997). Language, identity, and the ownership of English. *TESOL Quarterly, 31*, 409–29.

Norton, B. (2000). *Identity and Language Learning: Gender, Ethnicity and Educational Change*. Harlow: Pearson Education/Longman.

Norton, B. (2001). Non-participation, imagined communities, and the language classroom. In M. Breen (Ed.), *Learner Contributions to Language Learning: New Directions in Research* (pp. 159–71). London: Pearson.

Norton, B. (2005). Towards a model of critical language teacher education. *Language Issues, 17*, 12–17.

Norton, B. (2013). *Identity and Language Learning. Extending the Conversation* (2nd ed.). Bristol: Multilingual Matters.

Norton, B., & Pavlenko, A. (2004). Addressing gender in the ESL/EFL classroom. *TESOL Quarterly, 38*(3), 504–14.

Norton, B., & Toohey, K. (2004). Critical pedagogies and language learning: An introduction. In B. Norton & K. Toohey (Eds), *Critical Pedagogies and Language Learning* (pp. 1–17). Cambridge: Cambridge University Press.

Norton, B., & Toohey, K. (2011). Identity, language learning, and social change. *Language Teaching, 44*(4), 412–46.

O'Mochain, R. (2006). Discussing gender and sexuality in a context-appropriating way: Queer narratives in an EFL college classroom in Japan. *Journal of Language, Identity, and Education, 5*(1), 51–66.

OECD (2004). *Anwerbung, berufliche Entwicklung und Verbleib von qualifizierten Lehrerinnen und Lehrern*: Länderbericht: Deutschland. Retrieved from: www.kmk.org/fileadmin/Dateien/pdf/PresseUndAktuelles/2004/Germany_Country_Note_Endfassung_deutsch.pdf.

OECD (2020). The impact of COVID-19 on student equity and inclusion: Supporting vulnerable students during school closures and school re-openings. *OECD Policy Responses to Coronavirus (COVID-19)*. Paris: OECD Publishing.

Ollis, D., Harrison, L. & Maharaj, C. (2013). *Sexuality Education Matters: Preparing Pre-service Teachers to Teach Sexuality Education*. Burwood: Deakin University.

OUT LGBT Well-being (2016). Hate Crimes against Lesbian, gay, bisexual and transgender (LGBT) people in South Africa, 2016. Retrieved from: https://out.org.za/wp-content/uploads/2020/10/Hate-Crimes-Against-LGBT-People-in-South-Africa-21-November-2016-Web.pdf (accessed 18 April 2020).

Owens, J., & Massey, D. S. (2011). Stereotype threat and college academic performance: A latent variables approach. *Social Science Research, 40*(1), 150–66.

Paiz, J. M. (2017). Queering ESL teaching: Pedagogical and materials creation issues. *ESOL Journal, 9*(2), 348–67.

Paiz, J. M. (2019). Queering practice: LGBTQ+ diversity and inclusion in English language teaching. *Journal of Language, Identity & Education, 18*(4), 266–75.

Paiz, J. M. (2020). *Queering the English Language Classroom: A practical guide for teachers*. Sheffield: Equinox.

Paiz, J. M. (2021). Opening the conversation on intersectional issues in LGBTQ+ studies in applied linguistics. In Paiz J. M. & J. E. Coda (Eds), *Intersectional Perspectives on LGBTQ+ Issues in Modern Language Teaching and Learning* (pp. 1–22). Cham: Palgrave.

Paiz, J., & Coda, J. (Eds) (2021). *Intersectional Perspectives on LGBTQ+ Issues in Modern Language Teaching and Learning*. Cham: Palgrave.

Pakuła, L. (Ed.) (2021). *Linguistic Perspectives on Sexuality in Education: Representations, Constructions and Negotiations*. Cham: Palgrave.

Pakula, L., Pawelczyk, J. & Sunderland, J. (2015). *Gender and Sexuality in English Language Education: Focus on Poland*. London: British Council.

Pandya, J. Z., Hansuvadha, N., & Pagdilao, K. A. C. (2018). Digital literacies through an intersectional lens: The case of Javier. *English Teaching: Practice & Critique, 17*(4), 387–99.

Pandya, J. Z., Pagdilao, K. C., & Kim, E. A. (2015). Transational children orchestrating competing voices in multimodal, digital autobiographies. *Teachers College Record, 117*(7), 1–32.

Pennington, C. R. (2016). The Effects of Stereotype Threat on Females' Mathematical Performance: A Multi-Faceted Situational Phenomenon? Unpublished Doctoral Thesis. Edge Hill University, United Kingdom.

Pennycook, A. (1994). Incommensurable discourses? *Applied Linguistics, 15*(2), 115–38.

Pennycook, A. (1999). Introduction: Critical Approaches to TESOL. *TESOL Quarterly, 33*(3), 329–48.

Pennycook, A. (2001). *Critical Applied Linguistics: A Critical Introduction.* Mahwah: Lawrence Erlbaum.

Pennycook, A. (2004). Critical moments in a TESOL praxicum. In B. Norton & K. Toohey (Eds), *Critical Pedagogies and Language Learning.* (pp. 327–45). Cambridge: Cambridge University Press.

Peräkylä, A., & Vehviläinen, S. (2003). Conversation analysis and the professional stocks of interactional knowledge. *Discourse & Society, 14*(6), 727–50.

Piller, I. (2016). *Linguistic Diversity and Social Justice: An Introduction to Applied Sociolinguistics.* New York: Oxford University Press.

Rahman, S. (2017). Women, English and empowerment: Voices from rural Bangladesh. *Script Journal: Journal of Linguistics & English Teaching, 2*(2), 191–202.

Rajagopalan, K. (2003). *Por Uma Lingüística Crítica: Linguagem, Identidade e a Questão Etica.* San Pablo: Parabola.

Ranker, J. (2008). Composing across multiple media: A case study of digital video production in a fifth grade classroom. *Written Communication, 25*(2), 196–234.

Ranker, J. (2015). The affordances of blogs and digital video: New potentials for exploring topics and representation. *Journal of Adolescent & Adult Literacy, 58*(7), 568–78.

Rhodes, C. M., & Coda, J. (2017). It's not in the curriculum: Adult English language teachers and LGBQ topics. *Adult Learning, 28*, 99–106.

Richards, C. (2020). Gender and Sexuality in English language teaching (ELT) coursebooks: What teachers think. *ELT Research, 35*, 11–13.

Richards, J. C. (2014). The ELT textbook. In Garton S. & Graves K. (Eds), *International Perspectives on Materials in ELT* (pp. 19–36). Basingstoke: Palgrave Macmillan.

Ringrose, J. (2007). Successful girls? Complicating post-feminist, neoliberal discourses of educational achievement and gender equality. *Gender and Education, 19*(4), 471–89.

Roberts, C., Davies, E. & Jupp, T. C. (1992). *Language and Discrimination: A Study of Communication in Multi-ethnic Workplaces.* London: Longman.

Robinson, K. H., & Ferfolja, T. (2008). Playing it up, playing it down, playing it safe: Queering teacher education. *Teaching & Teacher Education, 24*, 846–58.

Rogers, R., & Mosley Wetzel, M. (2014). *Designing Critical Literacy Education through Critical Discourse Analysis: Pedagogical & Research Tools for Teacher Researchers.* Abingdon/New York: Routledge.

Rosa, J., & Flores, N. (2017). Unsettling race and language: Toward a raciolinguistic perspective. *Language in Society, 46*, 621–47.

Rosaldo, M. (1974). Woman, culture, and society: A theoretical overview. In M. Rosaldo & L. Lamphere (Eds), *Woman, Culture and Society* (pp. 17–42). Stanford: Stanford University Press

Ross, H. A., Shah, P. P. & Wang, L. (2011). Situating empowerment for millennial schoolgirls in Gujarat, India and Shaanxi, China. *Feminist Formations, 23*(3), 23–47.

Rousselle, D. (2020). *Gender, Sexuality and Subjectivity: A Lacanian Perspective on Identity, Language and Queer Theory*. London: Routledge.

Ruiz-Cecilia, R., Guijarro-Ojeda, J. R. & Marín-Macías, C. (2021). Analysis of heteronormativity and gender roles in EFL textbooks. *Sustainability, 13*, 220.

Ruohotie-Lyhty, M., & Moate, J. (2016). Who and how? Preservice teachers as active agents developing professional identities. *Teaching & Teacher Education, 55*, 318–27.

Sadiqi, F. (2003). *Women, Gender and Language in Morocco*. Leiden: Brill

Salzinger, L. (2016). Re-marking men: Masculinity as a terrain of the neoliberal economy. *Critical Historical Studies, 3*(1), 1–25.

Sandretto, S. (2018). A case for critical literacy with queer intent. *Journal of LGBT Youth, 15*(3), 197–211.

Sano, F., Ida, M. & Hardy, T. (2001). Gender representations in Japanese EFL textbooks. JALT 2001 Conference Proceedings.

Sauntson, H. (2018). *Language, Sexuality and Education*. Cambridge: Cambridge University Press.

Sauntson, H. (2020). Language-based discrimination in schools. Intersections of gender and sexuality. In C. R. Caldas-Coulthard (Ed.), *Innovations and Challenges. Women, Language and Sexism* (pp. 144–158). London: Routledge.

Sauntson, H. (2021a). Applying queer theory to language, gender, and sexuality research in schools. In J. Angouri & J. Baxter (Eds), *The Routledge Handbook of Language, Gender, and Sexuality* (pp. 339–53). London/New York: Routledge.

Sauntson, H. (2021b). Rethinking gender and sexuality in the classroom: A corpus-based discourse analysis of classroom interaction. A plenary lecture given at *7th Young Linguists' Meeting Conference*, Faculty of English, Adam Mickiewicz University, Poznań, April 2021.

Schmader, T., Johns, M. & Barquissau, M. (2004). The costs of accepting gender differences: The role of stereotype endorsement in women's experience in the math domain. *Sex Roles, 50*(11–12), 835–50.

Schmenk, B. (2004). Language learning: A feminine domain? The role of stereotyping in constructing gendered learner identities. *TESOL Quarterly, 38*(3), 514–24.

Schütze, F. (1983). Biographieforschung und narratives Interview. *Neue Praxis, 3*(13), 283–93.

Scottish Government (2019). *LGBT Inclusive Education Implementation Group: Terms of Reference*. Scottish Government: Scotland. Retrieved from: https://www.gov.scot/publications/lgbt-inclusive-education-implementation-group-terms-of-reference/ (accessed 12 November 2020).

Seburn, T. (2019). This post will make you gay (or your mats anyway). Retrieved from: http://fourc.ca/lgbtqia2-coursebook/ (accessed 5 February 2021).

Sen, A. K. (1985). Well-being, agency and freedom. *The Journal of Philosophy, 82*, 169–221.

Sen, A. K. (1999). *Development as Freedom*. New York: Anchor Books.

Serafini, F. (2014). *Reading the Visual. An Introduction to Teaching Multimodal Literacy*. New York: Colombia University Teachers College Press.

Shapiro, J. R. (2011). Different groups, different threats: A multi-threat approach to the experience of stereotype threats. *Personality and Social Psychology Bulletin, 37*(4), 464–80.

Sharma, B. K., & Phyak, P. (2017). Criticality as ideological becoming: Developing English teachers for critical pedagogy in Nepal. *Critical Inquiry in Language Studies, 14*, 210–38.

Sims Bishop, R. (1990). Mirrors, windows & sliding glass doors. *Perspectives: Choosing and Using Books for the Classroom, 6*(3), ix–xi.

Sindland, L. K. F., & Birketveit, A. (2020). Development of intercultural competence among a class of 5th graders using a picture book. *Nordic Journal of Modern Language Methodology, 8*(2), 113–39.

Sipe, L. R. (2002). Picturebooks as aesthetic objects. *Literacy Teaching and Learning, 6*(1), 23–42.

Soars, J., & Soars, L. (2003). *New Headway* (The Third ed., Elementary). Oxford: Oxford University Press.

Soars, J., & Soars, L. (2006). *New Headway Plus* (The Midde Eastern ed., Elementary). Oxford: Oxford University Press.

Soars, J., & Soars, L. (2011). *New Headway Plus* (Special Edition ed., Elementary). Oxford: Oxford University Press.

Spencer, S. J., Steele, C. M., & Quinn, D. M. (1999). Stereotype threat and women's math performance. *Journal of Experimental Social Psychology, 35*(1), 4–28.

Steele, C. M., & Aronson, J. (1995). Stereotype threat and the intellectual test performance of African Americans. *Journal of Personality and Social Psychology, 69*(5), 797.

Stein, P. (2008). *Multimodal Pedagogies in Diverse Classrooms. Representation, Rights and Resources*. New York: NY: Routledge.

Stoet, G., Bailey, D. H., Moore, A. M., & Geary, D. C. (2016). Countries with higher levels of gender equality show larger national sex differences in mathematics anxiety and relatively lower parental mathematics valuation for girls. *PloS One, 11*(4), 1–24.

Stone, K., & Farrar, J. (2021). Advancing an LGBTI-inclusive curriculum in Scotland through critical literacy. *Improving Schools, 24*(2), 99–111.

Stornaiuolo, A. (2015). Literacy as worldmaking: Multimodality, creativity and cosmopolitanism. In J. Rowsell & K. Pahl (Eds), *The Routledge Handbook of Literacy Studies* (pp. 561–71). New York: Routledge.

Sunderland, J., & McGlashan (2015). Heteronormativity in EFL textbooks and in two genres of children's literature (Harry Potter and same-sex parent family picturebooks). *Language Issues, 23*(2), 17–26.

Sunderland, J. (1994). *Exploring Gender: Questions and Implications for English Language Education*. Prentice Hall.

Sunderland, J. (2000). Issues of language and gender in second and foreign language education. *Language Teaching, 33*, 203–23.

Sunderland, J. (2004). *Gendered Discourses*. New York: Palgrave Macmillan.

Sunderland, J. (2021). Review of Queering the English Language Classroom: a Practical Guide for Teachers by Paiz, J. *ELT Journal, 75*(2), 216–19.

Sunderland, J., Cowley, M., Rahim, F., Leontzakou, C. & Shattuck, J. (2002). From representation towards discursive practices: Gender in the foreign language. In L. Litosseliti & J. Sunderland (Eds), *Gender Identity and Discourse Analysis* (pp. 223–56). Amsterdam and Philadelphia: John Benjamin Publishing.

Sunderland, J., & Litosseliti, L. (2002). Gender identity and discourse analysis: Theoretical and empirical considerations. In L. Litosseliti & J. Sunderland (Eds), *Gender Identity and Discourse Analysis* (pp. 3–41). Amsterdam/Philadelphia: John Benjamin.

Swennen, A., Jones, K. & Volman, M. (2010). Teacher educators: Their identities, sub-identities and implications for professional development. *Professional Development in Education, 36*, 131–48.

Tajeddin, Z., & Teimournezhad, S. (2015). Exploring the hidden agenda in the representation of culture in international & localised ELT textbooks. *Language Learning Journal, 43*(2), 180–93.

Talmy, S., & Richards, K. (2011). Theorizing qualitative research interviews in applied linguistics. *Applied Linguistics, 32*, 1–5.

Tandon, N. (2006). Information and Communication Technologies in Bangladesh: Trends, Opportunities and Options for Women Workers. New York: USAID.

Taylor, J., & Coimbra, I. (2019). *Raise Up!: A Diverse & Inclusive View of English. Taylor Made English*. Madrid: TaylorMade English.

Terhart, E. (2011). Lehrerberuf und Professionalität. Gewandeltes Begriffsverständnis – neue Herausforderungen. *Zeitschrift für Pädagogik, 57*, 202–24.

The Glasgow Guardian. (2020). Scottish LGBTQ+ charity responds to homophobic backlash. University of Glasgow. Retrieved from: https://glasgowguardian.co.uk/2020/07/09/scottish-lgbtq-charity-responds-to-homophobic-backlash/ (accessed 18 December 2020).

The New London Group (1996). A pedagogy of multiliteracies: Designing social futures. *Harvard Educational Review, 66*(1), 60–92.

Thornbury, S. (1999). Window-dressing vs. cross-dressing in the EFL sub-culture. *Folio, 5*(2), 15–17.

Threlkeld, A. (2014). A critical queer literacy approach to teaching children's literature about same-sex parenting. In S. Lawrence (Ed.), *Critical Practice in P-12 Education: Transformative Teaching and Learning* (pp. 223–42). Hershey: IGI Global.

Tinto V. (2012). *Completing College: Rethinking Institutional Action*. Chicago: University of Chicago Press.

Tinto, V. (1973). Dropout in higher education: A review of recent research. A Report prepared for the Office of Planning, Budgeting and Evaluation, U.S. Office of Education, Washington, D.C.

Tinto, V. (1992). Collaborative learning: A sourcebook for higher education (with A. Goodsell and M. Maher), National Center on Postsecondary Teaching, Learning, and Assessment, Pennsylvania State University.

Trans Student Educational Resources (n.d.). *The Gender Unicorn*. Graphic by Landyn Pan and Anna Moore.

Treacy, M., & Nohilly, M. (2020). Teacher education and child protection: Complying with requirements or putting children first? *Children & Youth Services Review*, 113.

Tuchman, G. (1981). The symbolic annihilation of women by the mass media. In S. Cohen & J. Young (Eds), *The Manufacture of News: Social Problems, Deviance, and the Mass Media* (pp. 169–85). London: Constable.

Tyers, A. (2012). A gender digital divide? Women learning English through ICTs in Bangladesh Alexandra Tyers British Council Bangladesh / Institute of Education. University of London. Retrieved from: http://ceur-ws.org/Vol-955/papers/paper_16.pdf.

UCLES. (2015). *Preliminary English Tests (PET)*. Retrieved from: https://www.cambridgeenglish.org/exams-and-tests/preliminary/exam-format/ (accessed 17 April 2020).

UNDP (November 2007). *Human Development Report 2007/2008*. Available at www.hdr.undp.org.

UNESCO (2019a). *Bringing it out in the Open: Monitoring School Violence Based on Sexual Orientation, Gender Identity or Gender Expression in National and International Surveys*. Paris: United Nations Educational, Scientific & Cultural Organization.

UNESCO (2019b). *Behind the Numbers: Ending School Violence and Bullying*. Paris: United Nations Educational, Scientific & Cultural Organization.

Ussher, J., Hunter, M. & Brown, S. (2000). Good, bad or dangerous to know: Representations of femininity in narrative accounts of PMS. In C. Squire (Ed.), *Culture in Psychology* (pp. 85–96). London: Routledge.

Van der Toorn, J., Pliskin, R. & Morgenroth, T. (2020). Not quite over the rainbow: The unrelenting and insidious nature of heteronormative ideology. *Current Opinion in Behavioral Sciences*, 34, 160–65.

Van Leent, L., & Mills, K. (2017). A queer critical media literacies framework in a digital age. *Journal of Adolescent & Adult Literacy*, 61(4), 401–11.

Van Leeuwen, T. (2008). *Discourse & Practice: New Tools for Critical Discourse Analysis*. Oxford: Oxford University Press.

Van Leeuwen, T. (2011). *The Language of Colour: An Introduction*. London: Routledge.

Vandrick, S. (1997). The role of hidden identities in the postsecondary ESL classroom. *TESOL Quarterly, 31*, 153–7.

Varghese, M. (2017). Language teacher educator identity and language teacher identity. In G. Barkhuizen (Ed.), *Reflections on Language Teacher Identity Research* (pp. 42–48). New York: Routledge.

Vasquez, V. M., Janks, H. & Comber, B. (2019). Critical literacy as a way of being & doing. *Language Arts, 96*(5), 300–11.

Vasquez, V. M., Tate, S. L. & Harste, J. C. (2013). *Negotiating Critical Literacies with Teachers: Theoretical Foundations & Pedagogical Resources for Pre-service & In-service Contexts*. London: Routledge.

Vasudevan, L., Schultz, K. & Bateman, J. (2010). Rethinking composing in a digital age: Authoring literate identities through multimodal storytelling. *Written Communication, 27*(4), 442–68.

Vavrus, M. (2009). Sexuality, schooling, and teacher identity formation: A critical pedagogy for teacher education. *Teaching & Teacher Education, 25*, 383–90.

Vincent, L., & Howell, S. (2014). 'Unnatural', 'un-African' and 'ungodly': Homophobic discourse in democratic South Africa. *Sexualities, 17*(4), 472–83.

Walker, C., & Roberts, S. (2017). Masculinity, labour & neoliberalism: Reviewing the field. In C. Walker & S. Roberts (Eds), *Masculinity, Labour and Neoliberalism: Working Class Men in International Perspective* (pp. 1–28). London: Palgrave.

Watkins, N., & Ostenson, J. (2015). Navigating the text selection gauntlet: exploring factors that influence English teachers' choices. *English Education, 47*(3), 245–75.

Wenger, E. (1998). *Communities of Practice: Learning, Meaning, and Identity*. New York: Cambridge University Press.

West, C., & Zimmerman, D. H. (1987). Doing gender. *Gender & Society, 1*(2), 125–51.

Whitelaw, J. (2017). Beyond the bedtime story: In search of epistemic possibilities and the innovative potential of disquieting picturebooks. *Bookbird: A Journal of International Children's Literature, 55*(1), 33–41.

Whitelaw, J. (2019). *Arts-Based Teaching and Learning in the Literacy Classroom*. London: Routledge.

Widodo, H. P., Fang, F. & Elyas, T. (2020). The construction of language teacher professional identity in the Global Englishes territory: 'We are legitimate language teachers'. *Asian Englishes*, 1–8.

Wissman, K. K. (2019). Reading radiantly: Embracing the power of picturebooks to cultivate the social imagination. *Bookbird: A Journal of International Children's Literature, 57*(1), 14–25.

Wodak, R. (2015). Gender and language: Cultural concerns. In J. Wright (Ed.), *International Encyclopaedia of the Social & Behavioural Sciences* (pp. 698–703). Oxford: Elsevier.

Wong, A. (2016). How does oppression work? Insights from Hong Kong lesbians' labeling practices. In E. Levon & R. B. Mendes (Eds), *Language, Sexuality, and Power* (pp. 19–38). Oxford: Oxford University Press.

Wood, W., & Eagly, A. H. (2009). Gender identity. In M. R. Leary & R. H. Hoyle (Eds), *Handbook of Individual Differences in Social Behavior* (pp. 109–25). London: Routledge.

Woolard, K., & Schieffelin, B. (1994). Language ideology. *Annual Review of Anthropology, 23*, 55–82.

World Bank. (2020). *How countries are using edtech (including online learning, radio, television, texting) to support access to remote learning during the COVID-19 pandemic.* World Bank. Retrieved from:https://www.worldbank.org/en/topic/edutech/brief/how-countries-are-using-edtech-to-support-remote-learning-during-the-covid-19-pandemic (accessed 20 November 2020).

Wout, D., Danso, H., Jackson, J. & Spencer, S. (2008). The many faces of stereotype threat: Group-and self-threat. *Journal of Experimental Social Psychology, 44*(3), 792–9.

Wozolek, B., & Mitchell, R. P. (2018). Plastic or phalloplasty? Negotiating masculinity and (cis)gender norms in schools & the academy. *Journal of Curriculum & Pedagogy, 15*(3), 318–22.

Xue, J. (2014). Cultivating intercultural communicative competence through culture learning. *Theory and Practice in Language Studies, 4*(7), 1492–8.

Zeichner, K. (2009). *Teacher Education and the Struggle for Social Justice.* New York: Routledge.

Zeichner, K. (2011). Teacher education for social justice. In M. R. Hawkins (Ed.), *Social Justice Language Teacher Education* (pp. 7–22). Bristol: Multilingual Matters.

Zembylas, M. (2007). Emotional ecology: The intersection of emotional knowledge & pedagogical content knowledge in teaching. *Teaching & Teacher Education, 23*, 355–67.

Index

access 6, 68, 85–6, 105–8, 111–16, 119–20, 151, 193
action
  LGBT Action Plan 15
  political 68
  social 45–8, 53, 59–61, 105
actualizing 48, 50–4
agency
  definition 197
  teacher 81, 146, 151, 190–1, 202–6
  women 207–9
anxiety 37, 85, 90, 93, 98–102
autoethnography 12, 18–20

bisexual 105, 111–15

COVID-19 36, 193–4, 198, 208
critical discourse analysis 24, 67, 110, 145, 178
critical literacy 25, 57, 59, 136, 189
cross-cultural 36, 41, 148

dating 105, 108, 110–12
digital inclusion 195
disruption 17–20
diversity
  definition 31, 52–3,
  gender and sexual 2–5, 11, 25, 55, 135, 197, 212

EFL (English as a foreign language). *See* English language teaching
ELT. *See* English language teaching
ELT coursebook erasure. *See under* English language teaching
empathy 21, 50, 53, 55, 59
English as a foreign language. *See* English language teaching
English education 120, 207
English language teaching
  erasure 49
  lessons 50, 66–9, 81, 87, 100, 214
English learning 106–7, 111, 119
equity 7, 43
erasure 109, 170. *See also* English language teaching

family 66, 70–7, 87

gender
  definition 62
  diversity. *See under* diversity
  equality 51–2, 102
  inequality 177, 193
  non-conforming 2, 48–50, 53
  queer characters 20, 47, 50, 57
  representation 142, 162
global citizen 143–4, 156
globalization 68, 86, 142–3, 147, 157
glocal 143–4, 148–50, 154
glocalization 142. *See also* glocal
group work 36, 38

heteronormativity 65–8, 71–2, 112, 124, 136, 163–4, 177, 211–14
heterosexuality 16–17, 65, 67, 112, 124, 163, 212
homosexuality 22, 26–7, 112, 138, 163

identity
  construction 9, 56, 108, 115, 148, 151–2, 178, 189
  gender and sexual 5, 14, 30, 65, 67, 96, 123–4, 167
inclusion 17, 27, 52, 136, 165, 195, 216
inequality 178, 188, 206, 209. *See also* gender
inequity. *See* equity
intercultural competence 29, 86

language ideology 106, 108
language learning 30, 41, 61, 65–8, 86, 106, 184, 213
language teacher education 2, 175, 177–8, 188, 190
legitimate peripheral participation 106
Lesbian, gay, bisexual, and transgender (LGBT) 11–15, 27, 39, 43, 49, 124, 138, 159–64, 189, 211
LGBT. *See* Lesbian, gay, bisexual, and transgender
listening performance 87, 89, 94–9
lived realities 11, 47, 50, 165

materials
  course 36, 160, 166, 168
  textbook 65, 68–72, 141–4, 152–3. *See also* English language teaching
mediation 47–8, 50, 55–7, 99, 102
multimodal literacy 125
multimodality 124, 131, 135–6, 145, 166, 213, 216

non-binary 5, 45, 116

online English teaching 198–9

patriarchal 193, 197
picturebooks 46–50, 52, 57, 60
primary 34, 44, 46, 48, 54–6

queer
  critical literacies 11, 215
  queerness 45–8
  theory 2, 4, 19, 45, 106, 130, 215

self-efficacy 85, 91, 93, 98–100
sexual orientation
  sexual orientations, gender identities and gender expressions (SOGIE) 49
  understanding 33, 41, 51, 88, 111
sexuality
  definitions 2, 4, 17, 33, 64, 124, 130
  education 13, 22, 30, 51, 106, 163
social justice 11, 48, 212
social media 138, 200–1, 204
SOGIE. *See under* sexual orientation
space 46, 48, 53–4, 56, 59, 82, 137, 148, 194, 198
stereotype threat 86–7
student teacher 51, 61, 177, 189–90. *See also* teacher trainee

teacher educator 6, 45, 175–9, 181–3, 188
teacher trainee 179, 182, 187. *See also* student teacher
technology 9, 33, 41, 194–6, 202, 204–8
textbooks. *See under* materials
transgender 2, 5, 15, 31, 45, 48, 54–5, 68, 124
transnationality
  educational approaches 6, 12, 26–8
  understanding 4, 6–7, 212

university student 33, 85
usualizing 48, 50–3, 56, 61

women 23–4, 31, 33, 40–1, 85, 88, 95, 133–7, 145–7, 149, 162, 169, 193, 198, 207

www.ingramcontent.com/pod-product-compliance
Lightning Source LLC
Chambersburg PA
CBHW062129300426
44115CB00012BA/1860